34.98

Ben

Logs and Lumber:
The Development of the Lumber Industry in Michigan's Lower Peninsula, 1837–1870

A
Clarke Historical Library
Sesquicentennial Publication

Logs and Lumber:
The Development of the Lumber Industry in Michigan's Lower Peninsula, 1837–1870

Barbara E. Benson

Mount Pleasant:

Clarke Historical Library
Central Michigan University
1989

To my mother, Eleanor L. Benson, and
the memory of my father, Olander A. Benson
—a man who loved wood.

ISBN: 0-916699-14-5

Acknowledgements

The debts incurred over the years that I have worked on this project are numerous, and the mere listing of names does not do justice to the kind and generous support that I received from many individuals and institutions.

My first debt is to Irene D. Neu, Professor of History Emeritus, Indiana University, who guided this project through its dissertation stage. Her patient encouragement spurred me on and her careful reading improved content and style immeasurably.

A second and equal debt is owed to William H. Mulligan, Jr., Director of the Clarke Historical Library, Central Michigan University. Without his interest and support, this volume would not have been published.

Friends and colleagues from the Eleutherian Mills-Hagley Foundation and the University of Delaware have always been uniformly helpful. I especially want to acknowledge Eugene S. Ferguson, Lynwood Bryant, Richmond D. Williams, Daniel T. Muir, and Robert A. Howard. They shared insights into the technologies of logging and lumber manufacturing, read manuscript drafts, and provided support when it was most needed.

In addition to the Eleutherian Mills-Hagely Foundation, I gratefully acknowledge professional assistance from Indiana University Library, Clarke Historical Library of Central Michigan University, Detroit Public Library, the Baker Library of Harvard University, Bentley Historical Library of the University of Michigan, the Chicago Historical Society, the Bureau of Land Management, and the Library of Michigan. Whether in-person or by mail, I always received prompt, courteous, and thoughtful service from archivists and librarians at all of these repositories.

Ella Phillips and Marie Perrone typed many drafts of this manuscript. There must be a special place for typists and editors who have the patience, tact, and good cheer to bring projects to fruition.

Finally, my thanks go to those who have always stood with me. Carol E. Hoffecker, friend and critic, has helped in more ways than she can ever know. I am particularly grateful to her, as I am to my family, whose support has never failed me.

Table of Contents

Introduction   xi
Chapter 1   Geographic and Economic Setting   1
Chapter 2   Lumbermen Acquire an Inland
             Empire   15
Chapter 3   Sawmills and Settlement:
             Territorial Michigan   37
Chapter 4   Commercial Lumbering of the
             Michigan Forests: Regional
             Beginnings, 1837–1855   57
Chapter 5   The Development of a
             Commercial Lumber Industry,
             1837–1855: Logging   81
Chapter 6   The Development of a
             Commercial Lumber Industry,
             1837–1855: Milling   101
Chapter 7   The Development of a
             Commercial Lumber Industry,
             1837–1855: Marketing   121
Chapter 8   Logging in the Pre-Railroad Era,
             1855–1870   139
Chapter 9   Commercial Lumber Manufacturing
             in Michigan, 1855–1870   157
Chapter 10   Commercial Marketing in the
             Pre-Railroad Era, 1855–1870   181
Chapter 11   Laborers and Businessmen,
             1837–1870   195
Conclusion   221
Notes   225
Bibliography   307

Maps

1. Primary Rivers and Streams of Michigan's
   Lower Peninsula   3
2. Limits of White Pine Forest and Line of
   Settlement in 1850   7
3. Organized Counties in the Lower Peninsula
   in 1852   60
4. Organized Counties in the Lower Peninsula
   in 1860   61
5. Organized Counties in the Lower Peninsula
   in 1872   165

Tables

1. Birthplace of Territorial Michigan
   Lumbermen   53
2. Previous Occupational Experience   53
3. Ownership Arrangement   54
4. Additional Business Interests   54
5. Early Population Growth in Michigan   58
6. Population and Sawmills for Michigan's
   Commercial Lumbering Counties in 1850   58
7. Lumber Manufacturing for Selected
   Counties, 1840–1854   63
8. Lumber Manufacturing in St. Clair
   County to 1854   67
9. Logging in Ottawa and St. Clair
   Counties, 1880   84
10. Size and Specialization of Logging Crew   92
11. Log Prices for Selected Michigan
    Counties, 1850   97
12. Selected Leading Industries in Michigan,
    1850   102
13. Growth of Sawmills, 1837–1855   104
14. Aggregate Capital Invested in Lumber

Manufacturing in Selected Counties,
1840 and 1850   106
15. Capital Invested in Lumber Manufacturing
in Selected Counties, 1850   107
16. Water Mills and Steam-Powered Mills
for Selected Counties, 1850   117
17. Lumber Received and Shipped, 1847–1855,
Chicago   123
18. Lumber Prices for Selected Counties   137
19. Log Prices for Selected Michigan
Counties, 1860 and 1870   155
20. Selected Leading Industries in Lower
Michigan, 1860   158
21. Selected Leading Industries in Lower
Michigan, 1870   159
22. Leading Lumber-Producing States,
1850–1870   161
23. Sawmills in Michigan, 1860–1870   166
24. Water-Powered and Steam-Powered
Sawmills for Selected Counties, 1860   171
25. Water-Powered and Steam-Powered
Saw nills for Selected Counties, 1870   172
26. Aggregate Capital Invested in Lumber
Manufacturing for Selected Counties,
1860 and 1870   173
27. Capital Invested in Manufacturing for
Selected Counties, 1860   175
28. Capital Invested in Manufacturing for
Selected Counties, 1870   176
29. Federal Appropriations for River and
Harbor Improvements, 1866–1870   191
30. Number Employed in Sawmills for
Selected Counties, 1850–1870   199
31. Average Monthly Wage for Sawmill
Employees for Selected Counties,
1850–1870   208

32. Annual Average Wage for Selected
    Industries in Michigan, 1850–1870   212
33. Place of Birth for Lumber Manufacturers
    Entering the Industry Before 1856   213
34. Previous Occupational Experience for
    Lumber Manufacturers Entering the
    Industry Before 1856   214
35. Place of Birth for Lumber Manufacturers
    Entering the Industry Between
    1856 and 1870   216
36. Previous Occupational Experience for
    Lumber Manufacturers Entering the
    Industry Between 1856 and 1870   217

Introduction

From the days of the earliest settlers, America's forests
were important for lumber as well as for masts, spars,
and naval stores. By the time of the Civil War, lumbering ranked as one of the nation's largest industries,
standing third behind cotton goods and flour milling by
value added by manufacture.[1] One of the leading centers
of the industry during most of the nineteenth century
was Michigan. *Logs and Lumber* examines the development of this industry in lower Michigan from the time of
statehood in 1837 until 1870, the year in which Michigan became the nation's leading producer of lumber.

In order to make this study manageable, some limits
had to be set. The term "lumber industry" means in this
book to the primary, or first-stage, processing of the natural resource; that is, the transformation of logs to rough
boards. It is further restricted to pine, because throughout most of the nineteenth century this wood, light, soft,
easily workable—"the cream of the conifers" and "the
joy of the carpenter," as one author lyrically put it—was
most commonly used for general construction work.[2] Finally, the circumstance of time and space made it necessary to set some geographical limits to this study for
Michigan, where the industry's development was limited
to the Lower Peninsula until well after the middle of the
nineteenth century.

In a sense, *Logs and Lumber* can be considered frontier history, for lumbering coincided with, and in many
instances anticipated, the line of settlement in Michi-

gan's lower peninsula. Most individuals living in early-nineteenth-century Michigan would no doubt have agreed, although less poetically, with Henry Thoreau that lumber activity and lumber towns were "like a star on the edge of the night . . . ." To them, the lumber industry was not exploitive nor environmentally dangerous; it was a mark of progress. Environmental considerations arose only at a later date and are not a factor for this volume.

Logs and Lumber is frontier history in the larger metaphorical frame of "a flexible period of initial activity" to borrow a phrase that Margaret Walsh used in her work on early manufacturing in Wisconsin.[3] During the first half century of American settlement of the state of Michigan, from 1818 to 1870, the lumber industry expanded from small, scattered sawmills operating in restricted local areas, often on a custom basis, to large, complex manufacturing units producing for a national market. The sawmill, like the gristmill, was a harbinger of permanent settlement and commercial development, producing the timbers and boards necessary for houses, barns, fences, and stores. But lumbering in Michigan was more than the handmaiden of settlement: it dominated the economy of the state. In terms of number of establishments, number employed, and the value added in the manufacturing process, lumber ranked first among the state's industries by a large margin throughout most of the period studied in this work. Fully a third of the men employed in Michigan worked in its sawmills, whose output increased from approximately 25 percent of the state's total value added by manufacture in 1850 to 40 percent in 1870.[4]

Logs and Lumber is primarily institutional business history, for its major focus is on the development of the industry: the changing structure, strategies, and techniques of land acquisition, logging, manufacturing, and marketing. The commercial potential of Michigan's rich forest resources attracted manufacturers and investors from the state's earliest days of settlement. The problems they encountered—plant location, transportation, lack of capital, and the search for markets—were typical of what lumbermen faced throughout America, as were their solutions. Like frontier manufacturers everywhere, they were usually poorly financed, but their initial successes generated income that permitted self-financing and also attracted outside investment into the state.

In the early days, sawmilling was not a difficult or complex operation, and output was neither large nor constant. The early reliance on steam power and the adoption of a succession of new machines clearly indicate the drive to rationalize the manufacturing process and expand production. Technological innovation and adaptation played a large role in the transformation of lumber production from a custom to a commercial basis. In addition to improvements in manufacturing, lumbermen showed concern for maximizing efficiency and reducing costs in the acquisition and handling of the raw material. Expansion of the work force, division of labor, increasing separation between logging camp and mill, and the creation of special log-handling intermediaries characterized the changes in woods operations over the years.

Historians and economists point to the lumber industry as an example of nearly classical competition, unlike most industries where expansion brought concentration of ownership.[5] This was certainly true in Michigan, where small and large firms coexisted in all regions. Although the number of highly capitalized firms increased, small mills with a capital investment of less than $5,000 still accounted, in 1870, for nearly 20 percent of the total number of mills in Saginaw County, the leading lumber center of the state.[6] At least through the late 1860s the availability of good timberlands at modest prices insured ease of entry, while the dispersed patterns of pinelands and the physical geography of the state encouraged decentralization of manufacturing.

The organizational pattern of the industry meant that lumber manufacturers were unable to control production and had to operate in an unrationalized market. The inability to control supply in relation to demand was exacerbated by the optimism of the lumber entrepreneurs. Their efforts to increase production demonstrated their sanguine outlook for the future. The increased investment in physical plant and equipment as well as the generally limited reserves of working capital led the industry into a cycle of high demand and high prices followed by overproduction and falling prices through the 1850s. Only when eastern and western markets steadily increased in the 1860s could lumber manufacturers utilize the full capacity of their mills.

In some other respects the lumber industry typifies expanding American enterprises of the nineteenth century. Largescale lumbermen responded to growth by integrating vertically, assuming all stages of production from owning the raw materials, either as land or stumpage, through manufacturing it into lumber, to marketing it. The movement toward full integration increased after about 1850 in Michigan, particularly among major producers, and it was largely a reflection of increasing nationwide demand for lumber. Manufacturers responded to the challenge, and the history of the industry in the formative years is in large measure one of expanding markets to the regional and then national level. Particularly in the days before the railroad, geography dictated that the major marketing centers would be along the Great Lakes, west to Chicago and east to Ohio and New York. Over the years, sales at the mill and through local merchants gave way to branch yards, specialized commission dealers, and traveling buyers as the leading methods of distribution.

The men of the lumber industry differed little from those in other mid-nineteenth-century industries. Although *Logs and Lumber* is neither labor nor entrepreneurial history, those two topics are considered within the context of this study. Through the 1860s workers and owners were largely native-born. The industry's major need was for unskilled labor, drawn primarily from the agricultural population of the state or the surrounding region. Lumber workers acquired the skills they needed through on-the-job training. Entrepreneurs came from diverse backgrounds and brought various skills to their new business. In the first decades of the industry in Michigan most manufacturers came from mercantile and agricultural backgrounds, but by 1870 the majority came with previous lumber experience. Whatever their background and training, their decisions governed the growth of the industry, which in turn helped shape the development of the State of Michigan.

CHAPTER 1

Geographic and Economic Setting

The German philosopher Johann G. Herder once re-
marked that "history is geography set into motion."[1]
Such words certainly ring true to anyone looking at the
forest history of Michigan's lower peninsula, for here location, geological structure, topography, climate, soil,
and vegetation combined to produce a physical environment favorable to the growth of a great lumber industry,
which in turn affected the settlement and development
of the state.

Circumscribed roughly between 42° and 48° north
latitude and 82° and 90° west longitude, Michigan contains approximately 56,800 square miles. Its lower peninsula, a land mass of 26,500,000 acres that looks
remarkably like a mitten, lies slightly southeast of the
continent's geographical center within boundaries some
200 to 300 miles at its maximum width and length. En-
circled on the west, north, and east by lakes Michigan,
Huron, and Erie, the lower peninsula has one of the
longest shorelines of any area in the United States. Direct
land contact is limited to common borders with Indiana
and Ohio, both to the south.[2]

Given its latitude, lower Michigan's weather should be
similar to that of the northeastern United States, but the
Great Lakes exert a strong moderating influence on seasons, temperature, and precipitation. They make for

1

longer summers and briefer winters, more rain but less
snow, and lesser extremes in temperature than the Northeast. Annual rainfall averages thirty-one inches, distributed quite evenly throughout the year. Snowfall shows
greater variation, ranging from thirty inches in the
southeast to 100 inches in parts of the Northwest. Such
levels of precipitation minimize the dangers of drought
and flood, the twin nemeses of water-powered mills. The
threat of floods in Michigan exists primarily in the late
winter and early spring when rain can combine with
melting snow. The peninsula has a definite weather cycle
determined by high- and low-pressure masses that pass
at two- to five-day intervals. Mild weather with rain or
snow alternates with cooler, clear weather. Dangerous
and damaging storms are rare. Few climates were more
ideal for the lumber industry.[3]

Michigan is fully within the range of glaciation, the
most important geological element in landform development. During their icy ebbs and flows, the glaciers
molded the peninsula's surface features, leaving a complex configuration dominated by moraines and till and
outwash plains. Elevation ranges from 580 to 1,600 feet,
with almost all areas above 1,000 feet located in the
northern half of lower Michigan.[4]

The peninsula's glacially molded terrain significantly
affected its internal water system. From a central table-
land watershed extending the length of the peninsula,
streams and rivers follow topographically determined
serpentine courses either east into lakes Erie and Huron
or west into Lake Michigan. Thirty primary rivers and
streams with extensive branches form an estimated
16,000 miles of internal waterways (see map 1). In addition to great length, stable volume and even flow generally characterize lower Michigan's river system.[5]

The Black River and its tributaries, especially the Elk
and the Mill, wind through present-day Lapeer, Sanilac,
and St. Clair counties before emptying into the St. Clair

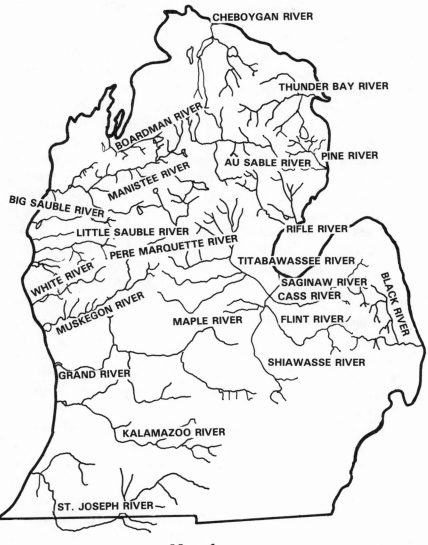

Map 1

Primary rivers and streams of Michigan's lower peninsula

River. The rivers of St. Clair County, the first to be used
by lumbermen in Michigan, were good logging streams,
with gentle banks and a moderate flow. To the west of
the Black lies the most important river system of the
eastern half of the Lower Peninsula. The Saginaw River
and its branches drain an area of over 6,000 square miles
before emptying into Saginaw Bay and Lake Huron.
Four main tributaries joining the river within a few
miles of each other feed the Saginaw, an unimposingly
sluggish and short stream. In contrast, the tributaries—
the Cass, the Flint, the Shiawassee, and the
Tittabawassee—swiftly descend 300 to 600 feet over
their forty- to eighty-mile courses. The Pine, the Chippewa, the Tobacco, and the Cedar rivers, in turn, supply
the Tittabawassee River, the Saginaw's largest tributary.[6]

Rivers of the northeastern region, the area north from
Saginaw Bay to the Straits of Mackinac, provide a sharp
contrast to the more gentle and integrated river system
of the Saginaw Valley and the Thumb. The major rivers
of this area, the Rifle, the Au Gres, the Au Sable, the
Thunder Bay, and the Cheboygan, all rise in the central
highlands but follow independent courses through rugged terrain to Saginaw Bay, Lake Huron or the Straits of
Mackinac. Steep banks and rapids mark the tortuous
courses pursued by these, the peninsula's swiftest
streams.[7]

The St. Joseph, the Kalamazoo, and the Grand rivers,
the main rivers of southwestern Michigan, all rise in
close proximity but pursue very divergent courses to their
outlets on Lake Michigan. All three rivers share the common characteristics of great length, extremely winding
courses, multiplicity of branches, and relative uniformity of current. As the most complex system in the western
half of the state, the Grand River and its six primary
tributaries share certain similarities with the Saginaw
complex. One is size of territory; the Grand River system
drains an area of almost 6,000 square miles. The swift

flow of the sharply falling affluents slows after joining with the Grand, as the latter moves through flat terrain. Such low lying ground means that both the Grand and Saginaw river areas occasionally experience flooding.[8]

The Muskegon River, the largest and longest river of the state, dominates the central portion of western Michigan, passing through present-day Missaukee, Roscommon, Clare, Osceola, Mecosta, Newaygo, and Muskegon counties. Other important rivers of the region, including the White, the Pentwater, the Pere Marquette, the Little Sauble, and the Big Sauble, follow relatively short, independent courses before emptying directly into Lake Michigan. North of the Muskegon area lies the Manistee River district. Fed by numerous small branches and two principal tributaries, the Pine River and Bear Creek, the Manistee flows through five counties before emptying into Lake Michigan. Its winding course, steep banks, and swift movement make it as dangerous a river as the Au Sable to the east. The remainder of the northwestern waterways are short rivers that traverse a variety of terrains.[9]

In addition to an extensive and well-distributed river network, lower Michigan's internal water system includes over 5,000 lakes formed as a result of the ice age. Scattered throughout the peninsula, particularly where irregularity of terrain prevails, and varying greatly in size up to 30.8 square miles, they aid in stabilizing river flow and volume. No lakes exist along the peninsula's eastern shore, but seven of the western rivers—the Kalamazoo, Grand, Muskegon, White, Pere Marquette, Big Sauble, and Manistee—flow into lakes that, in turn, empty into Lake Michigan.[10]

Michigan soils exhibit a diversity as great as the state's topography and rivers. Although all are classified as forest soil, twenty varieties have been identified and grouped according to the predominating element of sand, clay, or lime. True podzol, or fully leached acidic soil that is deficient in fertility and waterholding capacity, is found north of an approximate line from Muskegon to Saginaw. To the south, gray-brown podzolic soil predominates. This soil easily supports continuous agriculture.[11]

Soil, topography, and climate determined vegetation. In variety and abundance of flora, Michigan surpassed any other region of the northeastern United States. Botanists have been able to identify ninety-five types of trees and shrubs as indigenous to the state. With the exception of the southwestern corner, which was covered with prairie grass, coniferous and deciduous forests provided over 90 percent of the original vegetation of the lower peninsula.[12] Although some studies locate conifers, especially the white pine, throughout the entire lower peninsula, most place its southern limit roughly along the forty-third parallel, or the southern limit of podzol soil. A more precise demarcation would follow a line moving northward from Lake Michigan in the extreme southwest of the peninsula along the coast of Berrien County, through the northern part of Van Buren County and the eastern part of Allegan County and then eastward through the centers of Kent, Ionia, Clinton, and Shiawassee counties before dipping through the southwestern corner of Genesee County and across the middle of Oakland and Macomb counties to the northern tip of Lake St. Clair (see Map 2). Thus, pine forests, dominated by the magnificent white pine, ranged through more than two-thirds of the lower peninsula.[13]

Knowledge of the pine tree dates back to antiquity, but not until 1753 did the Swedish botanist Carolus Linnaeus identify *Pinus Strobus L.* (white pine) as one of the more than 100 species within the genus. White pine, Norway pine, and jack pine are the only species indigenous to Michigan, and all three represent mature species at their highest level of evolution. In addition to the genus *Pinus*, species of six other genera within the Pinacae

Map 2

——————— **Southern limit of white pine forest**

— — — — **Line of settlement in 1850**

family compose the remainder of lower Michigan's coniferous forest.[14]

A rugged tree, the white pine can thrive on small
amounts of water and nutrients, on a wide variety of
soils from sand to clay, within a wide range of elevation,
and on a minimum of direct sunlight. When full grown
it attains heights of sixty to 175 feet with trunk diameters
ranging between two and seven feet. The development of
a sophisticated resin-producing system makes it strongly
resistant to physical damage after the first several years
of growth, and a thick bark also serves as a buffer
against physical injury and fire damage.[15] The white
pine yields a wood that is compact, light, soft, not brit-
tle, straight-grained and easily workable, characteristics
that established its pre-eminence in lumber manufacturing and in economic value.[16] It was the "standard of
measurement" for all woods, and, until its exhaustion, suffered no rival as the nation's basic building materials.[17]

In the northern part of the lower peninsula, the forests
were exclusively evergreens, but in the middle part coniferous and deciduous forms intermingled. These mixed
stands were the most mature forests in the state and contained the best white pine. Pines grow in small, scattered
clusters, with the white pine predominating on the
ridges and the upper elevations. Although "superior"
pine stands were dispersed throughout the peninsula, in
terms of quality and quantity, central Michigan's "super
pine belt" supplied the best pine, commonly known as
"cork" or "pumpkin" pine.[18] Less than 20 percent of the
peninsula's pine was classified as cork. These mature
trees rose at least 125 feet, had a diameter of at least two
feet, and were without limbs (and therefore knots) for at
least 100 feet. Most of Michigan's white pines had less
height and girth but were still considered fine timber
prospects.[19]

If raw materials, water supplies, power resources, and natural transportation routes constitute the most important physical factors affecting industrial location, lower Michigan's physical environment obviously endowed it with the prerequisites essential to the development of a great lumber industry. Pine forests stretching over two-thirds of the peninsula merely suggest the natural reservoir of raw material. The size of that reservoir can never be precisely known, but an estimate of 150,000,000,000 feet of standing pine for the entire state, made in 1835, proved to be far too conservative when the saws finally finished the cutting process.[20]

Michigan's extensive forest resources possessed the virtue of accessibility. The gentle terrain of the forests and their general proximity to lakes and rivers assured a maximum return on logging efforts. Throughout the first three-quarters of the nineteenth century, when logs were transported to mills by water, proximity to rivers and streams determined the value of timberlands. According to one estimate, some 6,000 square miles, or nearly 4,000,000 acres, of pineland lay adjacent to water routes.[21]

In addition to transportation, the peninsula's water system provided industrial power. Abundant precipitation, river elevations, and uniformity of flow assured a dependable power supply, estimated at over 330,000 horsepower, which could be harnessed at numerous potential mill sites. Manufacturing could, and did, develop all along the rivers, but the major milling and marketing centers rose at or near the coast. Mills sprang up along the Saginaw from the confluence of the Titabawassee, Shiawassee, and Flint rivers to Saginaw Bay and on the Muskegon River from its mouth along Muskegon Lake to Lake Michigan. The state's location on the Great Lakes provided it with an unrivaled water network. The importance of good transportation routes cannot really be overstressed, for in their absence an industry based on a heavy and cumbersome raw material must, of necessity, develop only close to the source of supply.[22]

Resources of the physical environment, no matter how plentiful and attractive, remain "latent resources" until man wants them or needs them—and possesses the technological ability to exploit them. Michigan's changing position in relation to potential markets proved most advantageous in the development of the lumber industry. The increasing lumber needs of an urbanizing East coupled with migration westward, especially onto the treeless plains, steadily enhanced the value of the peninsula's location for lumbermen and investors in pinelands. It was only a question of time until man and axe came to conquer Michigan's forests.[23]

Throughout nearly two centuries of French and then British control, Michigan's timber resources remained largely untouched. The unbroken forests filled the French "with wonder and admiration," but the French crown confined its interest to fur-bearing animals. Military rather than economic concerns determined British policy, although the government made some use of the pine near the mouth of the St. Clair River in the construction of military vessels. A systematic development of the timber resources, however, interested neither country. The earliest value of the peninsula's pineries lay solely in serving the very limited needs of a provincial population numbering less than 3,000. Throughout the eighteenth century, Detroit, the single settlement of any size, afforded the only market, small as it was.[24]

Michigan was part of the territory ceded to the United States by Great Britain under the terms of the Treaty of Paris in 1783, but actual control did not pass to the United States until the signing of the Jay Treaty in 1796. At that time the lower peninsula remained wilderness, sparsely populated around the perimeter. Initially a part of Indiana Territory, Michigan received separate territorial status in 1805 and was officially opened to settlers in 1818. Its population stood at only 4,762 in 1810 and 8,896 in 1820. During the following decade, especially after the opening of the Erie Canal in 1825, steady settlement began, and by 1830 the territory had 31,639 inhabitants. The most spectacular decade of growth came in the 1830s, when the population increased over 570 percent to reach 212,267. When Michigan entered the Union in 1837, it contained nearly 175,000 people, all but approximately 1,000 of them in the lower peninsula.[25]

As Michigan's population grew, so did the need for building materials for dwellings and agricultural uses. By 1830 a strong demand for pine lumber existed within the territory. The earliest mills located in the St. Clair, Saginaw, Grand, and Muskegon valleys were established to supply the needs of this expanding home market, which remained lower Michigan's largest consumer of lumber until after 1840. Throughout the territorial period, Detroit continued to be the largest center of population. The town grew in number from 1,650 in 1820 to 2,200 in 1830, and finally to 8,273 in 1837. Although its relative share of the territory's total population decreased from one-third to one/twenty-third during the same period, its importance as a trading center, a "central place," as geographers would label it, did not diminish. In addition to Detroit, during the late 1820s settlements in the interior of the southern tiers of counties began to develop and assume local importance.[26]

By the mid-1830s lumbermen began to seek markets beyond the boundaries of the territory. The expansion of this distribution area began slowly. Initial demand for Michigan pine came from the west. As Chicago and the midwestern prairies increased in population, so did their need for lumber for fences, barns, homes, and stores. A small outpost of less than a hundred inhabitants in 1830, Chicago had a population of over 10,000 in 1845, rising to 80,000 by 1855. As early as 1836 the city was importing lumber, almost exclusively from Michigan, for local consumption as well as to supply interior settlements. At first all the trade with the interior was by wagon, and the expensiveness of this form of transportation limited the size of the market area. The opening of the Illinois and Michigan Canal in 1848 and the subsequent construction of railroads radiating from Chicago in the 1850s fully opened the interior of Illinois and adjacent areas to Michigan pine. The relentlessly westward movement of settlement onto the treeless prairies and plains of Illinois, Iowa, Missouri, Kansas, and Nebraska assured the development of a great interior lumber market. According to one estimate, Iowa's fencing requirements alone in the mid-1850s could totally consume Michigan's output of pine.[27]

A growing realization of the rapid exhaustion of eastern pine forests in the face of an expanding market prompted an interest in the pine resources of Michigan in advance of actual need, and as early as 1835 lumbermen and investors from Maine and New York began investigating and purchasing pinelands in the lower peninsula. Attempts to extend the state's distribution network eastward also began at an early date, but met with little initial success. The first cargo of Michigan pine went to Albany in 1840, in what proved to be an unprofitable venture. The success of the second attempt to penetrate the Albany market in 1847 marked the real beginnings of entry into the New York lumber trade. The demand for the high-grade dry pine required by the urban East continued to increase as the supply of good pine from Maine and New York neared depletion. By 1856, Buffalo and Albany, the most important eastern lumber centers, drew a large and ever-increasing part of their stocks from Michigan.[28]

By physical endowment and location, Michigan was destined to become the center of a great lumber industry.

The state possessed perhaps the best forest in the nation as well as a climate and terrain ideal for this year-round primary-processing industry. It received, on average, the right amounts of snow and rain for logging, driving, and manufacturing; its extensive river system provided a transportation network and was a source of power for industry. In addition, Michigan was well located in relation to the pattern of population expansion and developing lumber distribution centers. The *Merchants' Magazine* observed as early as 1848 that "Generations will cease to live before this [lumber industry of Michigan] will cease to be a branch of commerce, a vast resource."[29] The journal's error was in underestimating the speed at which the industry would develop and the swiftness with which the forest resources would be consumed.

CHAPTER 2

Lumbermen Acquire
An Inland Empire

While the Union Jack still flew over Detroit and Mackinac, the Congress of the United States had already begun formulating land policies that would apply to the disposal of over 35,000,000 acres in what was to become the state of Michigan. Much of the land in that state, as elsewhere, was rich in minerals or timber, but it was the agricultural qualities of land that almost exclusively, and in retrospect myopically, concerned the federal government. Certainly there was no official recognition of timber as a unique resource during the years when the lands of Michigan passed into private ownership.

Once Indian title could be removed and surveying undertaken, the national government placed its Michigan holdings on the market under laws reflecting an agrarian philosophy. Although the Harrison Act of 1800, as modified in 1804, governed the earliest land sales after the Presidential proclamation opened the territory to settlement in 1818, the Act of 1820 was to govern the bulk of cash sales. This new act reduced the minimum price per acre to $1.25 and the minimum lot to eighty acres. It also eliminated purchasing on credit, placing the public auction and subsequent private entry system on a strictly cash basis. Minimum purchase was ultimately reduced to forty acres in 1832. But this earliest public-land legis-

lation designed to encourage small, independent family
farm units failed to foster sufficient agricultural settlement and development. Congress in 1830 began granting
specific pre-emption rights to individuals or families
who settled on public land before it was put up for sale.
A general pre-emption law was subsequently adopted in
1841, which allowed a settler a one-year period between
filing and payment. As early as 1824 Thomas Hart Ben-
ton of Missouri began to champion legislation that
would reduce the price of unsold public lands over a period of years. Finally, in 1854, Congress passed the
Graduation Act. Supposedly designed to encourage actual settlement, the law tied the minimum cost of land
per acre to the number of years it was on the market,
reducing the price for every five years the land remained
unsold. Lands unclaimed after twenty years could be
purchased for fifty cents an acre, while the cost dropped
to just twelve and one-half cents an acre if the land was
still unclaimed after another ten years. The capstone of
agrarian-oriented legislation came in the Homestead Act
of 1862, which granted 160 acres to actual settlers for a
mere filing fee after five years of residency on the claim.[1]

No matter how well they actually worked, the laws
governing the sale of the public domain in Michigan
were designed to dispose of agricultural lands. They
failed totally to deal with its timberlands. Lawmakers
reflected prevailing popular opinion when they failed to
consider the commercial value of timber. The essentially
arable nature of the lands previously settled south of the
forest region of the Great Lakes and the contemporary
belief in the inexhaustibility of the nation's vast woodland resources encouraged indifference. Forests were
often considered "as much an injury . . . as a benefit" to
settlement.[2] Congress followed a policy of "default and
drift" when placing Michigan's public lands on the market, a policy that allowed, actually obliged, timberland

transactions to be made according to land laws of agricultural intent.[3]

The lack of any substantative federal forest policy continued into the 1870s, when the need to deal with non-agricultural lands and diminishing timber resources began to confront Congress. In 1874 the General Land Office initiated proposals for improvements in government land classification and disposal, and the subsequent passage in 1878 of the Timber and Stone Act acknowledged this need for separate agricultural and timber lands regulations. Under the terms of this law, timbered lands unfit for cultivation in Washington, Oregon, Nevada, and California could be purchased in lots up to 160 acres at $2.50 an acre. The extension of the act's coverage to Michigan did not come until 1892. By that date the state's valuable timberlands had already passed into private hands. Late nineteenth-century timber laws, however, did not prevent speculation in timberlands nor large-scale holdings.[4]

Frontier attitudes aided and abetted the federal government's policy, or nonpolicy, on the disposal of timberlands. Settlers considered heavily wooded areas a natural barrier to an advancing agricultural frontier, for timber in excess of modest personal or family requirements presented an obstacle to cultivation that was costly and time-consuming to remove. Because of the paucity and distance of markets and poor transportation, the forests of Michigan held little, if any, commercial value for an early settler concerned with crop production and land improvement. The frontier farmer considered natural resources such as land and timber inexhaustible and valueless unless needed and improved, a priority arrangement that accounts for the large-scale destruction of timber through cutting and burning.[5]

Frontier attitudes coincided with the needs of lumbermen. The individualistic spirit of the settlers and their

lack of concern for timber resources made it easier for
lumbermen to acquire large tracts of forest land. Indeed,
some lumbermen felt little need to buy land when there
was so much unwanted timber on unclaimed lands.
They might actually have been able to convince themselves that logging public land was a commendable act,
since they were making the lands more attractive to agricultural settlers. David Oliver, one of the first lumbermen north of Saginaw, recalled that such illegal logging
was a common practice until the early 1850s. Timber
stealing, or "moonshine lumbering" as it was sometimes
called, was condoned by the settlers, and when the government finally moved against the moonshiners, they
often met fierce opposition from farmers as well as lumbermen. One federal agent complained that associations
of loggers actively harrassed and sabotaged enforcement
efforts.[6]

The courts had held in *U.S.* v. *Briggs* in 1832 that the
federal government had the power to protect all timber
on public lands, but government timber agents, under
the jurisdiction of the Department of the Treasury, were
too few to be effective. In 1854 enforcement responsibilities passed to the Department of the Interior, but no
completely satisfactory system of enforcement was devised during the years that the public domain in Michigan was passing into private hands. In 1853 and 1854
federal officers did crack down on timber depredators in
the state, arresting a number of leading lumbermen and
seizing sizable amounts of lumber and logs, but moon-
shining was never completely suppressed. After the raids
of 1853 and 1854, however, lumbermen were more likely
to buy the land they logged than had earlier been the
case.[7]

For lumbermen the best government policy would
have provided for an arrangement whereby lumber interests could have purchased standing timber without acquiring title to the land. This would have eliminated

problems of cutover land maintenance and disposal that private ownership entailed, but the idea of government as landlord ran counter to prevailing ideas. In actual operation, federal law bore no relationship to this ideal arrangement and worked to the disadvantage of both the lumberman and the government. Lumbermen in Michigan could not acquire valuable timberlands except under agriculturally oriented disposal laws; therefore, statutes intended to encourage small, independent farm units were used to amass great forest holdings. Thus there was a discrepency between ends and means that encouraged and inevitably resulted in extensive and flagrant acts of speculation and fraud.[8]

The General Land Office found public auction, private entry, pre-emption, and homesteading to be the legal procedures involving cash payments most often used to obtain timberlands from the public domain. Newspapers throughout Michigan and the nation advertised forthcoming land auctions in the state, supplying the location, date, and site of the sale. While public auctions were customarily held only in the autumn, they were announced the previous spring to allow potential buyers to inspect the land under optimum traveling conditions. All lands not sold at auction became subject to private entry at the minimum price.[9] Through the combination of public auction and private entry, lumbermen acquired large quantities of superior pinelands at or near the minimum figure. A survey of the records of the General Land Office for 147 townships in forty-nine counties of the lower peninsula revealed that only a small number of purchases in the land mania of 1836 exceeded the minimum of $1.25 an acre.[10]

Although in retrospect the General Land Office blamed the low per-acre price of timberland in the antebellum years on collusion among timbermen's rings, fraudulent tactics probably played a less important role than did the immensity of the land area in relation to demand for it. Only in the late 1860s and early 1870s did competitive bidding drive prices dramatically higher. Lands in T18N; R3W of Clare County, Michigan, for example, which had been unsold when withdrawn from the market in 1867 brought as much as $12 an acre when returned for sale in 1869.[11]

Lumbermen and speculators used pre-emption laws, intended to encourage bona fide agricultural settlement, to their advantage, since the pre-empting of timber tracts was within the letter, if not the spirit, of the law. During the late 1830s a few nascent lumbering concerns, including the Newaygo Lumber Company, the Grand Haven Company, and the Muskegon Steam Mill Company, acquired small amounts of timberland by pre-emption, primarily in the southwestern portion of the lower peninsula.[12] Later lumbermen also made use of this method of land acquisition. Charles Mears, an important lumberman of western Michigan and Chicago, noted in a single diary entry in 1859 the filing of nineteen pre-emption declarations. This had been part of a coordinated plan that he arranged with Thomas H. Wood, the resident manager of one of his mills in Michigan. On May 31, 1859, Mears had directed Woods to pick men who might actually settle on the land once it were cut over and then have them file their claims as a group.[13]

Pineland pre-emptions were often fraudulent. A lumberman could enter a tract and cut off the marketable timber during the one-year grace period before payment was due. He then relinquished his claim, having exploited a valuable woodland for the mere cost of the fifty-cent filing fee. Although the pervasiveness of fraud cannot be determined precisely, the commissioner of the General Land Office termed this practice "fairly common" in Michigan, where fraudulent entries apparently outnumbered legitimate settlement claims under this act.[14]

Neither lumbermen nor speculators made extensive use of the Graduation Act of 1854 in acquiring lands in Michigan. Only eight of the 320 lumbermen or speculators identified in the 147 townships surveyed purchased land under the act. Between 1854 and 1860 they bought 1,744.44 acres in tracts of forty to 320 acres. To those interested in lumbering, even fine interior stands of timber were useless unless they were located near transportation routes. By the time the interior and northern pinelands had commercial value, the Graduation Act was no longer in effect.[15]

Abuse and fraud increased with the application of the Homestead Act to timberlands, for here again action directly contravened the spirit of the law. Companies or individuals employed "dummies" to enter forest lands and then rapidly stripped an area of its valuable timber before allowing the claim to lapse. Between 1863 and 1870 over 12,000 entries, totalling nearly 1,500,000 acres, were made in Michigan under this act, yet less than half the applications were completed.[16] The survey of townships in the lower peninsula reveals a particularly high incidence of cancelled homestead claims in eight townships of Bay and Midland counties, two important lumbering centers.[17] In addition, the Homestead Act contained a commutation provision that permitted the homesteader to buy his land at $1.25 an acre after six months of residence. The General Land Office discovered the highest incidence of homestead commutations in connection with timberlands and attributed his correlation to speculation.[18]

Although much of the timberland in the lower peninsula was alienated from the public domain by methods involving a cash consideration, the extent to which such methods were used depended upon the lumberman and the times. Timber purchases in Michigan remained small throughout the 1840s, when cash sales constituted the only means of acquisition. After the middle of the century, and coinciding with an increasing market for Michigan pine, new and cheaper ways to acquire land became available. Those who continued to purchase exclusively by cash methods tended to be smaller operators, "one horse concerns," as Michigan lumberman and politician Henry H. Crapo rather contemptuously referred to them. Those operating on a larger scale often, if not usually, combined cash purchases with the use of warrants and scrip to obtain land from the federal government. Between 1852 and 1868, Eber B. Ward, a shipper, industrialist, and lumberman, purchased 22,907.87 acres of timberland in the 147 townships studied, less than 30 percent of it for cash. Francis Palms, perhaps the largest speculator in pinelands in Michigan, used cash to purchase just over 26 percent of the 10,443.20 acres he bought in the selected townships. Others paid in cash less frequently. Both Mars and Charles Merrill, a Maine lumberman who transferred his operations to Michigan in the 1850s, paid cash for only 6 percent of the lands that they each purchased in these counties.

The federal government provided land bonuses for military service as early as the Revolutionary War, but military bounty warrants could at first be located only within designated tracts. Since Michigan contained no such district, bounty holders could not select lands within its borders until the right of location was extended in 1842 to all public lands then on the market. Wholesale traffic in military bounties, however, did not begin until 1852, when Congress made all warrants assignable.[20] The land warrant then became "the most tempting means of its time for land speculation," with fully 90 percent being used in that manner, according to the estimate of the Commissioner of the General Land Office.[21] During the heyday of the warrants, stock exchange reports and newspaper financial columns quoted their price. Detroit's commercial journal, the *Detroit Daily Advertiser*, carried such information. A comparison of prices during the two-year period 1859–1860 shows that land could be obtained for considerably less than the government minimum of $1.25, particularly during depressed times. The price per acre on a forty-acre warrant dropped as low as $1.025, while 160 acres could be had for as little as $.712 an acre in mid 1860.[22]

Both before and after the Civil War, buyers of land in Michigan used military bounty warrants extensively, primarily in the acquisition of pinelands. Dallas L. Jones, the leading student of the disposal of the public domain in Michigan, found that during the period 1849 to 1854 selections by warrant exceeded cash sales by a margin of more than three to one.[23] In the 147 townships I surveyed, timberland buyers large and small obtained twice as much land by warrant as through cash sales. In the years before 1870, the proportion varied, of course, for each individual. For Mears and Merrill, warrant selections accounted for more than 93 percent of their holdings in these counties, while Ward and Palms acquired approximately 65 percent of their totals through warrants. One of Michigan's largest pineland investors, David Ward, cousin of Eber B., asserted that he obtained most of his lands through warrants purchased at a maximum cost of $1 an acre.[24] Michigan lumbermen could purchase warrants from brokers within the state or directly and indirectly from eastern sources. Some of the more prosperous large-scale operators, such as Mears or David Ward, traveled east to buy warrants, but others purchased through agents. Crapo noted in his diary the names of several men in Massachusetts who would supply him with warrants, but those without special contacts could look to men such as Daniel Ball, a lawyer and landlooker of Kalamazoo, who operated a business in warrants in the early 1850s.[25]

The Morrill Land Grant Act of 1862 provided yet another means for lumbermen and speculators to obtain government land in Michigan inexpensively. Under the

terms of this legislation, designed to encourage agricultural and mechanical education, each state was to receive 30,000 acres of public lands for each of its
congressional representatives and senators. States with
no public domain were to receive assignable scrip for
lands to be located elsewhere. The maximum number of
acres that could be located by scrip within any state was
1,000,000 acres, an allotment Michigan reached by
1868, primarily because of the popularity of its timberlands. Through the late 1860s, agricultural college scrip
could generally be purchased at sales for approximately
fifty-five cents an acre, making the cost of a forty-acre
tract very inexpensive, just over $20.00.[26] In the town-
ships studied forty-eight of 320 men or companies,
largely the bigger operators, acquired over 40,000 acres
with agricultural-college scrip. Eber B. Ward and Palms
used scrip to pay for about 7 percent of their total holdings in these townships. David Ward and David Rust of
Saginaw made greater use of it, paying for from 20 percent to 38 percent of the lands they purchased from the
federal government in the townships surveyed with such
scrip. According to the calculations of Anita Goodstein,
the large Bay County firm of Sage & McGraw secured
most of its 75,000 acres in the lower peninsula with agricultural scrip obtained at a cost of fifty-five to sixty cents
an acre.[27]

Michigan's pinelands were purchased not only by men
interested in logging and manufacturing, but also by investors, often termed "speculators." The federal government's "practice in default of policy" on timberlands
provided such buyers with a cheap way to acquire large
forest holdings.[28] Despite the hostility to speculation in
popular and official rhetoric, no national or state action
interfered with large-scale acquisitions. Little speculation occurred during Michigan's territorial period, but
the fledgling state became "the El Dorado of the West".
at the pinnacle of the country's manic land speculation

craze in 1836.[29] Although there are no exact figures on the acreage that speculators acquired during this boom, research supports the contemporary belief that the percentage was "very large."[30] A variety of reasons, including the increasing scarcity of Eastern lands coupled with the accessibility and quality of those available in Michigan, explain the boom within the state.

Speculative interest in the 1830s centered on agricultural lands, but some expert landlookers encouraged their clients to buy pinelands. John M. Gordon of New York noted in his diary in 1836 that his landlooker recommended pinelands around Saginaw, because "plank will be immensely valuable." Gordon, however, worried too much about the danger of forest fires and decided to purchase agricultural lands.[31] John Ball received the same advice when he went land hunting in Ottawa County in 1836. Unlike Gordon, Ball followed the advice and purchased a 2,500-acre tract of pinelands in that county.[32] The land entries of Charles and William Carroll of New York demonstrate the pattern of purchase among large-scale land speculators. During the 1830s father and son selected both agricultural and timber lands in large units and in many counties. One entry of 1836 alone was for 40,000 acres.[33] In the counties surveyed, the Carrolls made extensive purchases in Bay, Gladwin, Gratiot, Midland, Saginaw, and St. Clair, all areas with fine pinelands. The 1830s was also a period of speculation in town sites, but only a few promoters, such as the Grand Haven Company in Ottawa County or the Boston Company in Allegan, were interested in the acquisition and exploitation of pineland as a part of a larger scheme.[34]

The Panic of 1837 ended the first wave of aggressive land speculation in Michigan for nearly a decade. Throughout the 1840s land sales and settlement exhibited a high correlation, according to Jones' research, but by the latter part of the 1840s Michigan businessmen,

Eastern speculators, and foresighted lumbermen, such as Merrill and Newell Avery of Maine, again invested in Michigan pinelands. Soon the momentum accelerated to a rush.[35] Ira Davenport, a New York speculator, observed in 1849: "The west has good [agricultural] land that won't be sold in 20 years, but there is no pine timber this side of Oregon, but will have an owner short of that time."[36]

Pineland speculators were encouraged by the lack of aggressive purchasing on the part of Michigan's lumbermen. In the 1850s manufacturers failed to anticipate the scale of development of the industry and the consequence for raw materials. In 1851 James Fraser tried to discourage David Ward from buying pinelands, which Fraser thought could never become valuable. Ward also later recalled that other operators thought him "foolish" for buying lands in areas that they could not believe would be logged within their lifetimes.[37] Ward was not the only individual who perceived future needs. Thomas D. Gilbert, a lumberman and businessman of Ottawa County, conceived a most grandiose timberland scheme when around 1850 he prematurely and unsuccessfully attempted to raise $2,000,000 to $3,000,000 for military warrants from eastern sources, to be used to corner all the pinelands of western Michigan.[38] Most lumbermen in the 1850s, and even the early 1860s, were content to buy only the most accessible stands of timber to meet their short-term needs.

Lumbermen and speculators seldom, if ever, bought pinelands without careful study. Aided by the notes of government surveyors, some lumbermen, like David Ward, Ami W. Wright, and Crapo, personally inspected and selected their own lands, but most buyers hired an experienced landlooker or timber cruiser for this task.[39] In the early years of the lumber industry in Michigan, landlooking was little more than a crude guess based on a man's walking through a property, but as timber became more valuable, more accurate appraisals became necessary. Lumber cruisers measured parts of the tract and included topographical considerations in their analyses. The papers of the Michigan Pine Lands Association contain several such detailed reports from cruisers. S. S. Hastings measured the trees every twenty rods, taking sixteen samples for a forty-acre lot. His summary included a detailed section on the quality and size of the trees and an estimate on the number of logs per tree.[40] The landlooker was usually a "semi-independent agent" rather than a salaried employee and often employed his own crew.[41] Usually he investigated tracts of land selected by his backer, although occasionally the cruiser might locate a fine timber tract on his own and then attempt to obtain capital for its purchase. His payment was either stipulated sum per acre or per day, or, more commonly, a percentage of the land located. David Ward, who began his career as a cruiser, recalls being paid at a daily rate that included board, but usually the landlooker received one-quarter of the tract he had located for his services.[42]

Lumbermen and investors were most concerned with the quality of the timber, the quantity of it, and its location. Before the railroad, logs moved exclusively by water, and lands within a mile and one-half of a river were considered the most valuable. Purchasers, especially manufacturers, chose lands carefully, often in units as small as forty acres. This led to a scattered holding pattern, particularly in the early days when there was a large amount of land from which to choose.[43]

Approximately two-thirds of the public lands in Michigan were sold directly by the federal government. Title to the remaining third, including much timberland, passed to the state as Congress liberally diverted more than twelve million acres of its most abundant asset to aid state and private corporative projects.[44] These grantees, in turn, free to formulate their own policies, became important sources of pinelands for manufacturers and investors by the mid-1850s. According to the calculations of Charles Wolfe, Hannah, Lay & Company, one of the largest lumber concerns of western Michigan, purchased almost 70 percent of their total 44,799 acres from sources other than the national government.[45]

The state of Michigan itself served as one important conduit through which great tracts of timber passed into private hands. The pineland operator and investor showed especial interest in its swamplands and school lands. As the federal government's junior partner, as it were, in landholding and disposal, Michigan displayed little more foresight than had Congress concerning the distinctive quality and value of its timberland holdings. Nor could the state be commended for originality in land legislation, preferring to pattern its land disposal laws on federal statutes. It is not surprising, therefore, that state laws were as much abused as federal land laws had been.

Only in the area of price did Michigan begin to demonstrate some recognition of the value of pinelands, but here again, the legislation produced uneven results as the cost per acre established by statute varied for each grant. The acceptance at face value of depreciated state warrants selling at thirty cents to forty cents on the dollar for all state lands except public school lands helped to offset any legislated increase in the price per acre. Following Washington's lead, Lansing rejected any special leasing or licensing arrangement in favor of immediate direct sale, and by 1877 the state had liquidated some two-thirds of its holdings. The land disposal procedure sanctioned by state statute produced the same purchase-log-default cycle encountered by the federal government, and only belatedly did the legislature attempt to eliminate the loophole by eliminating credit provisions for timberland purchases.[46]

The largest grant to the state came from the Swamp Land Act of 1850.[46] By accepting those lands considered unfit for cultivation on the basis of General Land Office field notes, Michigan received title to over 7,000,000 acres. Since most government surveying took place during the wet periods of spring and fall, when the swamps were most extensive, the grant contained much good land, including timberlands. Initially the state placed these lands on the market under especially attractive terms, hoping to sell the land as rapidly as possible. The land was to be sold in multiples of forty-acre units, first at public auction and then by private entry at a minimum price of seventy-five cents an acre. Although subsequent legislation raised the price first to $5 and then to $8 an acre, the state adopted a liberal credit system that required a down payment of only 25 percent and allowed the balance to be spread over a ten-year period. Not surprisingly, state swamplands sold briskly to settlers, investors, and lumbermen; by 1860 nearly 70 percent of the 7,000,000 acres had passed into private ownership.[48]

In addition to swamplands, Michigan received from the federal government more than 1,000,000 acres in educational grants to pay for public schools, universities, seminaries, and normal schools. The state legislature vested the responsibility for selling these holdings with the superintendent of public instruction, under the usual public auction-private entry arrangement. Michigan set the minimum price of its school lands at $8.00 an acre and its university lands at $20.00 an acre in the late 1830s, but a progressive reduction in prices to $4.00 and $12.00 respectively coupled with liberal credit provisions ranging from 50 percent to 90 percent over the decade of the 1840s increased their attractiveness. Again, abuse and fraud in timberland transactions flourished under the credit system, which allowed men to make a small payment, harvest the timber, and then abandon it. Initially the state demonstrated no greater awareness of the value of its forest holdings than did the federal govern-

ment, but by 1863 the situation had changed. In an effort to stop the stripping of pine from school lands, the
legislature required full payment for timberlands.[49]

When Congress transferred an additional 240,000
acres to Michigan under the terms of the Morrill Land
Grant Act of 1862, state legislation governing sale of the
land reflected the increasing awareness of the value of
timberland. Agricultural lands were to sell at a minimum of $2.50 an acre, with a down payment of 25 per-
cent required. Timberlands were to be handled
differently. The legislature authorized the state land
commissioner to set the minimum payment for these
lands anywhere between 25 and 100 percent of the price.
In 1869 the state tightened its policy on timberlands selected under the Morrill Act by raising the price to $5
an acre and demanding full payment at the date of
purchase.[50]

Besides disposing of part of its domain by sale, Michigan made liberal use of its most available asset to pay for
state improvement projects, a practice that provided
lumbermen and investors with an additional opportunity to acquire timberlands. Andrew and David Squier,
young brothers who carried on lumbering operations in
Newaygo County, held a state bridge contract for which
they received the equivalent of $40,000, half in cash and
half in land scrip. With the $20,000 in scrip, they lo-
cated pinelands subsequently valued at $150,000.[51] Since
state land scrip was transferrable, there was lively trading in it. Swampland scrip, which usually sold at ninety
cents to a dollar an acre, was often used to acquire pinelands. In 1868 six or eight "speculators," as a newspaper
contemptuously referred to them, attempted to "grab"
some 30,000 to 40,000 acres with the use of swampland
scrip, but their action produced such a storm of protest
that they gave up the plan.[52]

A third way pineland operators acquired land from
the state was by taking advantage of tax sales. The rec-

ords of Hannah, Lay & Company show that lands sold for nonpayment of taxes could be bought at advantageous prices. At tax sales in 1864, for example, the company purchased 400 acres at an average cost of eighteen cents an acre. In all the company acquired nearly 4,500 acres, or one-tenth of its total holdings, in this way.[53]

The federal government also granted lands to the state to aid in railroad and canal construction. The state granted such land to corporations, which then could offer it for sale. Congress made its first grant to a state for an internal improvement in 1822 and its first grant for railroad construction in 1850. The state, and ultimately the railroad corporation, initially received six sections for each mile of road constructed, an allotment that was increased in 1864 to ten sections for every mile of track laid. By 1873 six corporations had received land for railroad construction in the Lower Peninsula: Amboy, Lansing & Traverse Bay Railroad, 716,372.19 acres; Grand Rapids & Indiana Railroad, 841,573.22 acres; Flint & Pere Marquette Railroad, 511,618.28 acres; Detroit & Milwaukee Railroad, 31,138.76; Port Huron & Milwaukee Railroad, 6,468.68 acres; and Chicago & Northwestern Railroad, 110,700.72 acres. The total amount of land eventually bestowed by the federal and state governments on private corporations for railroad construction in Michigan surpassed 5,000,000 acres.[54]

In this way private railroad corporations became important pineland holders. The Flint & Pere Marquette Railroad placed half of the 307,200 acres it had received by 1870 on the market as timberlands at a price of $5 to $10 an acre, depending on the quality and location of the timber. The company's lands did not sell as rapidly as it had hoped; by 1877 slightly more than half of its 511,502.20 acres remained unsold.[55] The Jackson, Lansing & Saginaw, which subsequently became part of the Michigan Central, and then New York Central, system, also placed its timberlands and farmlands on the market

as rapidly as the company received title. The land commissioner of the road was authorized to sell pinelands for
a 25 percent down payment, with the balance due in
three annual installments at a 7 percent rate of interest.
If Ogemaw County is at all representative, the Jackson,
Lansing & Saginaw experienced about the same rate of
sale as did the Flint & Pere Marquette. Between 1861
and 1875 the road was able to sell only about one-half of
the land it held in that county.[56]

Between 1852 and 1856 four Michigan canal corporations received over 1,250,000 acres through federal
grants to the state, but only one, the St. Mary's Falls
Ship Canal Company, received authorization to locate
750,000 acres in the lower peninsula.[57] Agents selected by
the company, appointed by the governor, and approved
by the Secretary of the Interior began selecting lands in
1853. Some fifty-five to seventy-five experienced landlookers, surveyors, and lumbermen, usually operating in
parties of three, searched the state's pinelands over a period of eighteen months to find the best available selections. In all, the company selected 560,000 acres of its
grant in timberlands, locating just under 500,000 of this
total in twenty-nine counties in the lower peninsula. One
hundred and ninety thousand acres of mineral lands in
the Upper Peninsula completed the grant. The company
prepared maps of the selections, opened a land office in
Detroit under the management of George S. Frost, a
former clerk in the office of the Surveyor General in Detroit, and began to advertise its holdings. The price of
timberlands ranged from $5 to $15 an acre, depending
upon location, quality, and quantity, with a minimum
down payment of 20 percent at the time of purchase.
The balance was payable over a four-year period with an
annual interest rate of 6 percent.[58]

Despite the fine quality of the canal company's holdings, early sales were very poor. By 1863 when Cyrus
Woodman, an experienced land dealer, became the St.

Mary's Falls Ship Canal Company's land agent, there were still about 500,000 acres of unsold land. Woodman immediately placed 124,000 acres on the Saginaw and Muskegon rivers up for auction at a minimum price of $3.00 an acre. The sale failed miserably, and the stockholders decided to divide the lands among themselves. The company's lands were grouped into 744 parcels of approximately equal value and auctioned to stockholders and the public, with stockholders entitled to pay for 90 percent of their purchase with canal stock. In this way, much of the canal-grant lands came into private hands. Some of the stockholders formed the Michigan Pine Lands Association to dispose of the lands that they had purchased, but others, such as Erastus Fairbanks of Johnsbury, Vermont, chose to manage and sell their lands independently.[59]

Other timberland owners began to put their lands on the market in the mid-1850s as individuals vied with corporations and state and federal governments to attract buyers. Eber B. Ward's 85,000 acres dominated the early blocs offered for sale, but by the mid-1860s it was not uncommon for large-scale owners and dealers to be advertising timberlands in excess of 100,000 acres.[60] In his catalog published in 1864, John Craig, a major broker in Detroit, listed 150,000 acres for sale in lots ranging from 800 acres to 40,000 acres in eighteen counties. Competition, particularly in the 1850s, was always keen. Crapo recorded in his notebook that eight owners or dealers actively sought to sell him pinelands in Michigan in the mid-1850s. He later complained to his son that the St. Mary's Falls Ship Canal Company had deliberately under-estimated the value of a competitor's tract to his partner in the hopes of selling some of their land.[61] David Ward found the lumber business more lucrative than buying and selling in pinelands in the 1850s, but the value of the latter continued to increase until by the late 1860s Sage began to find timber sales more profitable than manufacturing operations. Sage was a very shrewd investor. He bought lands in an area only after manufacturers committed themselves to large-scale operations there. This eliminated the risks and problems of long-term holding.[62]

Pinelands sold by private parties tended to bring a higher price than those sold by the federal, or even the state, government, probably because of their quality and location. In 1836 and 1837 Charles C. Trowbridge, a banker, speculator, and promoter, and his partners purchased over 5,000 acres of pineland in Allegan and Berrien counties from the federal government and individual owners for prices ranging from $1.25 to $5.25 an acre. Good buys were to be had in the depressed years of the 1840s, although well-located pinelands could still command a high price. It is not surprising that 160 acres on the Black River near Port Huron would sell for $3.125 an acre in 1845. All the available evidence indicates that the cost of privately held lands increased in the 1850s. David Ward and Charles Merrill sold a large tract on the White River in the early part of the decade for $3.50 an acre. By 1856 Crapo could not find good pinelands for less than $4.50 an acre. That same year Hannah, Lay & Company purchased just over 7,000 acres from the St. Mary's Falls Ship Canal Company at an average cost of $8 an acre. A price of $10 an acre does not appear to have been uncommon before the Panic of 1857. Land prices drifted lower in the next few years. In 1864 the Michigan Pine Lands Association sold nearly 55,000 acres in nineteen transactions at an average price of $4.05 an acre, with rates ranging from a low of eighty-five cents an acre to a high of $8.93 an acre.[63]

As long as cheap federal and state lands remained on the market, the number of private sales remained relatively small. According to one expert's report to the Bureau of Corporations in 1913–14, government timberlands were available in Michigan until the middle of the

1860s. Contemporary sources support his statement, for prices appear to have jumped after that date. By the late 1860s and early 1870s timberland sales at $15, $25, and even $50 an acre were being recorded. In a piece of promotional literature of the mid-1860s, Frost estimated that pinelands located directly on rivers cost between $15 and $50 an acre, while lands less advantageously located were priced at $5 to $15 an acre.[64] By the 1870s lumbermen and investors fully appreciated the implications of industrial growth and the disappearance of cheap lands. The race was on then to acquire holdings in anticipation of future needs and the increased value that scarcity would bring. The price of pinelands in Michigan continued to rise until the value of white pine lumber declined in the 1890s, when large quantities of southern yellow pine came on the market. In these decades, holdings came to be more concentrated, and the ownership of timberlands came to be more important than the manufacture of lumber. This was a mixed blessing for the millman. On the one hand, the increased value of his lands improved his financial situation, providing him with the credit he often needed. On the other hand, purchasing additional lands became an expensive proposition.[65]

Lumbermen in Michigan sought timber, not land, but the federal policy on public land disposal dictated that the two came as a legal package. Legislation in the form of the Land Act of 1820, the Preemption Act of 1841, the Graduation Act of 1854, the Homestead Act of 1862 took no cognizance of the needs or even the existence of buyers of timberlands, but this neglect allowed lumbermen and timber investors a certain latitude as they adapted the government's agrarian policies to their special needs. In addition to selling land directly to the individual, the federal government donated more than 12,000,000 acres to the state and to private corporations, who, in turn, sold the land on their own terms. While the lands of the federal government remained abundant in Michigan, prices were low, and for those who pursued a cut-and-run policy on lands bought on credit, the cost was even lower. Only in the late 1860s, when cheap state and federal timberlands were no longer available, did such lands undergo a sharp rise in prices. By that time individuals and companies had acquired the major part of the timberlands of the public domain in Michigan under very satisfactory terms, an arrangement supported by the prevailing philosophy of the time that supported the rapid transfer of land into private hands and the exploitation of forest resources to meet growing economic demands.

CHAPTER 3

Sawmills and Settlement: Territorial Michigan

The white man pushed into the Old Northwest Territory with axe as well as rifle. Trappers and traders felled trees for road clearing and shelter, but left unexploited the area's vast timber resources. Need for such a resource came only with settlement. A growing population demanded timber and lumber for houses, barns, fences, stores, and all the buildings that signify civilization. Mills played an integral role in that pageant of settlement as virgin wilderness gave way to cultivated fields. This classic frontier pattern of small mills arising to meet local needs is strikingly apparent in the southern third of the lower peninsula of Michigan during its territorial period.

For nearly two centuries French and then British colonial policies discouraged agricultural settlement. French interest in Michigan centered on exploiting rather than destroying the habitat of fur-bearing animals. This policy in part accounts for the very limited growth of settlement, which was concentrated around Detroit.[1] Yet sawmills of a most rudimentary nature date from the French period. Records indicate operation of mills for military purposes as early as 1690, but mills in connection with settlement date from the early 1740s. The French located their mills near the mouths of the Black,

Pine, and St. Clair rivers in what became lower St. Clair County, the pine region most accessible to Detroit.[2]

Michigan experienced little growth in population during the brief period of British rule, which began in 1763. Military defense and Indian unrest concerned Great Britain more than the promotion of westward expansion and settlement. Population, which never exceeded 4,000 during the period of British control, remained clustered around Detroit, and lumber from the lower St. Clair region continued to supply this population center.[3] Unfortunately, so little information has survived about colonial mills in Michigan that it is impossible to present more than a fragmentary sketch. In 1765 Patrick Sinclair obtained 3,759 acres of pineland near Fort Gratiot (present-day Port Huron in St. Clair County) from the Indians and established what was probably the largest sawmill of the period. Ownership passed through several hands before it was purchased in 1792 by Meldrun and Parks, one of Detroit's handful of fur-trading and mercantile firms. The addition of several more mills in the 1790s assured a steady and adequate supply of building materials to this enclave of population. When the United States obtained title to Michigan in 1783, the St. Clair area could boast of a fledgling lumbering community that was systematically tapping forest resources for a small but growing local market. By 1800 seven mills were operating in the county.[4]

The United States government's need for pine timber during the War of 1812 spurred the development of the lower St. Clair lumbering region and the small, slow-growing community of St. Clair. Yet the area remained remote and virtually isolated from contact with settlements only fifty miles to the south. As migration moved ever westward during the 1820s, the interior settlements of Pontiac, Tecumseh, Adrian, and St. Joseph gained reputations as regional lumbering towns.[5] By 1837 the state census placed the number of operating sawmills at nearly 450, with less than a dozen of the mills located in the pine area. Little is known about those small and rather primitive lumber enterprises. The Meldrun and Park concern at Port Huron, consisting of two sawmills, a gristmill, and workers' housing, was an exceptionally large and complex operation.[6]

Michigan changed little for some time after it became an American territory. By 1810 the population, which was concentrated in the area from present-day Port Huron to the Ohio border, had not reached 10,000, and furs remained the principal export. Significant population increase began with the commencement of land sales in 1818. Initially settlement was confined to the four most southeasterly counties bordering Lake Erie, but by 1830 the lower peninsula had a population exceeding 26,000 that spread over eleven counties in the three lowest tiers. The construction of the Erie Canal accelerated immigration and settlement of the interior. Practical considerations such as navigable streams and the availability of water power usually determined the selection of town sites. Census data emphasize quite clearly a horizontal migration pattern: settlers spread laterally across prairie and scattered hardwood areas in search of good farm lands. As long as that more easily clearable land remained available, the heavy pine forests to the north were preserved from agricultural exploitation. By 1840, after only three years of statehood, Michigan had a population of 212,267 spread over thirty-two counties, all but seven below or just bordering the pine forest line.[7]

Population growth stimulated demand for residential, agricultural, and commercial dwellings. Without processed lumber, construction remained simple. The sawmill, boasted a lumber trade paper, marked the "transition from the era of the log cabin to that of the frame house."[8] But obtaining more finished lumber presented a problem for early Michigan settlers. Even if roads or navigable waterways were available, lumber was expensive and difficult to transport over long distances. For example, transportation charges accounted for 50 percent of the lumber costs of a building erected in Saginaw in 1830 and 20 percent of the material costs for a warehouse constructed in Bay County in 1835.[9]

Sawmills and settlement were complementary threads in the fabric of development. It was a great advantage, even a necessity, for the settler to have a convenient source of lumber. The territory that a local mill could service depended largely upon its location. The most successful mills were those on navigable streams; those that depended on overland transportation served only a local market. Mills received logs from upstream and sent sawed boards, formed into rafts or cribs perhaps six feet wide and six feet deep, downstream.[10] Conforming to the colonial and frontier pattern, mills often preceded general stores and acted as magnets for settlers and commercial development. For example, in 1836 settlers came from a twenty-mile radius to help raise a mill building in Shiawassee County. Very often a frontier mill served a social as well as an economic function, for it was not at all uncommon for a sawmill, frequently in conjunction with a gristmill, to be the core of a community. Many frontier sawmills operated largely, if not exclusively, on a custom basis, processing logs to order. For this service the mill operator received cash, goods, or a portion of the lumber.[11]

The instability of firms and the paucity of business records and correspondence limit a description of the lumber industry during Michigan's territorial period, but some insights can be gleaned from fragmentary information for five of the largest undertakings scattered across the lower peninsula in the years before statehood. Those operations were atypical of the time, but the very ambitiousness of those enterprises represents the embryonic stage of large-scale commercial lumber development.

Early Michigan sawmills attracted investors in both Michigan and the East. In 1818 fifteen Detroit and Macomb County businessmen formed the Pontiac Company to purchase and exploit 1,280 acres on the Clinton River. The town of Pontiac, the successful product of their ambitious undertaking, was to become a political and commercial center. In 1819 the company sold water rights for $1,000 to Mack, Conant & Sibley. Mack, agent for the Pontiac Company, and Conant were Detroit merchants; Sibley was a Detroit lawyer and politician. These men constructed a dam and a mill and began large-scale lumbering. Their action set off a competition for pine, particularly with the mill at Waterford, which quickly depleted the area's supply. Conant retired in 1820, but Mack and his son continued to operate with Sibley as silent partner until the former's death in 1826.[12]

The development of Allegan in Allegan County, a less successful attempt at town building, is an example of Eastern investment. In 1833 Elisha Ely of New York purchased 20,000 acres of land for the Boston Company. In addition to Ely, the partners included Samuel Hubbard, Edmund Monroe, and Pliny Cutler of Boston, and Charles C. Trowbridge of Detroit. The company had the dual purpose of developing a town and manufacturing pine lumber. Ely, a man with lumber interests in New York State, selected the company's lands on the Kalamazoo River, which flows into Lake Michigan. The company built a dam and a mill, hired a resident manager and large crew, and commenced operations. The Boston Company floundered in the aftermath of the Panic of 1837, and in 1844 the five members agreed to a division of the property.[13]

While lumbering in the interior and on the western shore might be part of a town promotion scheme, on the eastern shore it was more often allied with a mercantile business. The firm of Howard and Wadhams began as a commercial lumber venture in 1827, when Ralph Wadhams, a Detroit merchant, purchased pinelands and a mill in St. Clair County from four of his fellow merchants. He then added two partners from New York State, W. S. DeZeng and Henry Howard, a former business associate. DeZeng played no active role during the five years of his association with Howard and Wadhams, but Howard moved to Detroit to manage the firm's mercantile interests. Wadhams took charge of the lumber business. The company distributed its product through sales at the mill and in Detroit, where lumber was sent by vessel and raft. It is impossible to determine whether lack of demand, poor management, or other problems plagued the business, but by 1835 outstanding obligations totaled more than $30,000. Serious financial trouble continued until 1839, when the partnership was dissolved. Wadham's father, a wealthy New York merchant, personally intervened to save the firm's investment.[14]

In 1833 another Detroit merchant, Francis P. Browning, began a large lumber operation in St. Clair County. His was probably the most ambitious enterprise of the period. Browning built a steam mill valued at $35,000, which contained two upright saws with a twelve-hour capacity of 10,000 feet. He also owned a steamboat that supplied his Detroit and Ohio stores with lumber. When Browning died in 1834, the inventory of his estate listed assets of $63,000 and debts of $60,333 owed to creditors in Detroit, New York, Albany, and Boston. Seven of the creditors from Detroit took over and expanded the lumber business, incorporated it as the Black River Steam Mill Company, and successfully operated it until 1855.[15]

In aggregate, these five enterprises tell us a good deal about the beginnings of Michigan's commercial lumber industry. Whether started as part of a town promotion scheme, as an aspect of a mercantile business, or simply as a venture in commercial lumbering, the mills were all large-scale operations intended to supply something more than a local market. Equally revealing are the patterns of ownership and sources of capital. Businessmen, particularly merchants, from outside the local area were partners in four of the five companies. They brought to their businesses the expertise of merchants, but most of them lacked experience in the lumber business. One partner in an enterprise usually assumed management responsibility. It appears that financing, like leadership, came principally from Detroit and eastern sources.

As early as the territorial period considerable vertical integration appeared in the Michigan lumber industry. The manufacturer often exercised all the functions of cutting, processing, and distributing. A sawmill could obtain its raw materials in three ways: it could conduct its own logging operations; it could make a contract with a logging jobber; it could purchase logs in individual transactions. From the very beginning some firms owned pinelands, an example of backward integration. The Boston and Grand Haven companies owned their own lands, but while the Boston Company apparently managed its own logging operations, the Grand Haven firm contracted for the work with independent jobbers. Records of the Black River Steam Mill Company indicate that it both hired loggers and purchased logs. In contrast, the large mill owned by Thomas Palmer in St. Clair County purchased its entire log supply from various local sources. Small-scale logging operations and the purchase of logs from individuals characterized the early period. Formal logging contracts came later.[16]

Raw materials presented no problem for the earliest sawmill operators, for trees literally grew in their own backyards. In time, immediate supplies were consumed, and logs had to be transported from ever-increasing distances. Since the transportation of logs by water proved more economical than overland hauling, logging operations began an upstream movement along the banks of the state's numerous rivers and streams, a pattern that would continue until the arrival of the railroad.

The numerical growth of sawmills in early Michigan indicates the lack of barriers to entry into the industry. Although there were a few large and highly capitalized firms, the vast majority of the territory's mills were crude, water-powered affairs of small capacity. Consequently, persons of modest financial resources could establish mills which could then generate their own capital.[17] A small single-saw mill with a daily capacity of 1,000 to 2,000 board feet required an investment of less than $1,000.[18] Since millsites, timber, and labor were plentiful and inexpensive, equipment consituted the major capital expense. Apparently equipment had to be brought from outside the territory until the Detroit Iron Company began manufacturing sawmill machinery in 1831.[19]

The requirements for working capital were small. Raw materials and labor accounted for the major operating expenses. During the territorial years the price per log delivered at the mill averaged around fifty cents. At an estimated average of 200 board feet per log, a mill with a daily capacity of 1,000 to 2,000 feet would need only five to ten logs a day.[20] Sawmills, especially the early ones, required but a small labor force. Often only the owner and one of his children or a relative could run the operation. Laborers, if needed, could be recruited from the local agricultural community, at the prevailing wage of fifty cents a day.[21]

To the would-be millman, ease of entry meant more than just the low cost of entry. The level of sawmill technology, unlike that of the iron industry, for example, was sufficiently simple and straightforward to be easily mastered. A sawyer could produce an acceptable product after a brief learning period. Experience with such common activities as land clearing and farming provided sufficient background and skills.

It is easier to discuss entry into sawmilling than it is to assess its profitability, especially in the face of fluctuating demand and frequent changes in ownership. Successful operation depended upon the selection of a site with sufficient water power, access to raw materials, and a developing local market. One traveler from New York in the mid-1830s concluded that the strong demand for lumber assured manufacturers an annual profit of 300 percent to 400 percent, but another observer asserted that the absence of a steady demand made the raising of livestock a less risky venture.[22] Such contemporary reports contradicted each other, but they illustrated that demand constituted the most important, if least certain, element for success.

Many manufacturing failures apparently stemmed from the inability of owners to construct mills with capacities adjusted to local needs. The Grand Haven Company, perhaps the largest and most ambitious operation begun on the western slope of Michigan during the territorial period, is one such example. The Rev. William H. Ferry, his brother-in-law, Nathan H. White, from Detroit, and Rix Robinson, western Michigan agent of the American Fur Company, formed the Grand Haven Company in 1833 for the purpose of buying lands, erecting mills, selling lumber, and developing a town. With Ferry as resident manager, the partners invested $100,000 in three mills and a large steam vessel. The ship was intended to transport lumber and passengers between western Michigan and Chicago, but its capacity, as well as that of the mills, far exceeded current demand. After six years of a precarious existence, the company was disbanded in 1840.[23] Sometimes unsuccessful mills ran on a part-time basis before being abandoned. In the mid-1830s Flint, Michigan, could boast of three mills, but when the mills ran at capacity, their product glutted the limited market, nearly causing all three firms to suspend operations.[24]

When manufacturers located their mills where strong local demand existed or developed, milling proved profitable. In the 1820s the number of settlers around Selby in Macomb County allowed Ira Preston to run his mill at full capacity, while the mill of Gardner and Ephriam Williams in Saginaw could not meet local demand even when operated at full production.[25]

Although the absence of company records makes it impossible to document numerically the rate of return of early sawmills, fragmentary information on lumber confirms its value at different times and places. Since lumber was a vital product on the frontier of settlement, it came to be an important barter item when money was in short supply. One pioneer recalled chopping timber for one week as payment for 700 feet of lumber in 1826.[26] Through the early 1830s Ira Preston of Mt. Clemens accepted goods and grain in lieu of cash for his lumber, while the Ann Arbor firm of Maynard and Guiteau offered to trade goods for lumber at their store in 1833.[27]

The price of lumber depended upon demand. Boards that had been selling for as low as $2.50 per thousand board feet [M] at the Williamses' mill in 1834 sold two years later for $12, an increase of nearly 500 percent. Prices appear to have ranged between $6 and $12 during the mid-1830s, depending on time, place, and grade, with common lumber averaging around $9.[28] Lack of information on transportation costs makes it difficult to assess the profitability of the earliest sales in Chicago, the first large out-of-state market, but the price received clearly indicates a good rate of return. In 1834, for example, a load of lumber from Michigan sold for $28 per M; by 1836 increased demand raised the price of a cargo to a reported high of $50 per M.[29]

Early Michigan mills often did custom work in addition to processing their own logs. Farmers hauled logs from their woodlots to the mill for sawing into boards. Although this function diminished and then ceased as the industry became more commercialized after the period of settlement, the processing of small orders of lumber for individuals was for a time very important to both the sawyer and the farmer.[30]

Sawmills of early nineteenth-century Michigan differed little from their New England counterparts of colonial days in either size or equipment. The sawpit was the first type of mill to appear on the frontier. Albert Miller, an early lumberman of the Saginaw Valley, left reminiscences of one such operation that he conducted with Francis Lull in the early 1830s. After adzing the sides, the two men rolled or hoisted a log over the pit. Then, one in the pit and one on top, they manually whipsawed the log into planks of the desired thickness (illustration 1). Cutting took place only on the downward stroke, while sawdust was expelled when the saw was pushed upward. It was a difficult, slow, and taxing job.[31]

The application of waterpower to sawmilling meant a great savings of both time and labor, which was especially important where raw materials were more abundant than labor. Victor Clark estimates that a waterpowered mill could produce the same amount of boards in a given time as twenty hand sawyers. Michigan's first waterpowered mills were of the sash or gate saw variety. Set within a frame, the saw was either pulled downward by a crank attached to the waterwheel and upward by a large elastic pole, or regulated by a weighted flywheel (illustration 2). As in the sawpit, cutting took place only on the downward stroke. Usually the log was carried, hoisted, or rolled onto a sliding wooden track known as the carriage and clamped into place by an iron arm called a "dog." The sawyer used a primitive gearing mechanism to align the log on the carriage and then set desired thickness (illustration 3). The saw's motion controlled the advance of the carriage. To prevent the saw from damage by contact with the metal dog, the sawyer had to reverse the movement of the carriage before the saw cut the complete length of the board. This was a slow process, so slow that one old-time sawyer claimed that he could "take a good nap while his saw went through the cut."[32] On the average, the sash mill could produce 1,000 feet a day, although by the 1830s some mills boasted of a 100 percent daily increase in production, to 2,000 feet.[33]

While increasing the speed of production, technological improvements in milling equipment also made a better finished product. Gang saws appeared in some Michigan mills by the early 1830s. In gang mills, one frame contained two or more sash saws set at the desired board thickness (illustration 4). Gang saws saved time by reducing the number of carriage runs needed to turn a log into boards.[34] The muley saw followed the sash and the gang saws. The muley saw was first used in America in the late eighteenth century, but the earliest reference found to its use in Michigan was in 1825.[35] A muley differed from a sash saw in that it was attached to steel rods rather than set in a frame, but both operated with an up-and-down motion. In the case of the muley saw, the reduction in weight increased sawing speed and output to up to 6,000 feet per day, but its greater kerf, or slit made in cutting increased the amount of waste.[36]

Experiments with steam-powered sawmills, which could expand production up to 50 percent, came late in the territorial period. According to a survey published by the federal government in 1839, Benjamin Wheelock installed Michigan's first steam engine in his mill in present-day Ottawa County in 1825. By 1837 there were twenty-two steam sawmills in the state. Of these, all but seven were located in Ottawa, Saginaw, St Clair, and

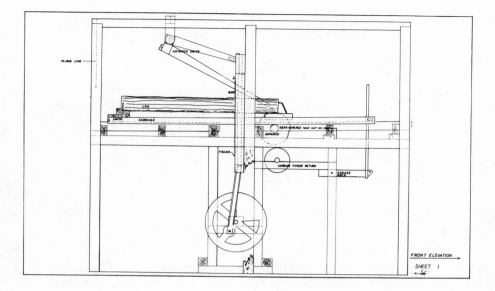

PLUMB LINE

ADVANCE DRIVE

SAW

LOG

CARRIAGE

GEAR ADVANCE rack not on m

ADVANCE

FRAME

CARRIAGE POWER RETURN

ENGAGE DRUM

FRONT ELEVATION

SHEET 1

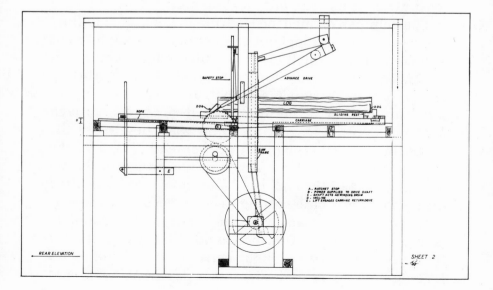

SAFETY STOP

ADVANCE DRIVE

ROPE

DOG

LOG

DOG

CARRIAGE

SLIDING REST

SAW FRAME

E

A - RATCHET STOP
B - POWER SUPPLIED TO DRIVE SHAFT
C - SHAFT ACTS AS WINDING DRUM
D - INCLINE
E - LIFT ENGAGES CARRIAGE RETURN DRIVE

REAR ELEVATION

SHEET 2

Wayne counties, leaders in lumber production. Little
was known about steam mills at the time, and these ventures appear to have been something less than successful
experiments by local mechanics and blacksmiths, who
added steam power to a sash mill. At least two of the
mills had engines taken from sunken steamboats and
adapted to milling. In addition to the millmen's lack of
technical expertise, the high cost of steam-powered sawmills slowed their adoption. Until the formation of the
Detroit Iron Company in 1831, all engines and boilers
had to be imported from the East.[37]

According to several reports, labor as well as machinery for Michigan's sawmills was imported, particularly
through the 1820s, and there is some evidence that a
shortage of labor in territorial Michigan did exist. Indeed, the traveler and author Charles Hoffman deemed
the demand for laborers in 1833 "excessive."[38] The very
scanty lumbering records available, however, do not indicate that the embryonic industry experienced great labor shortages. On the contrary, it appears that loggers
and millmen found an adequate pool of labor among the
local farming families and new immigrants.[39]

The number of men needed for logging and milling
remained small throughout the period. A work force of
two could run a small gate or muley mill; logging was
conducted by individuals or very small crews.[40] Work in
the lumber industry was seasonal. In the winter, it centered on logging, while mills ran from spring through
autumn, depending, of course, on water levels. By the
1850s there were many men who worked full time in the
lumber industry, logging in winter and in a mill during
the summer, but through the 1830s most labor was hired
on a short-term basis during peak periods. Winter logging provided farmers with an opportunity to supplement their incomes. A farmer could sell logs to a mill for
50 cents apiece, or he might earn up to $1 a day on a
logging crew. A rate of 50 cents a day, with room and

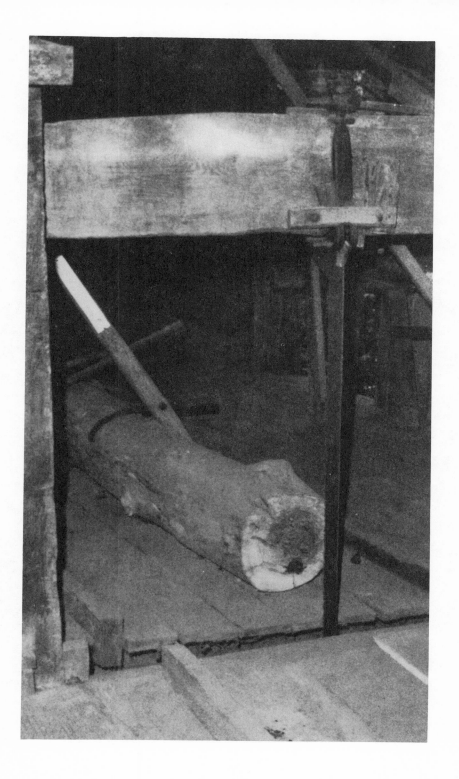

Virginian Saw-Mill (1650).

board provided, was probably the most common wage. Sawyers earned between $14 and $20 a month, which might include room and board. Especially in this early period, owners of mills in isolated areas had to provide boarding houses or dwellings for their men.[41]

Ownership and leadership in the lumber industry rested in the hands of men of limited technical experience and capital. Biographical data for fifty-one Michigan lumber entrepreneurs compiled from county histories, newspapers, trade journals, and secondary sources, although incomplete, allow us to make generalizations about Michigan's early mill owners. As Table 1 shows, only two of the men were foreign-born. Twenty-two, or just over half, came from the New England states, while fourteen came from the mid-Atlantic states, eleven of them from New York.

TABLE 1
Birthplace of Lumbermen in Michigan Lumber Industry

Massachusetts	9	New York	11	Virginia	2	Ireland	1
Connecticut	6	Pennsylvania	3	Ohio	1	Scotland	1
Vermont	4			Michigan	1		
New Hampshire	2						
Maine	1						

The early entrepreneurs came from diverse occupational backgrounds (see Table 2). While only 15 percent had previous experience in lumbering, nearly half the group had mercantile or agricultural experience. The

TABLE 2
Previous Occupational Experience

Mercantile	17	Teaching	2
Farming	6	Real Estate	2
Milling	5	Millwright	1
Lumbering	3	Minister	1
Mill Laboring	3	Clerk	1
Banking	3	Journalism	1
Transportation	2	Legal	1
Military	2	No Information	2
Medical	2		

early lumber manufacturer conducted his business as either a partnership or proprietorship, often in conjunction with other businesses, particularly mercantile, milling, or real estate ventures (see Tables 3 and 4).[42]

TABLE 3
Ownership Arrangement

Partnership	27
Proprietorship	19
Corporation	3
Lease	2
No Information	7

TABLE 4
Additional Business Interests of Michigan Lumbermen Before 1837

None	14
Real Estate	11
Milling	8
Mercantile	6
Banking	3
Farming	3
Unspecified	3
Medical	1
Shipping	1
No information	10

The background and career of Zephaniah Bunce provide a good example of a typical early Michigan millman. Born in Connecticut in 1787, Bunce was a small merchant in New York before going to Michigan in 1817. After a year as a clothing merchant in Detroit, he purchased land and erected a mill in the St. Clair region, which he ran for a decade. After a brief return to mercantile life he operated sawmills on contract until 1846 when he built a second mill.[43]

Through the 1830s Michigan's sawmills remained small primary processing industries with relatively simple distribution patterns. Rather than relying on commercial intermediaries, the manufacturer personally carried on the marketing function. The vast majority of the millmen in territorial Michigan ran small frontier mills which sold or graded lumber directly at the mill. The small number of other manufacturers, who were representative of a nascent commercial industry, had somewhat more complex distribution arrangements. Since many manufacturers were also merchants, they could sell lumber at their stores as well as at their mills. For example, The Black River Steam Mill Company, whose records are the best source for this time, sold in small quantity at the St. Clair mill, but the larger volume of its sales was through its Detroit store. This distribution arrangement prevailed on Michigan's eastern shore, where Detroit merchants often founded or purchased mills in the St. Clair area to meet an existing demand.[44]

The distribution pattern differed for the western shore of the lower peninsula. Here commercial intermediaries played a role from the beginning. Although the earliest mills, like those in eastern Michigan, were erected to meet local needs, excess capacity led manufacturers to seek additional markets. At this time, Chicago's marked growth made that city an increasingly avaricious consumer of wood. The sawmill operator of western Michigan either sold his stock at the mill or at the lake shore to an intermediary, or he personally transported it to Chicago. In 1835 Nathaniel J. Brown took one of the earliest shipments of pine lumber to Chicago from his mill in Kent County by schooner. Upon docking he discovered that the dealers of the city opposed sales of anything other than whitewood, but he eventually was allowed to purchase a selling permit. Later, the marketing of pine in Chicago became commonplace.[45]

As long as manufacturers sold their product locally there were few difficulties, but as the marketing area expanded so too did costs and problems. Since lumber is a heavy product in relation to its value, transportation costs represent a large part of the selling price. The easiest and least expensive way to transport lumber was by

water, and, fortunately, Michigan's river system provided maximum assistance. In those few areas, such as
Flint, where natural water transportation routes to distant markets or a distribution center were unavailable,
sawmilling faltered to the verge of failure. The most
common means of water transportation was rafting, but
this method presented problems. In addition to the
threat of loss through grounding, sinking, or theft, the
water itself soiled, bruised and split the boards. It was
for this reason that early sawmills produced only rough
lumber; there was no advantage to finishing and seasoning the wood. At times a load would arrive at its destination so damaged that it could be sold only at the
cheapest prices.[46]

A transportation pattern linking the mills with newly
settled towns and cities soon developed, and all along the
rivers the sight of passing lumber rafts became common.
From Detroit in 1833, F. P. Browning, drawing upon his
knowledge of the rafting of lumber on Lake Champlain,
instructed his assistant in transporting lumber down the
Black River and across Lake St. Clair. To cut costs, the
wood was to be sorted before rather than after shipment.[47] Usually the lumber was placed in cribs of timber
six to ten feet deep and then rafted and floated to its
destination. Lumber destined for Chicago had to be
rafted to the lake shore and then transferred to schooners. By the mid-1830s the Chicago market was considered sufficiently large to warrant construction of several
special lumber-carrying schooners.

Sawmills had come with the white man as he claimed
and conquered a new frontier. As population grew, so too
did the number of mills. By the end of the territorial
period, a growing demand from within and outside the
state assured continual development of the lumber industry and offered hopes of a bright future to those who
wished to transform the product of the forest into building supplies for man.

CHAPTER 4

Commercial Lumbering of the Michigan Forests: Regional Beginnings, 1837–1855

When Michigan entered the Union in 1837, three-quarters of the state remained an untouched, unspoiled primeval wilderness. Within a generation, the silence of the forest had given way to the steady sound of axe and saw as a number of men, armed with tools, machines, and seemingly boundless energy, took the wooded areas of Michigan swiftly, as a prize of conquest. Pursuing a "cut and run" policy, the lumbermen denuded the lower peninsula of the Wolverine state as deforestation outran settlement.

Unless an industry is based on a specific scientific or technological breakthrough, establishing its beginning is more difficult than narrating its growth. Yet the history of an industry remains incomplete without some grounding in time, however qualified and arbitrary. In Michigan large commercial sawmills did not supplant small service-oriented mills at any particular date; rather both types coexisted throughout the nineteenth century. But a case can be made for dating the rise of a large-scale lumber industry in the state from 1837, for by that date the elements of demand, supply, and capacity essential for integrated commercial development were present. By

1855 the industry's basic pattern and outline had been firmly established.[1]

Spurred initially by the feverish land race of the mid-1830s, Michigan's population increased rapidly during the remainder of the nineteenth century. In 1850 the number of people in the state stood at just under 400,000. Table 5 summarizes both the state's growth in

TABLE 5
Early Population Growth in Michigan

Date	Population	Percent Increase	Number of Organized Counties
1830	27,378	—	12
1840	212,267	675	33
1850	395,523	86	43

Sources: U.S., 22d Cong., 1 sess., House of Representative Doc. no. 269, *Abstract of the Returns of the Fifth Census*, 42; U.S., *Sixth Census or Enumeration of the Inhabitants of the United States as Corrected at the Department of State, in 1840* (Washington, 1841), 436–49; U.S., *The Seventh Census of the United States: 1850* (Washington, 1853), 882–83.

population and its geographic spread. Between 1830 and 1850 the number of organized counties increased from twelve to forty-three. By the latter date, the line of settlement extended from west to east across the lower peninsula at roughly the northern boundary of present-day

TABLE 6
Population and Sawmills in Michigan's
Commercial Lumbering Counties in 1850

County	Population	Sawmills
Wayne	42,756	31
Genesee	12,031	5
Kent	12,016	18
St. Clair	10,420	32
Lapeer	7,029	13
Ottawa	5,587	30
Allegan	5,125	22
Michilimackinac	3,598	15
Huron, Sanilac, Tuscola	2,613	13
Saginaw	2,609	8
Montcalm	891	6

Sources: *The Seventh Census of the United States: 1850*, 82–83; Manuscript Census for the State of Michigan, 1850.

Ottawa, Kent, Ionia, Clinton, Shiawassee, Genesee, Lapeer, and St. Clair counties (see map 3).[2]

It was at least in part to meet increasing intrastate
demand that the number of sawmills in Michigan expanded from 433 in 1837 to 922 in 1854.[3] Mills in the
pine-forested portion of the state, defined for our purposes as the area of commercial lumbering, increased 68
percent over the decade 1840–50, from 115 to 193, and
by another 68 percent in the subsequent four years to
315 (see Table 7). This is undoubtedly a low estimate,
since the figure for 1840 is probably inflated by the in-
clusion of all types of timber processors, while the state's
census for 1854 for some reason did not include the mills
of the Saginaw and northeastern regions.

Comparison in the location and size of mills provide a
better measure of a developing lumber industry than do
mere statistics on number. Unlike the small service mills
so characteristic of the earlier territorial period, sawmills
constructed after 1837 increasingly preceded the movement of settlers into the heavily pine-forested sections of
the state. From a few firms located in the southeastern
and southwestern corners of the state, lumber manufacturing spread over the lower peninsula according to the
industry's own requirements. Map 4 indicates the northern line of settlement in 1850 and the southern limit of
white pine growth. Of the eleven organized counties that
contained extensive pine forests and/or manufacturing
on a commercial scale, more than half, including Ottawa, Huron, Sanilac, Tuscola, Michilimackinac, Montcalm, and Saginaw, were located at least partly beyond
the line of settlement.

Table 6 lists population and number of sawmills in
Michigan's commercial lumbering counties in 1850.
Clearly, mills in those counties performed more than a
service function for the local area; they were frontier
manufacturing enterprises important in the state's economic development. Thirteen mills operated in the

Map 3

Organized counties in the lower peninsula in 1852

Map 4

Organized counties in the lower peninsula in 1860

Thumb counties, for instance, which had a population of only 2,613 people, while northernmost Michilimackinac had a population of just over 3,500 and fifteen mills. Allegan, with scarcely more than 5,000 people, had twenty-two sawmills. In Ottawa County the ratio of mills to people was even more indicative of a market-oriented industry: thirty sawmills in a population that hovered around 5,500.

Increases in capital investment, labor force, and amount or value of product, provide additional measures of Michigan's developing lumber industry. For the early years of the industry, federal and state census returns constitute the only sources for such information, but such data must be used with some caution. Not only are the records frustratingly incomplete, but the material that does exist is often incorrect.[4] With these caveats, however, the historian of the lumber industry can use the early censuses of manufacture as a driver uses road signs to keep moving safely in the right direction. Michigan's lumber industry did not develop at an even pace in the years after statehood. The Panic of 1837 had a prolonged retarding effect that lasted until the middle of the next decade. A reading of county histories and personal reminiscences suggests that a strong, steady expansion of the industry began about 1845 and accelerated after 1850. Federal and state census materials are available for the years 1840, 1850, and 1854, and the data compiled from them have been summarized in Table 7. Despite their incompleteness, which makes full comparisons impossible, the records clearly indicate substantial growth.

The number of mills in the lumber counties jumped from 115 in 1840 to 193 in 1850 and to 315 by 1854, an increase of nearly 175 percent in fourteen years. The size of the labor force also increased. There is no information available for 1840, but between 1850 and 1854 the number employed in lumber manufacturing expanded from just over 1,500 to about 2,700, allowing for errors in the

TABLE 7
Lumber Manufacturing for Selected Counties, 1840-1854

	Number of Mills			Average Capital Investment			Labor			Value of Product			Feet Produced, M		
	1840	1850	1854	1840	1850	1854	1840	1850	1854	1840	1850	1854	1840	1850	1854
Allegan	15	22	29	527	2,909	—	—	64	140	—	76,700	—	—	—	—
Genesee	10	5	26	1,350	4,140	—	—	89	122	—	33,225	—	—	5,200	12,095[e]
Huron															
Tuscola	—	13	22	—	5,631	—	—	76	219[d]	—	62,375	—	—	7,855	17,180
Sanilac															
Kent	18	18	36	1,167	2,103	—	—	72.5	181	15,000	55,475	—	—	10,825	13,650[e]
Lapeer	14	13	32	1,250	2,715	—	—	46	143	13,327	51,300	—	—	5,400	15,105
Michilimackinac[a]	—	15	19	—	9,531	—	—	218	222	—	109,550	—	—	20,250	20,171
Montcalm	—	6	13	—	4,500	—	—	80	95	—	26,000	—	—	5,101	7,000
Ottawa[c]	12	30	47	1,608	6,471	—	—	442	768	9,497	371,030	—	—	61,560	64,990
Saginaw[b]	6	8	2	3,000	12,950	—	—	95	8	—	64,050	—	—	6,975	1,500
St. Clair	16	32	39	1,312	7,254	—	—	335	445	27,900	301,620	—	—	34,263	46,320
Wayne	24	31	55	728	11,751	—	—	268	442	22,614	367,675	—	—	38,871	40,323[e]
Totals	115	193	315					1,785.5	2,785					196,300	241,439

Notes:
  a – The 1850 figure for Michilimackinac County includes the mills of the 21 unorganized counties of the lower peninsula, as well as a few mills of the Mackinac area. The figure for 1854 is the total of mills for Grand Traverse and Emmet Counties; there are no returns for the unorganized Northeastern areas.

  b – The 1854 figures for Saginaw County are incomplete.

  c – Ottawa County includes present day Ottawa, Muskegon, Newaygo, Oceana and Mason counties.

  d – This figure is too high—it should read 119.

  e – Based on incomplete returns.

Sources: *Compendium of the Inhabitants and Statistics of the United States*, Washington, 1841; Manuscript Census for the State of Michigan, 1850; *Census and Statistics of the State of Michigan, May 1854*, Lansing 1854.

census reports for Genesee County in 1850 and the
Thumb counties in 1854. By the latter date, there were
nine workers per mill, on average, which indicates a
commercial level of manufacturing.

Capital investment figures are another, perhaps more
useful, measure of growth. The state census in 1854 did
not provide information on capitalization, but the figures for 1840 and 1850 are clear. In Kent County, for
instance, the average capital investment in a sawmill almost doubled over the decade from $1,167 to $2,103.
The increases were greatest for Ottawa, Saginaw, St.
Clair, and Wayne counties, the leaders in the early years
of the industry. The level of capitalization by 1850 demonstrates the growing scale of manufacturing, which, in
turn, reflects increases in the capacity of mills, improvements in machinery, and specialization of labor. Mill
output showed a corresponding growth, from just under
200,000,000 feet in 1850 to over 240,000,000 feet in
1854. The increase would be significantly greater if the
returns for Genesee, Kent, Michilimackinac, Saginaw,
and Wayne counties were complete for 1854. By 1850
Michigan stood fifth among the states in the production
of lumber.[5]

As if feeding on itself, lumbering in Michigan moved
both to the north and into the interior with an ever-
increasing acceleration. A study of this industry, then, in
part must be a study in regional movement. The direction of the lumbering frontier was geographically determined by the lower peninsula's major drainage basins,
harbors, and shoreline. By 1855 the industry had spread
slowly up both coasts and almost tentatively into some
interior locations in a patchwork-quilt fashion. In the
formative years of commercial development, lumbering
penetrated into the St. Clair, Thumb, and Grand Traverse regions and the Saginaw, Thunder Bay, Black,
Grand, Muskegon, Pere Marquette, and Manistee river
basins.[6] The assaulting lumbermen found each region a

discrete entity that demanded new techniques and adaptations to the basic process of lumbering.

The lumbering activity of a region can be measured not only by the number and size of its mills but also by the amount of logging that is carried on there. As the two functions of logging and manufacturing became increasingly separated in early Michigan, specialization by location generally occurred. Eventually regions were divided into supply or logging areas and manufacturing or milling areas. For the lumberman the task was to cut logs at one point and market lumber at another, in what has been termed "the pipeline theory of production." The location of a mill played a leading role in the success of an enterprise, and the most important factor affecting sawmill placement was transportation. Mills could be, and were, constructed anywhere along the pipeline of water. For example, logs from the Black River might be manufactured along the river, at its mouth, or at a consuming point such as Toledo, Ohio, on Lake Erie. Interior counties long remained primarily log suppliers and did not become leading manufacturers of lumber. It was more economical to run logs to the larger, more efficient mills located near harbors for processing and shipment than it would have been to process them at the point of supply. Until the 1870s and the coming of the railroad, perhaps 90 percent of the sawmills in Michigan were located at or near the mouths of navigable streams.[7]

As the only important commercial lumber center outside the pine area, Detroit faced special problems. Always an important consumer of lumber, the city also became an early center for its distribution, servicing both a large hinterland and markets to the East. Initially merchants imported boards from the sawmills of St. Clair County, but they encountered difficulties with the separation of manufacturing and marketing. First there was the problem of securing an adequate supply. Some merchants, including James Abbott, solved this difficulty by purchasing a distant sawmill. But even if a merchant owned such a mill, the problem of coordination remained. Most importantly, the transportation of large quantities of lumber by raft across Lake St. Clair proved unsatisfactory, for the trip damaged the wood and reduced the merchant's profit. By the late 1830s Detroit's businessmen responded to a growing demand for lumber by establishing large-scale sawmills in the city. This strategy proved successful, and by 1848 sawmilling was one of Detroit's manufacturing activities.[8]

Detroit's mills ranked among the state's largest and most technologically advanced. Its manufacturers relied almost exclusively on steam power to run mills that contained multiple saws. According to one business magazine, the city's five steam mills in 1849 employed ninety men to produce 7,500,000 feet of lumber valued at $80,000. Data from the 1850 census of manufactures, however, indicate that these earlier figures are much too low. In 1850 the number of mills stood at nine and the number employed at 187. Total production exceeded 24,000,000 feet and was valued at $269,148. Detroit at mid-century was the largest lumber manufacturing center in Michigan,[9] containing five of the eleven mills in the state with minimum capital investments of $20,000.

Less than fifty miles north of Detroit rose the giant conifers of the St. Clair region. Settlers and lumbermen first tapped this area in the eighteenth century, and commercial-scale lumbering was firmly established there by 1837. Manufacturing centers grew up along the St. Clair River at Algonac, Marine City, St. Clair, and Port Huron. Logs from the Pine River supplied the village of St. Clair and below, while the raw materials for Port Huron's mills came down the Black River. In addition to Detroit, a consistent consumer of St. Clair logs and lumber, the region's product found markets in both the East and West during the 1840s. Over the next decade the percentage of pine from St. Clair County going westward decreased as markets in Ohio and the East increased.[10]

The commercial lumber industry in the St. Clair region expanded rapidly during the formative period. Sawmills increased both in number and size, from the early water-driven mills which were capable of producing considerably less than a million feet a year to steam-powered mills with a capacity of 2,500,000 feet of lumber annually. Indeed, the rate of growth prompted one local newspaper in 1848 to predict a swift end to the region's pine resources.[11] Between 1840 and 1850 the number of mills doubled from sixteen to thirty-two, while capacity per mill was enlarged by an increase in the number of saws per mill and the conversion of many mills to steam power.[12] Table 8 illustrates the dynamics of manufacturing growth in this region during an important period of expansion.

TABLE 8
Lumbering Manufacturing in St. Clair County to 1854

	1847	1850	1854
Total Mills	27	32	39
Steam Mills	7	11	16
Number of Saws	62	125	—
Annual Production (M)	21,060	34,263	46,320

Source: *Port Huron Observer*, Jan. 1, 1848; Manuscript Census for the State of Michigan, 1850; *Census and Statistics of the State of Michigan*, May 1854.

There was less manufacturing through the mid-1850s north of Port Huron in what is known as the "Thumb Region" than there was south of that point. The Thumb area, which includes present-day Sanilac, Huron, and Tuscola counties, is partially surrounded by the waters of Lake Huron and Saginaw Bay, but unlike the other pine-forested areas of Michigan, it lacks a network of streams, rivers, and harbors conducive to the location of large-scale commercial manufacturing. The feeder systems that do exist are tributaries of the Cass and Black rivers, whose outlets are at Saginaw in Saginaw County and

Port Huron in St. Clair County.[13] Lumbering enclaves did appear along the coast of Lake Huron from Worth to Port Austin in Sanilac and Huron counties, but these were small settlements, isolated from each other and without scheduled steamboat service to connect them with the outside world. Consequently, manufacturing developed slowly and remained on a small scale compared to other regions. By 1854 the sixteen small coastal mills in the Thumb Region produced only 13,330,000 feet.[14]

If geography determined that the Thumb counties would be primarily a logging rather than a manufacturing region, it further influenced its slow development as a logging area, for its forests remained relatively untouched as long as more accessible timber was available. Only when the timber was cleared close to the manufacturing centers in the 1850s did the logging frontier push swiftly into the Thumb.

West of St. Clair County, the Thread and Flint rivers flow through the mixed forests of Lapeer and Genesee counties before emptying into the Saginaw River some ten miles south of Saginaw. Thus, these two interior counties had the transportation network and motive power necessary for lumber manufacturing, and the industry became important to both counties. They served an extended market to the south, but their scale of operations remained small compared to that of Michigan's other lumbering counties. Mills appeared first in Lapeer County in the early 1830s, and by 1840 fourteen mills were scattered throughout the county. Of the thirteen mills in operation in 1850, all but two were capitalized at $2,500 or less, and aggregate production totaled only 5,400,000 feet. Strong industrial growth, however, began in the early 1850s. In 1854 thirty-two mills turned out 15,105,000 feet, almost triple the amount produced four years earlier.[15]

Unlike the dispersed pattern of mill locations in Lapeer County, a single manufacturing center, Flint, dominated Genesee County. After the construction of two mills in Flint in the late 1830s, business languished throughout the next decade. According to the 1850 census, Flint still had only two mills, although they produced well over half of the county's 5,200,000 feet of lumber. At that point, industrial development quickened just as it did in Lapeer. By 1854 the number of mills in Flint had increased to five, with a total capacity of 16,800,000 feet. But development of the industry brought the ruinous problem of excess capacity and overproduction. In 1854, for example, Flint's mills ran at less than half capacity. Transportation difficulties initially limited the range of markets to the south. In the 1840s individual lumbermen began to clear the river between Flint and Saginaw, but it was not until the mid-1860s and the coming of the railroad that the city had easy access to eastern and western markets.[16]

The premier lumber region of the eastern slope was Saginaw. Its pine lumber gained a national reputation for both quality of wood and of manufacture. A wide-reaching and complex network of streams and rivers opened 6,000 square miles of pine forests to the lumbermen of the region. Four main rivers, the Cass, the Flint, the Shiawassee, and the Tittabawassee flow into the Saginaw, which, in turn, empties into Saginaw Bay. In terms of political units, this river system touched at least sixteen counties. Manufacturing locations lay scattered along the rivers, but the natural and most important centers for manufacturing and distribution clustered along the Saginaw River at East Saginaw, Saginaw City, Bay City, and West Bay City.

The earliest development of the Saginaw area provided no clue to the spectacular growth that was to come. Some observers wondered why Gardner and Ephraim Williams, former agents of a fur trading company, bothered to build the first sawmill there in 1832 for a miniscule local market. Affluent Eastern speculators accounted for the greatest portion of early land purchases. Of these buyers, Norman Little of New York was the most important, for he had a great vision of the area's future. But he failed in his first attempt in 1836 to promote a region whose natural resources, he felt, guaranteed its success. Mackie, Oakley and Jennison, commission merchants of New York City, obviously agreed with Little about the potential of the area, for in the same year they built a mill and houses in an unsuccessful town promotion scheme. These early promoters were not lumbermen, and their plans were more grandiose than merely establishing a one-industry center.[17]

Left to itself after the Panic of 1837, the village of Saginaw and its hinterland languished. Well into the 1840s the half dozen small sawmills of the area that survived easily handled the local demand. Little lumber went beyond the local market. One county historian specifically dates the birth of Saginaw's commercial lumber industry from the first shipment of boards to the East in 1847. While such a categorical statement may be oversimplified, the nature of Saginaw's lumber industry did change markedly in the second half of the 1840s. The number and capacity of mills increased as market expanded. Men such as Curtis Emerson of Vermont and Detroit and Daniel Johnson of New York State moved into the Saginaw area to exploit the timber resources, building mills capable of large-scale production. In 1846, Emerson and Charles Grant bought the old Mackie, Oakley and Jennison mill for $6,000 and spent another $10,000 expanding its capacity to 3,000,000 board feet a year. The steam-powered mill contained three upright, one edger, and one butter saw. The *Detroit Free Press* predicted in 1849 that the Saginaw mills would cut 12,000,000 to 15,000,000 feet of lumber that year. Saginaw pine became prized cargoes in Chicago, Toledo, Cleveland, and even Albany. By 1851, for example, the Chicago lumberyard of Avery and Williams limited their stock to Saginaw lumber.[18]

Although the production of its eight mills in 1850 fell short by over half of the *Detroit Free Press'* brashly confident calculations of 1849, the lumber industry of the Saginaw Valley was just beginning to come into its own. According to production figures of the state's eleven lumber manufacturing counties in 1850, Saginaw ranked a poor seventh. This, however, gives only a fraction of the story. A more complete picture can be drawn from considering capital invested per mill. Here the Saginaw Valley ranked first, with an average investment of $12,950.[19] Unlike earlier developed areas such as St. Clair, Saginaw in 1850 was like a youngster poised at the brink of growth.

In the next half-decade Saginaw became a major center of Michigan's lumber industry. In 1854 Anson Rudd, a new settler at Saginaw, wrote to a friend in Pennsylvania about the great log rafts on the river, the large piles of lumber on the wharfs, and the many mills. According to his calculation, there were forty-one steam mills, operating two shifts, along the last seventeen miles of the Saginaw River. Between 1850 and 1855 the number of sawmills in the Saginaw Valley increased roughly 750 percent from eight to approximately sixty, while production expanded from slightly less than 7,000,000 feet to some 100,000,000 feet of lumber. The number of men working in the mills jumped from under 100 in 1850 to 843 in 1855. While some firms still employed only a few men to turn out under a million feet, the large-scale commercial mills usually hired work forces of between ten and thirty men and produced a correspondingly larger amount of lumber. The number of sawmills increased everywhere in the valley, but geography favored a more rapid growth of the lower Saginaw, from

Saginaw City to Bay City. Of the tributaries, lumbering developed earliest along the Cass River. By 1855 logs and lumber from the Cass' seven mills reached Saginaw in sizable quantity.[20]

Although some of the finest pine forests in Michigan were in the northern half of the lower peninsula, the area lay well beyond the lumbering frontier of the early 1850s. With a population of less than 4,000, this area had not yet been organized into counties. In time the major rivers of the northeastern region, the area north of Saginaw Bay to the Straits of Mackinac and between Lake Huron and the spine of the state, would each support major logging and manufacturing activities, but by 1855 only the barest beginnings had been made. The earliest forays into lumbering in the northeast were confined to the lower reaches of the Rifle, Au Gres, Au Sauble, Thunder Bay, and Cheboygan rivers. The first sawmill on the northern shore of Saginaw Bay was probably the one located at the mouth of the Pine River, begun in 1835. A case of premature enterprise, it had failed by 1840. Development of the area north to Oscoda dates from John Phillips's construction of a steam sawmill at the mouth of the Pine River in 1855.

Although Alpena at the mouth of the Thunder Bay River was to become the largest center of the Thunder Bay area, the two earliest lumbering experiments were conducted a dozen miles to the south at the mouth of the Devil River. Erected in 1844, the first mill failed after cutting less than a half-million feet. The second attempt to establish a sawmill on the site, sometime around 1850, clearly succeeded, for by 1852 two vessels were needed to carry the mill's lumber to market, primarily Cleveland. Nevertheless, the capacity of the small water-powered mill probably did not exceed 500,000 feet a year. Following the lead of the St. Mary's Falls Ship Canal Company, lumbermen from St. Clair and also from Canada began locating lands around Alpena about 1853. Their sawmills mark the beginnings of the lumber industry at Thunder Bay. Soon Alpena was the center for many flourishing and expanding lumbering operations. Archibald & Murray moved into the area about 1855 and began logging at least a million feet of logs annually, a large operation.[21]

Settlement began in Cheboygan County, in the northernmost tier of Michigan's lower peninsula, in 1840, but until well into the 1850s the area remained isolated, connected with the outside world only by irregular steamship service. By 1855 the population did not exceed 300. Lumbering was a primary activity of the area, but the scale of operations remained small into the 1860s. As early as 1844 the county's second settlers, A. and R. McLeod, came for the purpose of lumbering. Considering the location that they chose for their endeavor, the size of their operations was large. Their mill, valued at $14,000 in 1850, contained by that date, if not earlier, two upright saws and was producing some 1,500,000 feet annually. The McLeods employed a labor force of thirty. Little is known about the county's second mill, except that it was steam-powered and erected in 1847. From the date of their construction, the two mills in Cheboygan County produced 13,000,000 feet of lumber. Clearly they were the precursors of the "monster" mills of the next decade.[22]

Lumbering spread geographically up the western shore of Michigan in the same manner, although at a somewhat faster rate, as it did along the eastern coast. The steady exporting of lumber, particularly whitewood, from southwestern Michigan to Chicago began quite early, and by the early 1840s fair-sized manufacturing and distributing centers developed at New Buffalo and St. Joseph in Berrien County on the shore of Lake Michigan to handle this business. But the most important lumber area south of the Grand River was in Allegan County, which also bordered on the lake. According to one history of the county, the forests of Allegan, particularly the pine areas, were appreciated very early. During the territorial period a group of eastern capitalists formed the Boston Company in part to exploit the area's timber resources. Saugatuck, a lake port, became the area's marketing center, while that settlement shared manufacturing responsibilities with the village of Allegan, an early interior manufacturing center. This separation of manufacturing and marketing characterizes much of the industrial development of western Michigan and stands in sharp contrast to the more centralized pattern of the Huron shore.[23]

Allegan County contained fifteen mills in 1840, but a total capital investment figure of under $8,000 indicates their small scale. In the next decade and a half the scale of manufacturing increased. By 1854 there were twenty-nine mills, with an average capital investment of nearly $2,500. Allegan ranked fourth among lumbering counties by value of product, according to 1850 figures, but by 1854 it ranked only eighth in output. In terms of labor employed, also, manufacturing in Allegan County remained small compared to the major lumbering centers. Perhaps the county's limited supply of pinelands encouraged a steady but unspectacular development.[24]

From Grand Haven north the lumber frontier directly followed the fur-trading frontier and served as a magnet for, rather than an appendage of, agricultural and commercial development.[25] In 1850 Ottawa County included the territory bordering Lake Michigan north of Allegan County to the Manistee River and ranked as the largest lumber-producing county in the state. Four major rivers, the Grand, Muskegon, White, and Pere Marquette, serviced what would eventually become the six counties of Kent, Ottawa, Muskegon, Newaygo, Oceana, and Mason. Aggregate figures identify this area as the western shore's major lumbering region at mid-century, but it is misleading to consider it as a single manufacturing or marketing unit. To understand the development of the lumber industry of central Michigan requires an examination of the components rather than the whole. Fortunately, the census returns for Ottawa County in 1850 indicate the unorganized counties, so the data can be manipulated to reflect the geographical elements.

Like the Saginaw River system on the eastern slope, the Grand River and its tributaries form the most extensive water network emptying into Lake Michigan. Branch streams wind westward through five interior counties; the Grand River Valley drains an area of 6,000 square miles. Through the middle of the 1850s commercial lumbering operations on the Grand did not extend beyond Ottawa and Kent counties. Settlers built the first sawmills in the valley for their own needs during the territorial period. The beginnings of commercial lumbering, centering around Grand Rapids in Kent County, coincided with statehood. According to a report to the state board of internal improvements in 1837, eight mills in and around the city produced an estimated 3,000,000 feet of lumber annually. By 1851 the number of mills in the city and its vicinity had increased to fourteen, the majority of them steam-powered double mills capable of producing several million feet a year. Manufacturing remained largely an upriver operation, and rafts carried the lumber downriver to the distribution center at Grand Haven. Mills were erected near the coast at Grand Haven and Spring Lake in Ottawa County in 1840, but as late as 1854 the Grand Rapids area produced more than twice the amount of lumber than was manufactured at the mouth of the river. The Grand River region provides an example of successful long-distance separation of manufacturing and distribution during the formative years of the Michigan lumber industry.[26]

Manufacturing in the Grand River region developed rapidly during the 1840s and 1850s. Lumber exports

from the region alone totalled 4,000,000 feet in 1841 and
15,500,000 in 1848. Incomplete figures for production in
the 1850s preclude this measurement of growth over the
eighteen years following statehood, but the increase in
mills from twenty-three in 1850 to fifty-five in 1854
clearly suggests an ever-increasing output.[27]

For the lumber industry, Muskegon was to western
Michigan what Saginaw was to the eastern shore. Geographical elements combined there to produce a location
ideally suited to the rise of a large-scale manufacturing
and marketing center. The Muskegon River, the longest
river in the state, rises far in the interior and originally
traveled through a seemingly endless prize forest, drain-
ing an area of 2,880 square miles before emptying into
Lake Michigan through Lake Muskegon, a harbor that
never freezes. Enticed by this perfect setting, men came
early to exploit the area's timber resources. Logging and
lumbering operations began around Lake Muskegon in
the 1830s, antedating land sales, settlement, or outside
demand.[28]

Resident agents of the Muskegon Steam Mill Company
and the Buffalo and Black Rock companies began building the first mills on Lake Muskegon in 1837, and by
1840 a third mill had been added. Aggregate capacity of
these mills probably exceeded two million feet of lumber
a year, but limited demand either restricted production
or resulted in over-production. By 1845 all three mills
had changed ownership. Initially the entire lumbering
process on Lake Muskegon was simplified by a spatial
compression, but by the mid-1840s the narrow band of
prime pine forest adjacent to manufacturing sites was
depleted. Once the timber around the lake was exhausted the Muskegon River became an important conduit for logs. During the decade of the 1840s Muskegon
remained an isolated enclave of scattered clearings
around sawmills accessible only from Lake Michigan.[29]

In spite of problems of limited markets, excess capacity, and overproduction undoubtedly retarded the development of the Muskegon lumber industry, census figures indicate significant growth there in Michigan's first decade and a half of statehood. The number of mills increased from three in 1840 to ten by 1854. Capacity expanded at an even more rapid rate. In 1850 six mills produced 14,500,000 feet, while just four years later ten mills turned out 28,100,000 feet. Capital investment figures for 1850 confirm the increased scale of operations. Of the six working mills, four were capitalized at or above $10,000. By the mid-1850s Muskegon was well on its way to becoming the most important lumber manufacturing and marketing center of western Michigan.[30]

At the same time that lumbering began on Muskegon Lake, a similar development was taking place some twenty-five miles upriver in what later became Newaygo County. Excellent timber and ample waterways marked Newaygo as a lumber area, but the date of the earliest manufacturing there is somewhat surprising. If coastal sawmills faced serious marketing problems, the difficulties only increased for mills separated from their point of distribution. But such considerations apparently failed to weigh heavily with the enthusiastic and optimistic lumbermen who first settled Newaygo County. From their arrival in 1836 until the turn of the century, the lumber industry dominated the county and determined its pattern of settlement. Towns developed to supply logging operations, and by 1855 the village of Newaygo was the most important center north of Grand Rapids.[31]

As early as 1836 five Chicago "capitalists," hoping to realize big profits, had organized a land and timber company and begun establishing squatter's claims along all the rivers in western Michigan from the Grand to the Manistee. Members of that company, in what was apparently an independent venture, built the first sawmill in Newaygo County the same year. The mill shipped its first lumber to Chicago via Muskegon in 1837. Despite

this early flurry of activity, manufacturing developed
very slowly in Newaygo in the 1840s. The number of
mills and their output remained small, as the local supply of logs exceeded manufacturing needs. Frequent
changes in ownership indicate that sawmilling was not
yet a stable, profitable business. The problem of too
many logs prompted one manufacturer, John A. Brooks,
to experiment with log-running to the Muskegon mills.
This log drive in 1841, duly celebrated by whiskey and
rioting, marked the beginning of large-scale logging operations in Newaygo County.[32]

The size if not the number of sawmills increased in the
area that would become Newaygo County by 1850, and
total production for that year for the county's three mills
reached 6,500,000 feet. Indeed, if judged by capital invested, the individual mills of this county compared fa-
vorably with those of St. Clair County. The average
investment per mill in St. Clair was $7,254, while it was
$7,900 in Newaygo. Rapid growth in manufacturing be-
gan in Newaygo in the first half of the 1850s. State census returns for 1854 are incomplete, but it is clear that
the number of mills had increased by that time to eight
or ten. The rapid purchasing of pinelands in the county
during these same years insured that Newaygo's lumbering boom was yet to come.[33]

During the state's first decade and a half, small lumbering enclaves appeared at the various river outlets to
Lake Michigan, north of the mouth of the Muskegon
River. A number of lumbermen operated between the
Muskegon and the Pere Marquette rivers, but Charles
Mears was the dominant lumberman in the area. Between 1837 and 1850 Mears, a merchant from Massachusetts, established five mills and settlements along the
western shore of the lower peninsula. In the 1840s
he shipped his lumber to Chicago, Milwaukee, and
Kenosha, but by 1850 he had concentrated his marketing
at Chicago. The most important lumbering center of the

area was at the mouth of the White River where Mears erected the first mill in 1837. Although he discouraged competition, other lumbermen built at least two more sawmills there by 1850. After 1850 the scale of production greatly increased, and by 1854 there were eleven mills along the river, producing over 15,000,000 feet of lumber annually.[34]

Farther north in what later became Mason County, lay the Pere Marquette region. Lumbering along the Pere Marquette, Big Sauble, and Little Sabule did not begin as early nor expand as rapidly as in the regions to the south. Speculators began buying land in the county in 1840, but there were no settlements there until 1847. Nothing is known of the first sawmill except that it was built in 1845, burned the following year, and was not rebuilt. Commercial manufacturing dates from the construction of the second sawmill in 1849. This was a large operation, capitalized at $15,000 which employed twenty men, and produced 3,000,000 feet of lumber annually. During the 1850s Mears was the most important operator in the county's lumber industry, but large-scale manufacturing did not actually begin until the 1860s when Pere Marquette (later Ludington) became an important center.[35]

Still farther north, the Manistee River, the most dangerous river of western Michigan, swiftly runs its long, tortuous course to Manistee Lake at its mouth. This large lake, which empties directly into Lake Michigan, provides an ideal site for a lumber manufacturing and distribution center. This potential was recognized early, and lumbering at Manistee began with the Stronach mill of 1841. Steady development marked the decade: by 1850 there were five mills, with a total capital investment of $33,000 and a labor force of sixty men, producing 7,000,000 feet of lumber a year. These figures suggest that the mills of Manistee compared very favorably with the mills of the large manufacturing counties of the eastern shore. The average capital investment per mill was $6,700 in Manistee and $7,254 in St. Clair. Only Detroit, Saginaw, and Michilimackinac showed a larger investment per mill (see Table 7). The average number of men employed per mill in Manistee was twelve, which equalled the average work force in the Saginaw mills and was slightly higher than the 10.5 hands per mill in St. Clair.[36] Although the figure for capital invested was significantly lower in Manistee than in Saginaw, in number employed and annual production Manistee ranked alongside the eastern center.

During the 1850s the number of sawmills in Manistee County steadily increased, while the level of production jumped spectacularly. In 1854, for example, the county's seven mills turned out 13,900,000 feet of lumber, or 1,985,714 feet per mill—the highest production rate in the state (see Table 7)—and lumbering on the Manistee was still in its early stages; it would not reach its high point for another quarter of a century.[37]

North of the Manistee lay Grand Traverse, the northwestern tip of the lower peninsula. Unlike other lumber regions, Grand Traverse was a one-company area, and Traverse City is probably the best example of a one-company town in all of Michigan. In 1851 Hannah, Lay & Company, a newly organized Chicago firm, purchased a small mill that had been operating for three years, briskly expanded logging and manufacturing operations, and built Traverse City. In 1854 the company employed eighty-one men at its three Traverse City mills and produced over 5,500,000 feet of lumber for its own yard in Chicago.[38]

By 1855 Michigan's lumber industry had assumed a shape and direction that would remain unchanged until the coming of the railroad. The number of mills and camps would increase in succeeding years but the pattern of regional development would remain unchanged.

CHAPTER 5

The Development of a Commercial Lumber Industry, 1837–1855: Logging

A commercial lumber industry involves several separate but interrelated components. It is an industrial process that includes logging, driving, manufacturing, and marketing. The following three chapters examine the functioning of each of these components and evaluates the influence of increasing demand and technological innovation on each during the years between 1837 and 1855.

It required a two-step process of logging and driving to bring raw materials to the manufacturer. According to lumbermen's terminology, logging included felling a tree, cutting the trunk into logs, and banking or piling the logs along the edge of a river or a lake.[1] Driving referred to the floating of logs from the forest down a river to the mill. Both were exacting sciences and colorful arts complete with their own vocabulary, technology, and folklore.

Behind the romance of the woods lay the business of logging. Entrepreneurs in this phase of the industry can be grouped into three categories according to their manner of operation. Independent loggers owned land or stumpage and sold their logs on the market. Since that transaction generally took place at the mill, the independent logger assumed both logging and driving responsibilities. Many farmers logged on their own land during the winter season, a procedure that not only cleared their fields, but brought in what amounted to an off-season cash crop. The farmer-logger might employ a crew, but generally his operations were restricted to family. Thomas Jones and Richard Roberts of Muskegon were two such farmers who found winter lumbering "quite a profittable [sic] occupation" during the early 1850s.[2]

The size of independent logging businesses varied according to the amount of capital the logger had to invest in pinelands and the number of workers he could afford to employ. Many young men of limited means saw logging as the path of entry into the lumber industry. Some were unsuccessful. Hiram McCain, for example, invested his earnings from contract logging in pinelands, which he began cutting in 1840. His business had expanded into a two-camp operation before it failed in 1845 when log prices dropped precipitously. Others were more successful. Ami W. Wright, one of Michigan's wealthiest lumber barons, began his career in 1852 by logging his lands on the Cass River near present-day Caro. The largest independent loggers, epitomized by Delos A. Blodgett, bought timberlands in the thousands of acres and harvested them as their only or primary occupation.[3]

Born in New York in 1825, Blodgett migrated to the Middle West as a young man of twenty-one and after a year in the logging camps of Wisconsin decided to become a lumberman. He moved to Michigan in 1848 and began logging on the Muskegon River, first as an employee of a local logger and then in 1850 in a partnership with Thomas Stimson. Their business relationship was dissolved two years later, but Blodgett continued to buy and log pinelands. Blodgett's career is interesting in several respects. Apparently one of the earliest lumbermen to appreciate the value of the interior lands, he was in the vanguard of those moving in to exploit them. He did not integrate forward into manufacturing until 1871, although the size of his woods operations would have supported such a step much earlier.[4]

Contract loggers, in comparison, made no investment in either land or stumpage. Rather, they contracted to cut, bank, and mark a stipulated number of logs from timberland controlled by a manufacturer. The logger was usually paid a flat rate per thousand board feet of logs (M) or a portion of the timber cut.[5] He furnished men, supplies, and equipment and assumed the risks of the business. Since contract logging required only a modest investment in equipment and limited working-capital, its cost of entry was low. The technology of mid-nineteenth-century logging required no extensive or elaborate machinery. Basic hand tools such as axes and teams of oxen or horses constituted a logger's equipment.[6] The manufacturer or local merchants advanced credit for supplies and other operating expenses.[7] Of the thirty-two contract or independent loggers identified in the manuscript census of 1850, only six had a capital investment of more than $1,000.[8]

In addition, the census figures shed light on other aspects of the logging frontier of 1850. Loggers were few in number and were concentrated geographically in Ottawa and St. Clair counties, then the most developed area of lumbering activity. Yet even between those two counties significant differences in scale were observable. Table 9 indicates that in terms of capital invested and size of crew, logging was becoming a distinct branch of the industry in St. Clair County by 1850.

Logging could be part of a larger lumbering business if a manufacturer integrated backwards to control his source of raw materials. He then owned timberlands or stumpage, lumber camps and equipment, and directly employed a labor force in the woods. While this was a

TABLE 9
Logging in Ottawa and St. Clair Counties, 1850

County	Number of Loggers	Average Capital Invested	Total Capital Invested	Average Number Employed
St. Clair	12	3,358.33	40,300	7.33
Ottawa	20	557.50	11,150	4.40

Source: 1850 MS Census, Ottawa and St. Clair Counties.

common enough arrangement, particularly during the formative years, it was not a universal one. The availability of saw logs and later the problem of cutover lands undoubtedly prejudiced some manufacturers against logging. In his observations of the Saginaw lumber industry, Henry H. Crapo noted that only half of the mill owners furnished their own stock.[9] Even if the manufacturer assumed a logging function, he might at times need to supplement his supply of raw materials from outside sources by buying from an independent logger or by entering into a logging contract.

Logging provided one important path of entry into the manufacturing sector. Because the capital requirements of logging were low, successful contract loggers could save enough money to buy land and become independent loggers. The independent, in turn, could accumulate sufficient capital to buy a sawmill. Although there were many variations, the basic pattern of forward integration remained the same, as the following examples demonstrate. Samuel Rose worked for a season as a woods laborer before becoming a contract logger in 1837 at the age of twenty. Within four years he had accumulated enough capital to buy into the Muskegon mill that he supplied.[10] Amos G. Throop provides an even better "success" story. Born in 1811 in upper New York State, he moved to Michigan in 1832 and took a job as a woodsman for the Black River Steam Mill Company in St. Clair County. Within two years he and his brother, John E., began contract logging operations for various mills in

St. Clair County and Detroit. They put their earnings into pinelands that they then harvested. By 1845 the brothers had fully integrated forward, adding both manufacturing and marketing functions to their business operations.[11]

Logging was a part of the lumber industry's seasonal cycle, with transportation providing the key factor in the timing of work. Since it was easiest to move logs on snow-packed ground, logging was usually limited to the winter months. Depending on the weather and the amount to be cut, the logging season ran over a four-month period from mid-November to mid-March. While the cutting season itself was relatively brief, work continued over much of the year, with site preparation and camp construction occupying a skeleton crew from late summer until snowfall.[12]

The success of a logging venture, and therefore indirectly of the mill or mills to be supplied, depended primarily upon the weather. Loggers hoped for an early freeze, sustained snowfall, and a late thaw. A snow cover of one to two inches provided the optimum working conditions. Any less hampered the transportation of logs to the river bank, while an excess hindered swamping, chopping, sawing, and marking operations.[13] Newspapers of the lumbering regions offer the best testimony to the importance of weather. The *Port Huron Observer* reported in 1847–1848 that because of mild winter temperatures the mills of St. Clair County received only half of their anticipated log supply.[14] Such a shortage in a one-industry area created severe dislocations. By contrast, nature sometimes proved more cooperative, as in the winter of 1852–53 when a "good" snowfall late in the season saved the Saginaw loggers, mills, and community from a disastrous season.[15]

Woodsmen in Michigan borrowed their logging technology from New England, making only minor modifications. The single significant difference in logging

techniques between Maine and Michigan was that in the latter state a tree was cut into logs in the forest, while in Maine it was transported at full length to the mill.[16] No contemporary sources explained this adaptation, but it may have been that the trees in Michigan were too long to handle as single units. Small-scale logging prevailed into the middle of the nineteenth century and was considered a relatively easy undertaking as long as sites remained close to the rivers. According to one old-time lumberman, a Michigan logger usually "put in," or cut, less than a million feet per year, but other sources place an average season's production per logger at some 2,500,000 to 3,000,000 feet by the mid-1850s.[17]

Logging could begin only after a site had been selected, a camp constructed, paths cleared, and snow fell. Believing that the continent contained endless forest resources, the early loggers in Michigan, like their counterparts in the East, approached their work with great selectivity. As one contemporary observer, Theodore Winthrop, noted "a lumber campaign is like France after a *coup d'etat:* the bourgeoisie are as prosperous as ever, but the great men are all gone."[18] Along the Cass River, for example, early loggers harvested only cork pine; that is, pine that was of the highest quality.

After selection, a chopper used an axe to fell the trees, laying them parallel to a newly cut road. Felling was the most demanding job in terms of skill and precision and made the chopper the "aristocrat" of the camp.[19] Sawyers then took over, squaring the butt end and removing the branches with cross-saws. At this point the tree also might be "bucked," or cut into logs, although some operators waited to buck at the river bank. An "average" tree, according to the *Lumberman's Gazette,* measured 16 inches in diameter and 16 feet in length, contained 200 board feet, and weighed approximately 1,000 pounds. The early practice of selectively cutting only the largest and highest quality pine, however, meant that

many logs far exceeded the average.[20] If logging was going on within several miles of the river, it was possible to
"snake" or drag the log to the waterway using a simple
device known as a "go-devil," a "travois," usually made
from an angled intersection of two large branches. A log
was chained between the forked limbs, which were then
dragged along the ground. The go-devil gained its name
because it was as hard to keep balanced as a "tipsy Indian," in the words of one old woodsman.[21] Man-made
apparatuses were also used for short hauls. For longer
distances lumbermen built a sleigh, which consisted of a
bunk made of logs approximately four feet in length that
was mounted on iron runners. Teamsters used iron
wedges, chains, and cant hooks to load and unload the
sleighs, whose carrying capacity in the early days did not
exceed 700 feet. Sleighs required better road construction
and surface preparation than was needed for "snaking,"
and even under optimum conditions the sleighs were easily damaged, overturned, or immobilized. The teamster
who handled the go-devil or sleigh pulled by oxen was
probably the second most important member of the
early logging crew.[22]

Occupational specialization was limited during the
early years of the lumber industry. Logging teams remained small, and the organization of work was less specialized during the first half of the nineteenth century
than it was to be later. When crews numbered three or
four, each man had to perform a variety of tasks. Crews
had to be at least double that size before task differentiation was possible. Table 10 summarizes such specialization for a full-sized camp of the mid-nineteenth century.
At a minimum it consisted of ten men performing seven
specific jobs. Later crews would include additional cook-
ing staff, blacksmiths, and extra hands. Only four of the
thirty-two loggers listed in the manuscript census for
Michigan in 1850 employed a labor force of ten or more.
Most of the operations remained quite small, with the

TABLE 10
Size and Specialization of Logging Crews

Number	Name	Job
2	Chopper	Cut down trees
1	Barker	Remove branches and bark
1	Sled tender	Assist barker; assist teamster
1	Teamster	Load sled; lead oxen
1	Swamper	Prepare and maintain roads
2	Sawyer	Cut trees into logs
1	Cook	Prepare all meals
1	Extra hand	

Source: Compiled from Rector, 76.

owner and his family either living in or frequently visiting the camp.[23]

In the earliest years of lumber production in Michigan, logging and driving were thought of as a single operation to be carried on by a common pool of workers. As the distance between a mill and its timber source increased—and so, consequently, the difficulties and dangers—task specialization began. By the 1850s lumbermen considered driving a distinct operation to be contracted for separately.[24] The work of the logging crew was then considered complete once the logs were piled high along the river bank.

River driving was a brief, seasonal, and dangerous occupation. The driving season began with the spring thaw when workmen, commonly known as "river hogs," broke the banks of logs. As the freshet caused by the melting winter snows or spring rain raced past, it swept the newly released logs downriver to the mill. Since no boat could survive traveling in the midst of drive, workmen had to ride the logs, pushing stranded logs back into the current and loosening those that jammed. The only equipment a driver needed for this dangerous work was spiked shoes and a piked pole. Like all other lumbering operations, driving depended on the weather. Light snow the previous winter foretold a poor driving season—and consequently a poor milling season. Excessive snowfall meant flooding, which only increased the danger of the drive and the difficulty of keeping the logs together.[25]

If the logs had to be transported across a lake, rafts were prepared after the ice melted. The technology of log rafting had changed little since antiquity. The log rafts of White and Coffin, Detroit lumber manufacturers in the late 1840s, for example, were probably not so different from those that Solomon received from the King of Tyre.[26] Rafting was as slow as river driving was rapid, since water current provided the only motive power for the log rafts on Michigan's lakes. Even when rafting was carried on at night to take advantage of the strongest currents, it could take as long as four weeks to cross the twenty miles of Lake St. Clair, and storms or other disturbances would only further hamper and delay the trip.[27]

Problems of driving were by no means limited to the weather. The river hog lived with danger every mile of the downriver race, even if the trip eventually proved to be uneventful. It took a youthful and dexterous person to jump continually from one rapidly moving log to another. In addition, the spectre of the dreaded, deadly log jam always loomed as a possibility. Such occupational hazards help explain the raucous, even "lurid," spree that marked the end of a drive. The participants in the first drive that came down the Muskegon River in 1839 celebrated with a barrel of whiskey. That event became an "annual carousal" for nearly a quarter of a century, until Muskegon's city fathers built a jail and undertook a concerted campaign to "suppress" the revelers.[28]

Navigational obstructions often hindered the transportation of logs. Clearing rivers and lakes was a difficult, expensive, but necessary project that often proved to be beyond the limits of one individual.[29] The dramatic increase in the number of logs driven downriver in the 1850s magnified the problem of navigational hazards and eventually led to cooperative clearing projects. Even under optimum conditions, lumbermen counted on a certain loss, or "shrinkage," of logs in transportation. In addition to sinking, logs could be lost through rotting and theft. An attrition rate of approximately 10 percent was considered normal in the pineries of the Great Lakes.[30]

The importance of the river to the lumber manufacturer increased with the distance between logging site and mill. Landowners who claimed exclusive water rights opposed the lumbermen's increased usage of rivers and streams. That issue was finally resolved by a state court in 1853 in a case concerning the Pine River in St. Clair County. The court held that any stream with a capacity for floatage was navigable and that all persons using it had equal rights. That decision not only sanctioned existing practice, it also opened up the interior counties to full-scale lumbering.[31] In addition, lumbermen encountered resistance to the dams they needed to help regulate the flow of water for drives. Not surprisingly farmers whose lands might be flooded by such construction led the opposition, but here again lumbermen gained a victory. In 1851 the state legislature approved a bill that placed decision-making and police powers in the hands of county board of supervisors, groups that proved amenable to the industry's needs.[32]

As the pace of industrialization quickened in the state, the logs sent to the mill grew in number until they threatened to clog the rivers. The Black River was among the first to face such congestion, when in the spring of 1845 log and board rafts backed up eight miles from its mouth.[33] By 1854 log traffic on the Flint River threatened to block all navigation, prompting the *Genese Whig* to propose extensive construction that would create a new channel for navigation while leaving the old channel for log booms.[34] The increasing volume of logs also posed new problems for driving. By 1850 the old individualistic arrangement proved to be inadequate and expensive on the Muskegon River. Initially the lumbermen along the river undertook a mutual drive, with all log owners contributing men to the crew, but that arrangement only partially eliminated duplication of effort and costly confusion. Subsequently in 1852 the manufacturers and loggers using the Muskegon River formed the Log and Mill Owner's Association, a voluntary cooperative effort managed by a board of directors and maintained by an assessment on the value of each owner's logs handled by the Association's drivers. Sorting at the boom remained the individual owner's responsibility. For the next three years the Association functioned with reasonable success, eliminating many difficulties while reducing costs.[35]

Just as increased industrialization brought more complex organizational forms and task specialization to logging and driving, new responses were required at the mill end of the drive. As the logs of the various companies came down together in the spring freshet, some sorting process was needed at their destination. Booming works were created for this purpose near the mouth of the river, usually in a pond, secondary channel, or backwater area. Each owner had a section or pen. As the drive came by, his men would pick out the proper logs according to the marking and place them in the pen. From the pen the logs would be rafted, driven, or towed to the mill. As early as 1851 steam tows were being used at the Muskegon booming works, the only organized sorting grounds in the pre-1855 period.[36]

Aggregate production figures for logging in Michigan do not exist, perhaps because logs were not often considered in their own right but only as a part of the commercial lumbering process. Yet it is possible to draw an impressionistic picture of the expansion of logging on the local and state level. The demand for logs at the Muskegon mills increased from a lowly 9,000 in 1840 to 42,000 by 1850, while the loggers of St. Clair County had a market in local and Detroit mills for some 56,000 logs in 1845.[37] From the available data, it appears that the need for logs by Michigan's manufacturers rose from roughly 500,000 in 1840 to over 2,500,000 in 1855.[38]

Log prices have proven to be as difficult to determine as the level of production. Although their value fluctuated from place to place and from year to year—or, with changes in the weather, even within a season—prices appear to have risen as production increased. For example, a reporter in Port Huron, St. Clair County, placed the average cost of logs delivered to the mill in 1844 at a conservative figure of $2.00 per thousand board feet, or M. The next year the average value per log was placed at $5.00 M, which was also the prevailing rate in 1847, according to a correspondent of the *Merchant's Magazine.*[39] Ten years later the logging firm of Sweetser & Sanborn sold nearly 550,000 feet of pine logs to George D. Hill at $6.50 M.[40] Log prices at Saginaw, according to contemporary sources, followed the same pattern. The cost of logs delivered to the mill rose from $1.50 M in 1849 to $2.00–$4.50 M in the early 1850s, and to $6.00 M by 1855.[41] The price of logs on the western shore of Michigan appears to have been somewhat lower, although the evidence is too fragmentary to be more than suggestive. For example, in 1852–1853 Charles Mears paid an average of $2.00 M at Duck Lake, while the Gilbert brothers in Ottawa County sold their logs at $2.50.[42]

The only detailed source for log values in this period, the 1850 manuscript census, not only indicates that the figures cited above for St. Clair and Saginaw counties are on the low side, but it presents an opportunity for broader assessment. Although many firms reported log sales or purchases in board feet, there were sufficient entries based on logs to allow analysis.

As Table 11 immediately makes clear, log prices in 1850 varied widely, from an average of $2.00 in Michilimackinac County to $7.57 in St. Clair County. Price levels were indeed significantly higher along the eastern shore to Saginaw than in the northern and western areas. There are, no doubt, several reasons for this, but one of the most important must have been ease of access to the forest and relatively short length of the drive. More intensive cutting over a longer period had depleted the forests closest to the mills in St. Clair, Saginaw, Thumb, and the eastern interior counties, necessitating longer, more costly log runs. It would seem reasonable to infer from all of the data collected that log prices would continue to rise as demand increased, with western log prices rising more sharply as a reflection of the disappearance of the most accessible timber stands.

TABLE 11
Log Prices for Selected Michigan Counties, 1850

	Number of Firms[A]	Price Range Per M	Average Price
St. Clair	14	$6.00–9.75	$7.57
Wayne[B]	3	6.35–8.10	7.31
Lapeer	10	3.30–7.50	5.10
Sanilac, Tuscola, Huron	11	5.00–	5.00
Saginaw	7	2.50–6.65	4.40
Genesee	4	2.75–5.00	3.93
Montcalm	6	1.90–4.15	2.31
Ottawa	25	2.15–4.15	2.64
Michilimackinac	14	1.50–3.00	2.00

A. Manufacturing firms except for eighteen logging enterprises in Ottawa County.
B. Detroit mills only.

Source: 1850 Manuscript Census.

It is also impossible to assess precisely the profitability of logging in the early period of commercialization without additional data on production costs, although some generalizations can be made. Production costs equalled the sum of logging and driving expenses. In addition to labor, camp construction, road building, and mainte-

nance constituted the major expenses of logging. By the mid-1850s these costs varied between $1.50 and $3.00 M depending upon location and convenience of access.[43] If Rector is correct in holding that driving expenses exceeded those of logging, then the delivered cost of raw materials would have been in the range of $3.00 to $6.00 M. Some driving distances remained relatively short in the pre-1855 period, the lower assessment appears to be more reasonable. Comparing total cost figures with average selling price and volume of sales, it can be seen that logging could be a lucrative enterprise.

By 1855 the patterns of logging and driving were clearly established in Michigan's lumber industry. Stimulated by rising demand, manufacturing units expanded in size and production. This increasing output of lumber placed new demands on the procurement of raw materials, which were becoming steadily more distant from the manufacturing site. In response, logging and driving became better organized and standardized in business arrangements, camp organization, labor specialization, and technological operations. Log transport was similarly affected, but the ever-increasing volume began to place a heavy strain on individual operations. Early experiments with cooperative driving on the Muskegon River indicated the solution that would be adopted in the following years.

CHAPTER 6

The Development of a Commercial Lumber Industry, 1837–1855: Milling

Between 1837 and 1855 sawmills in Michigan increased in size, number, and complexity. With this growth came changes in function that altered the character of the business from custom processing to a commercial industry. Comparisons of industries based on census material help place lumber manufacturing within a state context. Number of firms, value added by manufacture, and number of hands employed provide three important measures of the relative importance of industries in ante-bellum Michigan.[1] These data, summarized in Table 12, present an industrial profile of Michigan. Industries processing natural resources dominated manufacturing, although household-craft consumer firms were of considerable importance. No industry, however, came close to challenging lumber. In terms of number of firms, value added by manufacture, and size of labor force, lumbering was far and away the largest, most important industry in Michigan at mid-century.

Initially, small sawmills served a processing or commercial function for a local area. Despite the prematurely grandiose visions of such men as Ralph Wadhams and Francis Browning, both operating in St. Clair County, most early mill owners entered the business with the limited ambition of meeting a localized need for

TABLE 12
Selected Leading Industries in Michigan, 1850

Industry	Number of Firms	Value Added	Percent Total	Number of Workers	Percent Total
Lumber	558	$ 736,728	36.80	2,730	32.26
Flour	220	435,304	21.74	624	7.37
Boots and Shoes	156	129,248	6.45	780	9.22
Leather	112	112,645	5.62	417	4.93
Liquors	35	97,195	4.85	120	1.42
Furniture	94	77,714	3.88	376	4.44
Blacksmiths	129	59,687	2.98	327	3.86
Minerals	103	56,966	2.84	191	2.25
Tin, Sheet Iron, Brass, Copper*	68	54,359*	2.71	912	10.78
Vehicles	89	45,369	2.26	357	4.22
Clothing	40	40,837	2.03	409	4.83
Wool	41	36,346	1.81	205	2.42
Tobacco	5	31,280	1.56	109	1.29
Iron and Copper Manufacturing	76	21,883	1.09	66	.78
Cooperage	77	20,771	1.03	239	2.82
Paper	4	20,769	1.03	30	.35
Food	14	17,219	.86	42	.50
Construction Materials	58	7,506	.37	298	3.52
Fisheries*	69	— *	—	231	2.73
Total	1,948	$2,001,826	100.00	8,462	100.00

*Information not available.

Source: *Abstract of the Statistics of Manufactures, 1850.*

lumber and finished boards. The mills of Albert Miller at Bay City and E. W. Perry at Tuscola are representative of a limited response to a specific need.[2] Under optimum conditions, their small water-powered mills could supply probably no more than 2,000 or 3,000 feet of lumber a year, yet even that capacity could exceed local demand. As the number of mills grew, production capacity enlarged, and costs rose. Under those circumstances, lumber manufacturing could not remain profitable without market expansion.

Correlating supply with demand was always the lumber industry's most difficult problem. Pioneer lumbermen reacted to the chronic dilemma of overproduction in several ways: some suspended or ceased operations;

some combined custom milling with commercial manufacturing; some sought to increase their markets. Albert
Miller of Bay City commenced business in 1836 and continued to manufacture into 1838. Since he could not
withstand the competition of other local mills or find
more distant markets where lumber could sell for something in excess of transportation costs, he ceased operations. His mill remained idle until he could sell it six
years later. His second attempt at sawmilling in 1847–
1848 proved no more successful. A poor market forced
Miller and his partner, James J. McCormick, to make an
assignment of their works to their creditors and finish
the season by contract milling.[3] E. W. Perry faced the
same problem but had somewhat better success in solv-
ing it. Although he began manufacturing in 1837 on the
Cass River at what later became Tuscola, an area then
beginning to attract settlers, inventory soon began to accumulate. Perry successfully rafted his surplus lumber in
small cribs down the treacherous Cass River to Saginaw,
only to find no market there. For reasons that remain
unknown, he then decided to ship his 60,000 feet of pine
boards to Cleveland, where he managed to find a buyer.
He sold subsequent loads at Detroit.[4]

George Hazelton encountered the same problem at
Flint as Miller and Perry had elsewhere. The local price
for lumber in 1838–1840 was $10.00 to $15.00 per thousand board feet, or M, but by the late 1840s excess capacity had dropped prices to $3.00 to $8.00 M. Hazelton
later recalled that the area's three mills "could not be
kept running for the want of a [local] market," which led
to a campaign to increase their area of service. Like
Perry, Hazelton looked to Saginaw. Expansion in this direction required removing obstructions from the Flint
River, a major expense shared with Charles Seymour, another millowner. Hazelton also sought to extend his market into the agricultural counties to the south and
southwest. In the latter direction he was particularly

successful, pushing his market more than 100 miles into the hinterland. The bulk of that overland business, however, was limited to the winter months when the ground was frozen.[5]

Whether built in anticipation of, in response to, or even in disregard of demand, the number of sawmills in the lower peninsula of Michigan expanded in the years following statehood from 433 in 1837 to 906 in 1854, an increase of 209 percent (see Table 13). There was no period of retarded growth, but a spurt came in the period

TABLE 13
Growth of Sawmills, 1837–1855

	1837	1840	1850	1854
Total mills, L.P.	433	491	558	906
Mills in Pine Belt	12*	115	193	315

*Estimated figure

Sources: Rector, 54; *Compendium of the Inhabitants and Statistics of the United States*, Washington, 1841; Manuscript Census for the State of Michigan, 1850; *Abstract of the Statistics of Manufactures, 1850; Census and Statistics of the State of Michigan, May, 1854*.

from 1850 to 1855. The figures, not surprisingly, are even more dramatic for the number of mills built in the pine belt. There the increase was from an estimated twelve in 1837 to 315 in 1854. In 1837 pine mills accounted for only 2.7 percent of the lower peninsula's sawmills, but this proportion steadily increased to 23.4 percent in 1840, 34.5 percent in 1850, and 35.7 percent in 1854. The growing number of mills clearly indicates that barriers to entry in the lumber industry remained very low throughout the entire period.

Figures for both individual undertakings and aggregated capitalization by county confirm the fact that a would-be entrepreneur with limited financial resources could easily enter into lumber manufacturing (see Table 7, chap. 4 and Table 15 below). Throughout the entire period of commercial development, small mills with limited capacity existed alongside their more complex, costly, and productive competitors. Small units were more important in the early years; by the 1850s the large sawmill was the dominant force.

For a lumber manufacturing operation, whatever its size, the basic costs were for site, physical plant, and machinery. Additional supporting facilities such as dams, docks, housing, and stores might also be needed. Information on cost of mill sites is difficult to find because such cost was usually considered a part of the construction bill. Since most mills in the pine region were located well in advance of settlement and with no competitive pressures, except perhaps in nascent lumbering centers, it seems reasonable to assume that location costs required only a modest capital investment.[6]

The amount of money necessary to build and equip a mill obviously varied greatly, as contemporary sources document, depending upon its size and machinery. Date of construction, however, was not a factor, for costs appear to have remained relatively stable in the years between 1838 and 1855. While there are passing references to mills built for $1,000 to $2,000, the average small mill, whether water- or steam-powered, with a sash or muley saw and a maximum capacity of 6,000 to 10,000 feet per twelve hours, cost somewhere between $4,000 and $6,000.[7] A mill with double that capacity would require, according to the experts of the day, a capital investment of approximately $10,000, while a manufactory with an annual capacity of 5,000,000 feet (up to five times that of the smallest, least efficient mill) would carry a $16,000 price tag.[8] There was an increasing number of mills of very high capitalization, costing $17,000 to $25,000, and even $50,000 in the 1850s.[9] Just what these larger sums bought is not known, but it seems reasonable to suppose that they included various support facilities as well as the plant itself.

The data available will not support any conclusions about the relative share of capital that went into equipment, but it is safe to say that the proportion of machinery costs to total investment probably declined in comparison to the pre-1837 period. For one thing, much equipment could be purchased locally as the number of mechanics and machine shops grew, and that meant reduced transportation costs. But the demand for increasingly complex equipment meant that machinery still accounted for one of the largest capital expenditures. In 1846 Curtis Emerson purchased a ten-year-old mill for $6,000 and then spent another $10,000 on restoring and replacing machinery, while in the early 1850s Gideon O. Whittemore and his partners invested just under $20,000 in a mill at Tawas City, which included over $5,000 in machinery brought from Detroit.[10]

Census data for eight counties where pine lumbering was conducted on a commercial basis, available for the years 1840 and 1850, have been tabulated in Table 14. This information in conjunction with average capital investment figures for the same year, summarized in Table 7, chap. 4, illustrates the story of manufacturing growth. Poor transportation plagued Genesee and Lapeer counties, while Kent faced the most limited reserve of raw materials. In the remaining counties there were

TABLE 14
Aggregate Capital Invested in Lumber Manufacturing
in Selected Counties, 1840 and 1850

County	1840	1850
Wayne	$ 17,475	$ 364,270
St. Clair	21,000	232,125
Ottawa	19,300	194,130
Saginaw	18,000	103,600
Allegan	7,900	64,000
Kent	21,000	37,850
Lapeer	17,500	35,300
Genesee	13,500	20,700
Total	$135,675	$1,051,975

Source: *Compendium of the Inhabitants and Statistics of the United States*, Washington, 1841; Manuscript Census for the State of Michigan, 1850.

few if any such restraints. In some cases the increase in capital invested over the decade is nothing short of spectacular and clearly indicates the shift to commercial manufacturing. Wayne, St. Clair, and Ottawa counties led in this development. The shift is most apparent in the Detroit area of Wayne County, the most advantageous location in terms of accessibility to capital sources and an established marketing network.

The number of highly capitalized forms provides further documentation of the changing dynamics of Michigan's lumber industry. While the number of enterprises operating on a small scale were most numerous, it was the growing number of highly capitalized firms that set the pace of industrial development. As Table 15 documents, these large businesses were concentrated in

TABLE 15
Capital Invested in Lumber Manufacturing
in Selected Counties, 1850

County	under $5,000	$5,000–$9,999	$10,000–$19,999	$20,000 +
Wayne*	23	0	3	5
St. Clair	13	10	7	2
Ottawa	12	13	4	1
Michilimackinac	3	8	3	1
Saginaw	6	0	1	1
Allegan	21	0	0	1
Sanilac, Tuscola, Huron	8	2	3	0
Kent	17	1	1	0
Lapeer	11	1	1	0
Montcalm	4	1	1	0
Genesee	3	1	1	0
Total	121	37	24	11

*Detroit area only

Source: Manuscript Census for the State of Michigan, 1850.

pockets—at Detroit, St. Clair, and Saginaw on the eastern shore and in Ottawa County on the western slope. Census data confirms scattered contemporary records and reminiscences: through the middle of the nineteenth century there was relatively easy entry for small manu-

facturers into an industry that was being transformed
into a big business.

In addition to his investment in property, buildings,
and machinery, a lumberman had to meet operating expenses. It was the ability to command working capital,
either cash or credit, that in large measure determined
the fate of a business.[11] For the lumberman, like most
antebellum manufacturers, the need for short-term capital was great, at times exceeding investment capital. This
money went for two basic expenses: logs and labor. Random examples of lumbermen's working capital requirements drawn from the 1850 manuscript census amply
demonstrate those propositions.[12] In that year Zephaniah
and Horace Bunce of St. Clair County produced 500,000
feet of lumber. The logs from which their lumber was
cut were valued at $1,500. They employed seven men at
a total monthly wage of $84, a low rate for that date.[13]
Based on an eight-month manufacturing season, their
operating expenses would have been slightly more than
$2,000, a figure two-thirds of their capital investment.
In Allegan County, Elias Streter paid three men a total
of $78 a month to mill 750,000 feet of logs valued at
$2,000. His expenses for an eight-month operation
would have been $2,624, more than his capital invest-
ment of $2,000. Ryerson and Morris, a much larger firm
in Ottawa County, capitalized at $20,000, employed a
labor force of twenty-five at a cost of $4,800 for eight
months to produce 2,300,000 feet of lumber from logs
valued at $5,000. Their total operating expenses for the
season amounted to $9,800. Smith and Dwight of De-
troit probably expended some $21,000 in 1850, or 42
percent of their $49,500 fixed investment. Aggregate fig-
ures confirm the random sampling. In 1850 the 558 sawmills in Michigan had raw material costs of $987,525
and labor costs of $740,076, for a total of $1,727,601, a
sum that nearly equalled the $1,880,875 in investment
capital.[15]

Sources of capital became more varied over time. In the territorial period, lumbermen could command only minimal financial support beyond their immediate families. The outside capital that could be tapped came primarily from Detroit and the East, as, for example, the resources brought to the Newaygo Lumber Company in 1853 by Amasa Brown Watson representing Eastern investors.[16] There might be a personal tie between the geographically separated borrower and creditor, for the merchants and other capitalists who lent money often had a previous acquaintanceship with the debtor or his family, or, less frequently, with the location of the enterprise. Occasional references to local financing make clear that this was an infrequent and most limited avenue of support.

For many manufacturers, the years of commercialization brought little change. Self financing remained a viable option. Once established, a mill could often generate its own capital. John L. Woods and Sweetzer and Sanborn were examples of successful firms in St. Clair county. Credit reporters estimated that the value of Woods's business climbed from $7,000–$8,000 in 1853 to $50,000–$60,000 by 1856, while that of Sweetzer and Sanborn jumped from $3,000 in 1851 to $200,000 in 1856.[17] There were others, of course, who were not as successful. George Ford of Pere Marquette, for example, had to seek outside help when he could no longer finance his own operations. Between 1849 and 1859 he borrowed a total of $69,849.71 in investment and working capital from James Ludington, a businessman and real estate investor in Milwaukee and partner in a Chicago lumberyard.[18]

For a man with business or technical skills but little or no money, a partnership with a capitalist was an attractive arrangement. L. C. Whiting, a Detroit dentist, supplied all the initial $17,000 investment for Whiting and Garrison of East Saginaw in 1854, while A. M. Hoyt, a successful businessman and speculator of New York City, was Charles Grant's silent partner from 1850 to 1855. George N. Fletcher, a Boston businessman and treasurer of the Old Colony Railroad, began in 1848 as the silent—and distant—partner in the St. Clair Lumbering Company. Fletcher's partner, G. P. Robinson, soon proved financially "irresponsible," forcing Fletcher to intervene to try and save the business.[19]

Advances from wholesalers to manufacturers against future production were sometimes of vital importance. The manufacturer who could command this backing was better able to withstand the vicissitudes of an industry where the bulk of sales, often on long-term credit, came only at the end of the season than one who had no outside support.[20] One firm that survived because of such advances was McEwan Brothers. The three brothers, Alexander, William, and John, were all machinists who came to Bay City in 1850 and built a mill. Their principal buyer was Shepherd, Sheriffs & Smith, a Chicago lumberyard that "whenever necessary" advanced them cash for stock deliverable later in the season, an arrangement providing them with "an advantage over some competitors."[21] Advances from wholesalers to manufacturers remained small, however, until independent lumber wholesalers became an important part of the marketing pattern later in the antebellum period.

There were no barriers that would have discouraged entry into the lumber industry in Michigan. In addition to ease of entry, power sources and raw materials remained abundant, and despite the increasing size of operations and complexity of machinery, the basic technology of sawmills remained relatively uncomplicated. Long years of apprenticeship and experience were not necessary, for a simple trial-and-error process could still result in a marketable product within an acceptable limit of time. The mid-nineteenth-century lumber industry remained one into which individuals with either general technical skills or business acumen could enter and hope to complete.

Just how successful individual lumber manufacturers were and how profitable the industry was remains as difficult to document for the decades of commercialization as it was for the territorial period. Continual changes in ownership and the consequent lack of reliable records make an assessment difficult, yet that revolving door of manufacturing proprietorships and partnerships suggests that exit remained at least as easy and common as entry. In 1845, L. M. Mason, N. D. Norton, and John L. Beebe built a mill on the Black River in St. Clair County. The next year Mason sold his share to Elisha B. Clark, and the business became Clark & Company. In 1849 came yet another change, with W. B. Hibbard buying out Clark and Beebe.[22] Likewise, between 1852 and 1859 a succession of six owners and leaseholders operated one mill on Rabbit Run in Allegan County.[23] One can only speculate on the reasons for this instability. For some, as we have seen, lumbering was merely a flirtation, often as transitory as the operator's stay in the county or state; for others it was a lure of high profits that never materialized. The Drakes came from Canada to West Bay City in 1851 with $15,000 to "engage in the lumber business," with which they had not the slightest experience. After only two years of operations they sold out because profits had not matched their expectations.[24] Yet for all the movement out of the industry, there were more who chose to enter.

Success in lumbering depended upon a variety of factors, of which demand remained the most important but least certain. While a business might survive without a first-rate product or even expert management, without sufficient demand it was doomed. One factor in success, then, lay in choosing the right manufacturing site. No theories of plant location existed to guide a manufacturer in the mid-nineteenth century; he had only instinct, common sense, and precedent on which to rely. In many cases these were enough. In general, lumbermen chose to build their mills in relation to markets rather than to raw materials. Mills in the interior counties were located on river routes, usually in towns. The size of their marketing area depended upon transportation, but the nearest lumber port was too far to make the rafting of lumber there at all profitable. The largest mills were generally located along the shore at or near the river's mouth, which then became a major distribution center. As for manufacturers who faltered, it was not so much that their location was wrong as that they located there prematurely.[25] In addition to site, success was largely dependent on adjusting output to demand. Throughout the antebellum period a clear differentiation was made between a mill's potential capacity and its actual production.[26] Success therefore depended in part upon developing more distant markets.

At the time of statehood virtually all of Michigan's sawmills were small frame structures located beside a stream or river. Through a relatively uncomplicated system of gears, a waterwheel transferred the power of falling water directly to the sawing mechanism and the log carriage, the mill's only equipment.[27] Mills in this period used some type of reciprocating saw, usually a sash (or gate), although there are scattered references to early uses of gang and muley saws. Most were single saw mills. Compared to mills just several decades later, the early mills were uncluttered, quiet, and slow. Production techniques matched the machinery in simplicity and speed. One such mill could produce no more than 2,000 to 5,000 feet per day, which in a good season with no floods, droughts, or mechanical failures would amount to roughly 500,000 to 1,000,000 feet of boards.

The level of technology and production of the single-sash sawmills proved, in most cases, more than adequate to meet the limited needs of a restricted local market. An increase in demand, or at least anticipation of it, led to improvements in equipment, power, and processing that expanded production. Greater speed and efficiency mark the sawmilling technology adopted by Michigan manufacturers in the years of commercialization.[28] Lumbering technology along the Great Lakes frontier differed little from that of the East. Similarities of terrain and forestation made the diffusion of technology rapid. Lumbermen could transfer their tools and techniques as easily as their capital.

The use of gang saws in Michigan dates from the early 1830s. A series of sash saws set within one frame, the gang saw represented only a modest technological advance. It still operated reciprocally, cutting only on the downward stroke. The early gangs, rather primitive in construction, were set in place by a local mechanic. Later versions improved upon this arrangement, as construction of the frame and the braces between the blades became standardized. The gang saw increased production by decreasing the number of carriage runs necessary to turn one log into boards, but the added weight of the additional saws within the frame reduced its speed of operation. Mills with gang saws required special construction; heavier foundations were needed to support the weight of the machinery.[29] Sash-saw blades, whether singly or in groups, had a narrow kerf, or cut, which meant that little of the wood was wasted as sawdust. Most early manufacturers, however, did not choose them for this economy; they chose them because they were time-saving.

In 1848 Solomon Johnson of the short-lived D. and S. Johnson Company of Zilwaukee, after a trip to various manufacturing centers in Maine, decided to put in gang saws at the company's mill. Without a trained mechanic's supervision the project failed; within a year the equipment had to be replaced. That experiment temporarily discouraged other local manufacturers from trying gangs, but the saw's advantages soon overcame any lingering prejudices.[30] Charles Merrill is credited by one trade journal with installing the first commercially successful gang saw in the state in the mid-1850s. Merrill no doubt had used such equipment in his sawmill in Maine, where a diminishing timber supply placed a premium on thin kerfs. He brought his expertise and equipment with him when he transferred his base of operations to Saginaw in 1854.[31]

The gradual adoption of the muley saw antedated the mid-century surge in demand for lumber. The muley saw had several desirable features that made it attractive, particularly to the small manufacturer. For one thing, it weighed less that the sash saw because it was not set in a heavy movable frame. This meant that it could be operated at greater speed for increased output. In addition, it cut an excellent product, boards that were straight and smooth. The muley saw with its wider kerf was more wasteful than the sash saw, but this must have seemed a small price to pay when the forest appeared limitless.[32] The speed of the muley saw necessitated changes in the linkage to the power source, particularly to the steam engine. Initially, mechanics connected the saw to the shaft from the power source, but the rapid motion of the saw quickly destroyed the engine. The solution to this problem lay in the development of independent gearing systems. Running at capacity, a muley saw could produce up to 3,000,000 board feet annually, although most turned out only half that amount. The muley saw's popularity as "the favorite among the mills" continued well into the 1860s.[33]

As important as the muley saw was, the circular saw must be considered the most important technological innovation adopted by lumber manufacturers in antebellum Michigan. With its circular motion, it represented the first departure from the reciprocating action that had characterized mechanical sawing up to that time.

Invented in Europe, the circular saw was transferred to America sometime between 1815 and 1820.[34] The earliest circular saws were crude, heavy devices of greater importance for their potential than for their actual performance. It required several decades of American adaptation before the circular saw proved satisfactory—and safe—in Michigan sawmills.

The circular saw posed major problems for mechanics and millwrights. It required additional power for operation and new linkages in gearing that would allow a temporary disconnection of the saw from the power source. Unlike up-and-down saws, which were secured at top and bottom, the circular saw could be fixed only at its center. Special engineering was therefore needed to reduce its tendency to wobble and produce a wide and uneven cut. Another difficulty lay in the design of the saw. In the earliest circular saws, the teeth were cut into the saw itself, but since this caused great repair problems and manufacturing delays, improvements were introduced. First a band of teeth was fitted around the saw, and finally in 1846 individual teeth were developed to fit into sockets around the edge of the saw. This final step minimized work delays, maximized safety, and made the circular saw a practical tool.[35]

It is difficult to say when the circular saw first made its appearance in Michigan. One trade journal places it as early as 1847, when James Fraser installed one in his Saginaw mill.[36] This claim seems plausible, given Fraser's flair for innovation, but if this dating is accurate, it was at least half a decade before the circular saw won popular acceptance.[37] In 1855 Wood, Smith & Wicks, a Genesee foundry, began manufacturing a circular saw with a special gearing arrangement designed by an unnamed Saginaw inventor. Manufacturers quickly adopted the Wood, Smith & Wicks saw, with its estimated capacity of 3,500 feet per hour.[38]

At an annual rate, a circular saw could produce between 8,000,000 and 10,000,000 feet of lumber, which was the key to its success. Once perfected, it could triple the output of a muley saw, using approximately the same amount of power. In addition to its speed, the circular saw produced a cleaner, higher-quality product, but the saw was the most wasteful one used in the antebellum period. With its broad gauge and widely spaced teeth, the saw insured that up to one-third of a log slab would be sacrificed as sawdust.[39] But if the circular saw was wasteful, it was also fast, and speed of production was what the manufacturers in Michigan sought.[40]

New technology was also applied to the sequence of manufacture, improving both speed and quality. Early milling was a three-step operation: slabbing, cutting, and butting a log. Slabbing consisted of removing the sides and squaring the log. The resulting slab was then cut into boards. Because the carriage had to be stopped short of the saw, each board had a butt end that had to be separately removed. This three-step process was a slow one in a mill with only one saw.[41] To increase production the manufacturing process had to be accelerated. This was done by adopting new equipment and by increasing the number of saws. Contemporary descriptions of virtually all the major mills operating after 1850 emphasize the diversity of equipment. Sash, gang, muley, circular, edging, and butting saws were used in a seemingly endless number of combinations. In this period slabbing was usually done with muley or sash saws, while gang and circulars were often chosen to cut the slab into boards.[42] The Emerson steam-powered mill at Buena Vista near Saginaw, considered one of the best in the state in the early 1850s, contained three uprights, an edger, and a butting saw.[43]

In addition to adopting improved machinery, lumber manufacturers rapidly replaced waterwheels with steam engines during the 1840s and 1850s. They could not afford to have their mills idled by either drought or flood;

they needed a steady, dependable source of power to operate the increased number of machines. Steam power had been applied to lumbering in Michigan as early as 1825, but the remote location of the mills, the high cost of engines, and the lack of technical expertise made steam-powered mills unfeasible, particularly when demand remained modest. Between 1838 and 1855, however, the picture altered: markets increased; knowledge and technology of steam power improved; and engines became more accessible and somewhat less expensive. Steam power still cost more than waterpower, but the dependability and increased production possible with steam tended to offset the cost difference.[44] If the small waterpowered mill was a sign of the pioneer settlement in Michigan, the steam-powered mill became a symbol of the commercial lumber industry.[45]

In 1838 there were only twenty-one steam-powered mills in the lumbering counties: eight in St. Clair, eight in Ottawa, two in Saginaw, and three in Wayne.[46] By 1850 the number had increased to sixty-one.[47] As Table

TABLE 16
Watermills and Steam-Powered Mills for Selected Counties, 1850

County	Number Water	Number Steam	Percent Steam	Percent Capital Invested In Steam Mills
Wayne*	1	8	88.8	93.0
St. Clair	11	21	65.6	73.0
Saginaw	3	5	62.5	62.7
Ottawa	16	14	46.6	62.0
Lapeer	11	2	15.4	47.6
Tuscola, Sanilac, Huron	10	3	23.1	46.0
Allegan	19	3	13.6	40.6
Michilimackinac	10	5	33.3	26.0
Kent	18	0	—	—
Montcalm	6	0	—	—
Genesee	5	0	—	—
Total	110	61	35.6	

*Detroit area only.

Source: Manuscript Census for the State of Michigan, 1850.

16 shows, only Genesee, Kent, and Montcalm counties had no steam-powered mills. By 1854 only Montcalm, the smallest lumbering county in number of mills and annual production, reported no steam mills.[48] The ratio of water- to steam-powered mills in other counties varied greatly. In 1850 the percentage of steam-powered mills ranged from a low of about 14 percent in Allegan County to a high of almost 90 percent around Detroit. In sum, 36 percent of the sawmills of Michigan's pine counties were steam-powered by mid-century. From Table 16 it can be seen that, with the possible exception of Michilimackinac County, steam mills absorbed greater sums of capital than their water-powered counterparts. The adoption of steam provides another measurement of the movement toward large-scale commercial lumbering.

Several technological problems remained unsolved throughout the years of increasing commercialization of lumbering. Inadequate boilers reduced the power and efficiency of mills. Edging, the process of smoothing the sides of a board, was still a bottleneck. No matter how strong or skillful a sawyer might be, the process of running both sides of a board through the edging machine was a slow one. The edger could not keep up with the output of the slabber and the circular saw operator. Finally, mechanical breakdowns presented a chronic problem. A malfunction of just one machine idled operations until repairs could be made or new parts brought in.[49]

Despite such difficulties, lumber manufacturers in Michigan eagerly adopted new technology, which is not surprising in an industry where labor constituted one of the largest costs of production. One authority on the lumber industry in the Great Lakes region has estimated that in the antebellum period one worker was required for every 1,000 feet of lumber produced daily, a reasonable calculation to judge from the available data.[50] But the manufacturers' goal was not to reduce the size of their work force; rather they strove to maximize its efficiency.

CHAPTER 7

The Development of a Commercial Lumber Industry, 1837–1855: Marketing

The years of commercialization posed new market problems for Michigan's lumbermen. Like the rippling from a pebble thrown into a pond, sales expanded ever outward from a local base to an interstate system. George W. Hotchkiss, the earliest chronicler of the lumber industry in the Midwest, estimated that in 1840 less than 5 percent of Michigan's output of 100,000,000 board feet of lumber was marketed beyond the borders of the state.[1] Domestic, commercial, and agricultural needs within the state claimed a full 95 percent of the lumber produced there. For all practical purposes, the producing territory and consuming territory were the same. Several complementary forces were soon in operation, however, ensuring that such geographical unity of mill and marketplace did not long endure. Supply rapidly exceeded local demand, while at approximately the same time, demand from outside the state began to increase. Thus, when the Michigan lumber manufacturer sought a wider market, he found some interest in his product. A newspaperman in St. Clair County dated the beginning of an interstate demand for Michigan lumber from 1843, while he said, before this date lumber was a "drug" on the market.[2] In 1847, 73,842,000 feet of lumber, valued at $520,864, was shipped from the state. In terms of value of product, lumber ranked as the state's third largest export, behind flour and wheat.[3] By 1855 the geographical separation between mill and market was almost complete, and a distribution system radiating south, west, and east from the pinelands of the lower peninsula had been formed.

Chicago became the largest and most important market for Michigan pine. That this would be the case could not have been apparent to the early lumbermen of St. Joseph, Saugatuck, Grand Haven, and other points along the western shore. Although they began shipping cargoes to Chicago as early as 1834, that was not because the Illinois lake port was a great trading center, but rather because it was the most accessible place at which they could hope to sell their excess lumber. Throughout the 1840s the city remained a small market. No good figures are available for the early history of Chicago, but Hotchkiss estimates that lumber imports in 1839 did not exceed 4,200,000 feet.[4] In this very narrow market, several cargoes—even small ones totaling no more than 30,000 to 50,000 feet—would swamp the market.

After 1836 Chicago began to supply the prairie settlements of Illinois, but because shipments could be carried only by wagon, much of the city's hinterland remained untapped. Consequently, the market for lumber grew slowly yet steadily, from just under 20,000,000 feet in 1844 to 32,118,225 by 1847.[5] But between 1848 and 1855 two major transportation improvements opened vast new market areas to Chicago, turning the small port into a thriving manufacturing and commercial center (see Table 17). The completion of the Illinois and Michigan Canal in 1848 and subsequent railroad construction provided Chicago with easy access to the Mississippi River and the plains states. Lumber receipts nearly dou-

TABLE 17
Lumber Received and Shipped, 1847–1855, Chicago

Year	Received	Lake	Canal	Railroad
			Shipped	
1847	32,118,225			
1848	60,009,250			
1849	73,259,553			
1850	100,364,779			
1851	125,056,437			
1852	147,816,232	—	49,095,181	21,645,090
1853	202,101,098	—	58,026,056	30,734,292
1854	228,326,732[a]	4,000	65,398,740	68,729,132
1855	306,553,467	5,500	81,040,328	134,539,526

Sources: *Annual Review of the Business of Chicago for the Year 1852* (Chicago, n.d.), 10; *The Railroads, History and Commerce of Chicago* (Chicago, 1854), 71; *Annual Review of the Commerce, Manufactures and Private Improvements of Chicago, for the Year 1855* (Chicago), 16. *The Lumberman's Gazette*, Mar. 30, 1881, recommends adding 50 percent to adjust for underreporting of shipments. See also, Wolfe, "Hannah, Lay and Company," 8.

Note a: Low estimate according to the *Annual Review of 1854*.

bled during the first year of the canal's operation, and with the exception of 1849, a slow year, increased some 20,000,000 to 25,000,000 feet per year. This annual rate of increase doubled in 1853, by which time a steadily growing network of railroad lines linked Chicago with all points on the compass. Two Michigan railroads, the Michigan Central and the Michigan Southern and Northern Indiana, reached the city in 1852, but they were not important lumber carriers since it was cheaper to ship lumber by water than by rail. The railroad was important, however, in supplying the west with lumber. By 1855 shipments of boards from Chicago by rail surpassed those by canal. This transportation network made it possible, for example, for John A. Westervelt of Saginaw to complete successfully in the St. Louis market against manufacturers on the upper Mississippi River.[6] By 1850 Chicago itself was a boom town. One student has calculated that in 1853 the city utilized over 114,000,000 feet of lumber, 12 percent more than it had exported.[7] Of the 202,000,000 feet of lumber imported

into Chicago in that year, it has been estimated that over
190,000,000 feet came from the pineries of Michigan.[8]
To look at it from the Michigan shore, by the mid-1850s
Chicago had become the largest, most important market
for the state's lumber. Of the 392,920,714 board feet
produced in the state in 1853, 57 percent was shipped to
Chicago.[9]

Important as Chicago was to lumber manufacturers in
Michigan, it alone could not handle all the lumber produced by the sawmills of the lower peninsula. According
to the *Saginaw Enterprise's* broadly rounded calculations for 1855, 40 percent of the state's 500 million-foot
output went to markets other than Chicago, a figure
that roughly corresponds with the estimate above. Half
of this amount, or 100,000,000 feet, the paper noted,
went to "lake ports" and Wisconsin.[10] Although the
wording is vague, it can be assumed that the author
meant such Wisconsin port cities as Racine, Kenosha,
and Milwaukee. Improbable as it first appears for a
great lumbering state, for a time Wisconsin was a major
consumer of Michigan lumber. Through at least the mid-
1850s, it was cheaper to ship lumber across Lake Michigan to Wisconsin's port cities than it was to transport it
from mills in the interior of that state. Lumber from
western Michigan reached eastern Wisconsin quite early,
and many observers believed that Milwaukee rather than
Chicago was destined to be the great transshipment center. Charles Mears, for example, operated a retail yard in
Milwaukee from 1837 to 1847, while James Ludington, a
Wisconsin capitalist, began investing in Michigan pinelands and sawmills in the early 1850s. Although Chicago
as the principle locus of trade became apparent in the
early 1850s, Milwaukee and the other ports of eastern
Wisconsin continued to be important markets for Michigan lumbermen.[11]

The remainder of the lumber produced in 1855 that
did not go to Chicago or Wisconsin went to "home con-

sumption [and] Eastern Markets."[12] Of this amount,
which probably totaled just over 150,000,000 feet, it is
safe to say that at least half remained within the state.
Michigan in the mid-nineteenth century was still young
and growing. Between 1840 and 1850 its population increased from 212,267 to 397,654; settlement pushed
northward and into the interior; and the number of organized counties increased by 11, to 43.[13] As early as
1849 interior counties in the southern agricultural belt of
the state were complaining that they could not get lumber as fast as they could use it.[14] Certainly the intrastate
demand on local and regional mills could not have been
less than 75,000,000 or 80,000,000 feet.

Probably less than 15 percent of Michigan's lumber
went to eastern markets in 1855. Attempts to extend the
state's marketing network eastward proceeded slowly,
primarily because eastern demand remained relatively
insignificant until the pineries of Maine, New York, and
Pennsylvania faced depletion after mid-century. Pine
lumber from Michigan first reached Ohio about 1840,
and by 1842 shipments to the Buckeye State totaled over
8,000,000 feet. It was only natural for manufacturers on
Michigan's eastern shore to seek a market at Toledo. The
Kelsey brothers of St. Clair County had such success in
the Ohio city that they decided to open a retail yard
there in 1845, and by 1853 they were doing a $100,000-
a-year business. George Hazelton also found Toledo to be
a good market when he was seeking an outlet for his
Flint mill's surplus in 1847. As in the case of Chicago,
Toledo's location made it a prime distribution center for
Michigan pine. From Toledo lumber could be sent
through the Miami and Erie Canal to Dayton, Cincinnati, and other places in the interior.[15] As long as Cincinnati could receive lumber from Pennsylvania by way of
the Ohio River, however, its need for Michigan lumber
was limited. By 1855, the amount the Queen City received from the lower peninsula probably did not exceed

2,000,000 feet.[16] In addition to Toledo, Sandusky, and Cleveland also became important markets. Wholesalers in Cleveland could move the lumber into the interior via the Ohio and Erie Canal. By the late 1840s a Cleveland newspaperman reported that virtually all lumber received in that city came from Michigan.[17]

According to one pioneer lumberman, early manufacturers along Michigan's eastern shore did not conceive of a lumber trade with Atlantic cities because they believed that the Eastern states contained more than enough pine to supply there own needs. The first attempt to market east of the Great Lakes was in 1840 when a cargo of pine was sent as a blind venture to Albany. In 1841 lumber exports to New York were valued at $100,000, making it Michigan's third largest revenue-producing export to that state behind flour and skins and furs.[18] Early shipments east of the Appalachians were apparently sporadic and not often successful. Most regional historians date the beginning of an eastern market for Michigan pine from the shipment consigned by Emerson and Eldridge to C. P. Williams and Company in Albany about 1848.[19] The high quality Saginaw Valley product was attractive to buyers who were beginning to experience shortages in some kinds of lumber from their suppliers in Maine, New York, and Pennsylvania.

Albany owed its position as the most important lumber distribution center in America in the early 1850s to the Erie Canal. Between 1850 and 1854 lumber shipments on the canal increased from 216,786,890 feet to 311,571,151 feet. In the latter year the New York capital's receipts of lumber exceeded Chicago's by 26 percent. Albany had begun as a distribution center for the surplus production of the mills in upper New York State, but as this supply dwindled, the city's lumber wholesalers sought Canadian and then Great Lakes pine.[20] One self-styled lumber expert and pamphleteer estimated that Michigan pine accounted for "more than 1/3" of the city's lumber receipts in the early 1850s.[21] Although this calculation, which would have amounted to over 100,000,000 feet in 1854, is far too high, it does demonstrate the growing importance Michigan lumbermen placed on the Albany market.

Not all Michigan pine bound for the east reached Albany. Some was distributed through Buffalo. A local market until 1850, Buffalo soon after became an important forwarding point and wholesale center for Michigan and Canadian lumber. Between 1846 and 1855 the city's lumber receipts more than doubled, increasing from 34,536,000 feet to 72,026,651 feet. Most of the lumber was transferred to canal boats for shipment to Albany, but an increasing amount was kept at Buffalo for home consumption or distribution. Throughout the decade, however, Buffalo remained a minor and less dependable market than Albany.[22]

Increased output resulting from technological changes and greater capital investment necessitated new market strategies. Most manufacturers expanded forward into marketing, adopting a variety of direct and indirect selling methods. Although there were to be refinements in the future, the basic arrangements devised by Michigan lumber manufacturers to dispose of their product had come into being by 1855. The simplest, most direct, and least costly way to sell lumber was at the point of manufacture, the mill, but this method satisfied only the custom sawyer or the producer content to operate on a small scale in a restricted setting. For those whose output exceeded local demand, additional distribution arrangements were necessary. One of the first responses was to seek some outlet already established. A natural but self-limiting solution was to sell to or through a merchant, a strategy that could expand the market area to a regional level.[23]

The connection between merchant and manufacturer was very close during the first two decades of Michigan's statehood. In some cases the merchant was a partner in or owner of a sawmill. Benjamin Luce, for example, was both a storekeeper in Lexington and manager and part owner of the Black River Steam Mill Company. Most of the mill's product was shipped to Detroit, but that which remained in St. Clair County was sold either at the mill or at Luce's general store. In many cases a merchant integrated backward to become a manufacturer. Smith, Dwight, & Glover, for instance, began as a mercantile firm in Detroit in 1837, but experienced such success in handling lumber, lath, and shingles that they added a sawmill in 1852. James Abbott, another Detroit merchant who owned a mill in St. Clair County, was not interested in becoming a manufacturer. He preferred to lease the mill under an arrangement that permitted him to control directly the quantity and quality of the stock he was to receive annually.[24]

For manufacturers interested in large operations within the state, full forward integration was necessary. These men established yards were lumber could be stored, stacked, and sold wholesale or retail. Unlike mills, which had to be located close to raw materials and water-power, yards could be situated with respect to demand. For this reason most of the lumber yards in Michigan in the antebellum years were in Detroit, Saginaw, St. Joseph, Grand Rapids, and other population or trading centers. John and James Bear, manufacturers in St. Clair County, understood the need to expand their market area and opened a yard in Detroit about 1846.[25] Lumberyards required an investment by the manufacturer, but they offered two positive advantages. First, they expanded the mill operators' marketing options, and, second, they permitted mill owners to increase production, sometimes to the limit of capacity. C. C. Haskell, a mill owner in Flint, explained his strategy to Henry H. Crapo in late 1855 or early 1856. He kept all of his lumber below top quality, he stated, at his yard in

Flint, which provided a steady outlet. His best lumber, however, he shipped to Saginaw, where it would sell more rapidly and bring a faster return on investment.[26]

Yards in Michigan in this period usually sold rough, green, unplaned lumber, although if the lumber were piled for a long period of time before it was sold, seasoning would occur naturally. Grading, or sorting and pricing according to quality, if used at all was very simplified and not uniform. Manufacturers often sold the product mill-run—directly as it came from the saw. Initially only a two-level classification of "common" and "clear" appears to have been used, but with time the system became more elaborate. By 1855 lumber might be classified into as many as three and four different qualities, including "cull," "common," "box," "select," and "clear."[27]

Regional and interregional distribution, particularly to the west and south, followed much the same pattern as manufacturers developed an increasingly complex and sophisticated selling system. The search for out-of-state buyers, particularly by lumbermen along the western shore, came quite early, propelled by a push-pull factor: lack of local demand, excess output, and the belief in the existence of more distant markets. Manufacturers looking to Chicago and the west responded to this set of circumstances in several ways. In the early years after statehood, some millowners simply sold their product on the docks at Chicago. Mears, a leading and not atypical Michigan lumber manufacturer, in the late 1840s ran his mill at White Lake with his assistant until they had cut 15,000 to 20,000 feet of lumber. The two sawyers then became sailors, loading Mears' ship *The Ranger* and sailing for Chicago. There they found empty dock space and began selling the cargo. If a Michigan manufacturer did not personally accompany his cargo, a lieutenant did. Daniel Ball hired young George Morton in 1840 to travel with his lumber to Chicago and arrange for its sale. Previously employed as a clerk, Morton was new to the lumber business.[28]

Loading a vessel with freshly cut boards was not always a simple operation. Harbors were sometimes too shallow to permit the passage of a loaded ship. For many years lumber manufactured at Manistee mills had to be rafted to vessels at anchor in Lake Michigan, and mills along the Saginaw River were forced to carry their product to ships out in the harbor. David Oliver encountered the same problem with sandbars when he began milling operations in 1851 at the mouth of Devil River in Thunder Bay. The only solution was to lighter, or ferry, the lumber out to the ship, but this was a slow and costly process. With a small vessel, it required five or ten trips to transfer the cargo. Hotchkiss estimates that transfer losses could amount to as much as 25 percent of the cargo value.[29] The Ferry mill at White Lake was in a particularly disadvantageous location. Since a loaded ship could not pass the mouth of the White River, the Ferrys had to either raft the lumber out to vessels in Lake Michigan or have the rafts towed by oxen from White River to Grand Haven for transfer to a boat. In 1855 the Ferrys built piers out into deeper water, which provided a costly but satisfactory solution to the problem.[30]

No lumber fleet existed on Lake Michigan for many years, so manufacturers had to provide their own transportation. This problem, which was particularly burdensome for the small-scale operator, led to the appearance of marketing middlemen who operated at the local level, aggregating small loads and selling them at Chicago. It would appear that the middlemen most often served as wholesalers rather than commission agents; that is, they purchased stocks outright rather than accepting consignments. None of these men in the period through 1855 could boast of any marketing connections in Chicago; they had to sell the same way as the manufacturer who took charge of his own transportation and with as little knowledge of the current state of the market. If the cases of Chauncey Davis and Thomas D. Gilbert are at all representative, middlemen realized the precariousness of their position. By the early 1850s Davis and Gilbert had joined lumber firms that controlled both manufacturing and marketing.[31]

Although evidence is fragmentary, it is clear that Michigan manufacturers were supplying western buyers with lumber on a contract basis quite early in the history of the lumbering industry. Contracts obligated the manufacturer to deliver a certain amount of lumber at a specified date for a prearranged price. Sometimes the agreement included specifications as to quality and length; at other times it was mill-run. William F. Ferry of Grand Haven and Samuel Rose of Muskegon were two early manufacturers disposing of a sizable portion of annual production through contracts. Ferry, for instance, delivered at least 2,000,000 feet of lumber on contract to two different Chicago lumberyards in 1845. In this early period the manufacturer assumed the responsibility for transporting the lumber from mill to buyer.[32]

Selling under contract sometimes proved as uncertain and as unsatisfactory as selling at the Chicago docks. Too often manufacturers discovered that prices had risen between the time a contract was negotiated and the delivery date.[33] The key problem for the lumberman was being sufficiently informed about current market conditions to be able to sell his product most efficiently and advantageously. When the market base was small, such as Chicago's was throughout most of the 1840s, several cargoes would swamp the market and drive prices down. Since the manufacturer usually needed to sell rapidly, he had no choice but to sell at a disadvantage.

Faced with a distribution problem common to antebellum manufacturers operating beyond a local market, many lumbermen responded by placing the marketing function in the hands of specialized middlemen. Somewhat surprisingly, commission agents and commission houses for lumber developed rather slowly at Chicago. Michigan manufacturers continued to accompany their cargoes to the Illinois city and to maintain personal control of marketing until well into the 1850s. Sometimes the cargoes sold so slowly that the manufacturer-merchant had to store his lumber at a local yard. The yardman was then entrusted with selling the remaining cargo as advantageously as possible. McClure & Larrabee and Walter & Allen appear to have been the earliest lumbermen in Chicago to serve in an intermediary capacity, beginning this role in the late 1830s in conjunction with their lumber storage facilities. Individual informal arrangements with yard dealers continued for over a decade. No commission agents specializing in lumber appear in the Chicago city directory until 1853, and Hotchkiss estimates that an independent commission lumber business was not firmly established until about 1855. By that date manufacturers were shipping full cargoes on assignment to a growing number of commission dealers.[34]

As Chicago grew in size and importance, a small number of Michigan millowners decided that there was sufficient concentration of trade there to warrant setting up their own lumberyards. In 1847 James F. Lord, a lumber manufacturer at St. Joseph, joined with Samuel F. Sutherland, a St. Joseph merchant, to form S. F. Sutherland & Company, a firm designed to sell the product of Lord's mill at Chicago. Their response was probably in response to the anticipated opening of the Illinois-Michigan Canal. The first year of operations was anything but auspicious. Without an office, the two men "operated from their lumber pile, . . . keeping their books in their hats."[35] They sold the stock remaining at the end of the season to another company. Undaunted, they returned to Chicago the next year and apparently began to prosper, for the firm continued in existence for a decade.[36] Mears provides another early example of forward integration. After trying to sell his lumber on the docks at Chicago, he decided that Milwaukee was a better place to open a lumberyard. He operated this yard with modest success for several years before shrewdly deciding in 1847 to move his marketing activities back to Chicago. He opened his new yard the following year, and by 1851 it required a labor force of twelve at peak season. Mears found it highly satisfactory to have control of both the manufacturing and selling functions. He had not only a steady outlet for his lumber but also constant contact with the market, which helped him adjust mill production to prevailing demands.[37]

Forward integration continued to attract manufacturers. Ryerson & Morris, Trowbridge & Swan, and James Fraser, large-scale producers at Muskegon and Kawkawlin in the Saginaw region, all found the demand at Chicago strong enough by the early 1850s to warrant their establishing their own yards.[38] Davis, Theodore Newell, and A. D. Loomis, all of Muskegon, formed a manufacturing and marketing partnership in 1850. In addition to their mill at Muskegon, they ran branch yards at Muskegon, Chicago, and Kenosha.[39] But A. H. Mershon expanded his operations farther than any other Michigan lumberman. With the help of Jesse Hoyt, a wealthy New York merchant, Mershon sold lumber from his Saginaw mill through branch yards in both Chicago and St. Joseph, Missouri.[40]

The advantageous combination of Michigan manufacturing and western marketing was as apparent to lumber dealers as to millmen. In 1848 Roswell Canfield, a dealer in Racine, Wisconsin, and his two sons bought pinelands around Manistee and built a mill there to supply their yard. Two years later they added a second mill at Manistee and another at Chicago. That same year Hannah, Lay and Company was formed. Initially a Chicago lumber business, the company had purchased its

entire stock by the cargo. As their trading sphere enlarged and volume increased, the partners decided to invest in pinelands and a mill at Grand Traverse,
Michigan. By 1852, just two years after its beginning,
Hannah, Lay and Company was operating as a fully integrated company. Beidler Brothers & Company was
another Chicago lumber business that moved into manufacturing at an early date. Two brothers, Jacob and
Henry, had opened a yard in that city in 1848, adding
two partners and a mill at Muskegon in 1854. By 1855
there were at least a dozen fully integrated lumber firms
manufacturing in Michigan and marketing at Chicago
or along the eastern shore of Wisconsin.[41]

If a manufacturer did not establish his own sales division, he might still be directly connected with what
amounted to one by a contract arrangement. W. M. Final of East Saginaw confided to Crapo that he found an
arrangement with a Chicago lumberyard to be most
profitable.[42] Contract sales and purchases by wholesale
or retail dealers at the mill became increasingly common
after 1850. Wilcox, Lyon & Company, for example,
hired a man in 1853 to buy lumber at Michigan and
Wisconsin mills for shipment to their Chicago yard.[43] As
the need for lumber accelerated, marketing arrangements were regularized. The manufacturer could no
longer simply pile his lumber cargoes on city piers—
indeed he seldom felt that need as buyers increasingly
sought him out.

Throughout the period of commercialization of Michigan's lumber industry, sales in the Chicago market followed no set pattern, for official inspections of cargoes
and a uniformly applied grading system did not yet exist.
Initially the manufacturer would pile his cargo mill-run,
although the very best stock might be stacked separately.
A simple two-class rating scale of "merchantable" and
"cull" was loosely applied. If a buyer demanded an inspection, it was usually confined to the surface of the

load. The lack of inspections initially worked to the advantage of the manufacturer, but in times of low demand and tight money, the broad grading classifications
benefited the buyer. Two contemporaries, one a millman
and the other a lumber dealer, agreed that culling could
be severe. Even a slight split at an end could cause a
good, clear board to be classed as a cull, which reduced
its value by at least one-half. Such difficulties with early
grading practices led to the gradual adoption of a three-
class rating system: "clear," "common," and "cull." By
1855 inspection at Chicago was commonly carried out
by specialized merchants, and classification of lumber by
grades was becoming more uniform.[44] In many respects,
the Chicago lumber market provides a paradigm of distribution techniques that were employed in other places.
This is certainly true for the Ohio market. Early bind
ventures led to direct sales at the docks, the development
of storage yards, contract sales, commission agents and
the establishment of manufacturers' yards.[45]

East of the Ohio there was less change. From Ralph
Waddams' first experimental cargo to New York in 1840,
distribution was in the hands of commission agents.
Michigan lumbermen found a systematized arrangement
of wholesalers operating in an established marketing network. Only one interesting exception to the pattern has
been found. In 1850 Thompson, Whitney & Coit, owners of a wholesale yard in Buffalo, invested in pinelands
in Michigan and built a mill at Bay City. Thomas Whitney, one of the partners, moved there to manage operations, sending "most" of the mill's production to the
Buffalo yard.[46]

Manufacturers who marketed in New York found
grading and selling procedures already deeply en-
trenched. Specialists completely and carefully examined
every cargo either before it left the mill or after its arrival at the wholesale yard. The lumber was then rated
on a five-point numerical scale as "good," "second," "se-

lect," "common" or "box," and "cull." The standardiza-
tion of practices and uniformity of application reflect the
well-established lumber market of Albany and Buffalo in
the mid-1850s.[47]

Contemporary sources show that Michigan lumbermen found manufacturing profitable as demand increased and the market area expanded. Although there is
no way to determine precise margins of profit without
complete financial records, a general assessment can be
attempted. As a first step, lumber prices have been
drawn from a variety of sources, such as commercial and
local newspapers, trade journals, and manuscript records.[48] In 1840 lumber was selling for $10.00 to $15.00 M
in Flint, $8.00 to $10.00 at Saginaw, $8.00 to $18.00 M
in Detroit, and $8.00 to $20.00 M in Chicago. As demand decreased after 1840, prices plummeted. By 1845
lumber hovered between $6.00 to $12.00 M along Michigan's eastern shores, although top grade might command
as high as $14.00 M in Detroit. Flint's lumbermen fared
no better. In 1846 their product was selling at only $3.00
to $8.00 M. Large-scale lumbering was less well devel-
oped on the western shore than on the eastern, but figures for Grand Haven and Muskegon in 1848 indicate
that prices for common grade there were about equal to
Detroit's and higher than those at St. Clair, Saginaw,
and Flint. Prices at Chicago by the end of the decade
had also declined to $6.50 to $8.00 M.

A somewhat different picture emerges from the 1850
census. As Table 18 shows, prices were lowest in the
western interior counties of Montcalm and Kent and
only slightly higher in the western shore county of Ottawa and the eastern interior counties of Genesee and
Lapeer. At the top of the scale stood Detroit, followed
closely by Saginaw and St. Clair counties.[49]

When demand declined, continued manufacturing,
even at a loss, was necessary in an attempt to meet current obligations. Such production then served to depress

TABLE 18
Lumber Prices for Selected Counties, 1850

Wayne*	10.21	Lapeer	6.16
Saginaw	8.15	Genesee	6.12
St. Clair	8.15	Ottawa	6.12
Tuscola, Sanilac, Huron		Allegan	6.10
Huron	7.45	Machilimackinac	5.45
Kent	6.16	Montcalm	4.33

*Detroit only

Source: 1850 Manuscript Census

further an already glutted market.[50] Contemporary sources record one result of this dilemma: the persistence of a barter economy. For example, when Joel W. Kelley and his brother could find no local buyer for their St. Clair lumber in the early 1840s, they shipped it to Cleveland and traded it for food.[51] Such exchanges remained common throughout the decade. In 1848 Hunt's *Merchant Magazine* estimated that two-thirds of the lumber brought to Chicago that year was paid for in feed and iron goods such as nails and mill castings.[52]

Prices slowly improved in the 1850s, reaching new heights by the middle of the decade. As Eli Bates wrote from Chicago in 1851 to his employer, Charles Mears, "prospects are brightening."[53] At Detroit lumber averaged $15.00 to $23.00 M by 1855, nearly double the price commanded a decade earlier, while at Chicago prices rose from a low of $4.50 M in 1847 to $13.00 to $28.00 M by 1855. The market at Flint and Saginaw also showed strong improvement, with lumber selling at $7.00 to $16.00 M in Flint and $8.00 to $22.00 M in Saginaw. The average price of lumber exports from Michigan in 1855 equalled almost $13.00 M.[54]

While the resurgence of demand was broadly based, it was the spectacular growth of the Chicago market that was most responsible for the improvement.[55] At the same time, improved lines of water and land transportation extended the market area and technological advances improved the product, making it more attractive to buyers, particularly in the East.[56]

The vigorous state of the lumber industry in Michigan by 1855 suggests that sawmilling could be very rewarding financially. Random and isolated bits of evidence for the years 1837 through 1855 confirm this assessment. According to one correspondent, St. Clair lumbermen of the mid-1840s "admitted" making a profit of $2.00 M, a 20 percent rate of return according to their own estimates.[57] Throop, Wait and Company, a moderately sized, fully integrated firm of Port Huron and Chicago, earned a profit of roughly $42,000 during the years 1846–48, a rather poor time for the industry.[58] In the early 1850s, Hannah, Lay & Company of Grand Traverse and Chicago averaged a $3.00 to $5.00 M margin over cost.[59] After surveying the Michigan lumber industry in the mid-1850s, the St. Mary's Falls Ship Canal Company reported that sawmills with a capacity of 3,000,000 to 5,000,000 feet netted $12,000 to $25,000 annually, a high rate of return on an estimated capital investment of $10,000 to $16,000.[60] This is not to suggest that all lumber manufacturers made great profits, for many did not, but for those who succeeded, the rewards were substantial.

CHAPTER 8

Logging in the Pre-Railroad Era, 1855–1870

By 1855 lumbering as a commercial enterprise was well established in Michigan. Techniques of supply, manufacturing, and marketing had been developed, and the state ranked fifth in national production. Fueled by both its own ever-increasing capacity and a somewhat less constant growth in demand, industrial expansion accelerated over the next fifteen years, until by 1870 Michigan ranked as the premier producer of lumber in terms of value added by manufacture as well as quality of product. The outstanding characteristic of the lumber industry in the period from 1855 to 1870 was this increasing scale of production, accomplished with few changes in business practices or significant technological breakthroughs. These were years of cautious experimentation and adaptation in an era of expansion and maturation.

Of the steps in the lumber cycle, logging remained least altered in structure or process. Through 1870 this aspect of the industry successfully responded to the challenge of increasing lumber production by continuing what it had been doing, only on a larger scale. By simply expanding the size of operations and enlarging the labor force, woodsmen were able to expand their output dramatically. Mechanical innovation was minimal; the nature of work and the life-style of the workers remained unaltered; and operations were, as always, fettered to the vagaries of the weather.

The business of logging in 1870 was not the same as it had been in 1855, however, for increasing the scale of production inevitably brought change in its wake. Expanded operations encouraged specialization, particularly in business arrangements. Manufacturers, independent loggers, and contract loggers still performed the logging function, but it appears that the amount of work undertaken by each of these three classes of entrepreneurs shifted over time, with manufacturers increasingly relying upon the independent and contract loggers to supply their mills.

Although there is no way to tabulate the number of manufacturers who actively engaged in logging, records and accounts of lumbermen suggest that by the end of the Civil War there were fewer large-scale operators than had been the case earlier maintaining sole responsibility for their own supply of logs. Smaller manufacturers, particularly those located close to the forest, were more likely to operate their own logging camps, but as the manufacturing unit increased in size, so did demands on the owners's time. For the millman, logging required not only a financial investment in land or stumpage but also a temporal investment in hiring, supplying, and supervising a sizable labor force. At the very minimum it meant numerous trips into the woods to inspect the camps. In a partnership such as Hannah, Lay & Company, where members of the firm assumed specific responsibilities, logging was a lesser problem than it was for an individual owner or manager. As Henry H. Crapo, a large lumber manufacturer and future governor of Michigan, ruefully discovered, logging was "of itself a most difficult and laborious as well as a distinct branch of the business, and would require all the time of any one man to look after."[1]

Crapo's observation on logging came through personal experience. When he decided to move in late 1855 from New Bedford, Massachusetts, to Flint to begin a lumber business, he talked to leading lumbermen in the Saginaw Valley. Following their advice, he hired logging contractors to cut and bank logs from his lands. After the first year, he decided to hire his own crews in the hopes of decreasing costs by directly controlling the operation. Over the next three years Crapo assumed full supervision of logging for his own mill. Occasionally he used log jobbers, but always took care to have his own men assigned to the best sections of the forest. For some reason, perhaps because of the increasing size of his operation or problems in other aspects of his business, particularly marketing, Crapo decided by 1860 to curtail his own logging responsibilities. Although he complained to his son that jobbers were "hard fellows" who could "not be depended on for the fulfillment of their contracts," he simplified his business by placing actual logging operations in the hands of contractors.[2]

Jobbing was an unpredictable business because ultimately the successful completion of a contract rested with the weather and not with the logger. Despite the risks, Crapo noted that twenty-one individuals or partnerships offered to take on his logging in 1856.[3] Certainly one of the reasons jobbing was so popular was its ease of entry. Census enumerators did not often list loggers, but the few cases reported in the 1860 census suggest that logging did not require a large investment. Less than one-fifth of the twenty-three loggers included in the census had a capital investment of $1,000 or more.[4] These data are incomplete and the investment figure probably too low, but they do indicate that contract logging remained an open business.

One way jobbers kept down overhead was by providing minimal accommodations for their workers. An old-

time logger complained that a former employer housed
his men in overcrowded and inadequate shacks to cut
costs. The jobber, he charged, was only "after the
money" and did not sufficiently care for his men or the
timber.[5] Jobbers were undoubtedly careless of the resources of the forest, but apparently this did not bother
the land or stumpage holder, for contract logging became increasingly popular. Of the eleven manufacturers
or independent loggers cutting their lands in the
Muskegon-Manistee area surveyed by C. Briggs for the
Michigan Pine Land Association in 1864, all used jobbers. Only one, James Ludington, also had his own
crews.[6] As the scale of logging increased, jobbers began
to subcontract part of their business. In 1870 Joseph
Procter agreed to cut and bank 2,500,000 feet of logs for
the jobbing partnership of Wilcox & Briggs. He had to
build his own camp, prepare sledding roads, and hire a
crew that reached eight in number at the peak of the
season.[7] Proctor's goal was to save enough money to buy
forty acres of land and become a farmer. Many other
jobbers undoubtedly had the same desire, but others saw
logging as the point of entry into the lumber industry.
Yet as the capital needed to become a large-scale lumberman increased, this option became less viable. Many jobbers stayed in their business for long years, becoming
specialists in an industry that was increasingly compli-
cated by the demands of expanding production.

Manufacturers also purchased logs from independent
loggers. Many independents bought and logged as little
as a quarter section at a time, but these small operators
found it difficult to compete with a growing number of
entrepreneurs who could command large amounts of
capital and credit for buying and logging many thousands of acres. The backgrounds and business careers of
five large-scale independent loggers reflect the industry
as a whole. These men were Russell Alger and Thomas
Merrill, who both operated in the Saginaw area; Robert

Moon and David Squier, who logged on the Muskegon River; and Horace A. Buttars, who worked in the Manistee region. Three of the men—Alger, Buttars, and Moon—began logging before the age of twenty-five, while the other two entered the business when they were middle-aged. All had previous experience either in Michigan or in the East. With the possible exception of Merrill, each of these men began on a small scale but rapidly expanded their business. Merrill and Alger had wealthy partners, which is reflected in their scale of operations— Alger and his associates bought in tens of thousands of acres. Although more limited in financial resources, the other three men used their early earnings to buy more pinelands. Squier, for example, started with only 140 acres but increased his holdings to over 8,000 acres. Two, Alger and Buttars, eventually became lumber manufacturers, while two others, Squier and Moon, remained in logging throughout their business careers. The fifth, Merrill, never owned a mill but did deal in lumber rather than logs whenever he found it advantageous.[8]

Whatever the business arrangements, the woods of Michigan literally reverberated with the sound of cutting and sawing during the logging season. "There is a *furor* to get off every Pine tree that can be reached," Crapo wrote to his son in 1860.[9] Between 1855 and 1870 the scale of logging jumped dramatically. A yearly cut of 1,000,000 to 3,000,000 feet, substantial in the mid-1850s, was considered small only a decade later. David Ward, perhaps the king of Michigan's lumbermen, began logging in 1857–58. In that year he cut some 1,700,000 feet of pine. His output expanded to 5,000,000 feet in 1860 and nearly 10,000,000 feet by 1870. Ward's operations in those years were not unusually large. Noble & Dexter, a logging firm in Grand Traverse, cut 3,000,000 to 4,000,000 feet in 1860, while the larger firm of Hannah & Lay got out 10,000,000 feet the same year. Briggs reported to Cyrus Woodman, agent for the

Michigan Pine Lands Association, in March of 1864 that Ludington hoped to stock 11,000,000 feet that season, while Charles Mears planned a winter cutting of 12,000,000 to 14,000,000 feet. Aggregate figures are equally impressive. The *Lumbermen's Gazette* calculated that logs rafted in the Saginaw district increased from 429,507,806 feet in 1867 to 623,397,353 by 1870, a sum greater than the total amount logged in the state in 1866.[10]

To achieve ever-higher levels of output, logging entrepreneurs had to expand their operations. This meant both increasing the size of the labor force and spreading activities over a wider area. Hannah, Lay & Company employed approximately one hundred laborers by the mid-1850s. Less than a decade later they hired some 150 to 200 men to work in eight camps located along the Boardman River. By the end of the 1860s, large operators, such as Ami Wright or Loud, Gay & Company, might have been running as many as twenty camps a season, with a total labor force of 300 to 400 men. The number of workers in each camp also rose. Some camps had a population as high as forty to sixty by 1870, but the normal unit was around twenty-five.[11] From the scant data available, it would appear that the logger could estimate an annual output of roughly 50,000 feet per hand. Expanded production could mean increased profits, but it also meant additional burdens of supervision, coordination, and logistics for the employer.

Between 1855 and 1870 logging spread rapidly northward and into the interior along the rivers of the lower peninsula. In the Thumb the best pine stands remained in Huron County and high up the Cass River in Tuscola County. The movement of loggers on the Cass was matched by the movement into the interior along all the streams of the Saginaw River system. When David Ward began logging on the Tittabawassee about 1860, there was little activity beyond Midland. By 1870 he had expanded his operations to the Tobacco, Pine, and Chippewa rivers, all tributaries of the Tittabawassee, which was by then being logged as far into the interior as Gladwin County. Camps were also being established on the Rifle and Au Gres rivers in Ogemaw and Iosco counties and on the Au Sauble, perhaps as far into the interior as Oscoda County. Some timber from Oscoda, Iosco, and Alcona counties was brought to Alpena via the Thunder River. At the northernmost tip of the lower peninsula, the Cheboygan River area, logging was just beginning.[12]

Activity on the state's western slope closely paralleled that of the eastern side. Loggers marched up the Muskegon River through Mecosta and Osceola counties into Missaukee County. By the time the Civil War ended, the interior village of Big Rapids in Mecosta County was a well-established center for loggers' supplies. To the north, cutting along the Pere Marquette River had moved into Lake County and along the Manistee River into Wexford County. In the lake counties of the northwest, Hannah & Lay continued to cut into the interior along the Boardman River.[13]

By 1870 logging had expanded into much of the forest of lower Michigan. Only those counties in the north central portion of the state, principally Clare, Roscommon, Crawford, Otsego, and Montmorency, remained untouched. Of these, Clare proved to be the best timbered but least accessible, situated as it was at the headwaters of both the Muskegon and Tittabawassee rivers, streams at that point too small and too rapid for easy handling of logs.[14] Swiftly and relentlessly the loggers of Michigan claimed the prize pine. Much timber would remain in the state after 1870, but little of it would be located along either its coasts or the banks of its many streams and rivers.

One element of logging that remained essentially unchanged despite expanding production was its depen-

dence on the weather. Woods work continued to be almost exclusively a winter operation, with the most
critical and least predictable element—as important as
investment capital or labor—the depth of the snow. In a
lumber region, "snow was what water was to the miners
of California."[15] Even the best calculations on output
could be ruined by either a mild or a harsh winter. What
loggers liked best was a solid freeze and then a wet, level,
and deep snow cover. A sledding season of fifty days was
considered sufficient to remove the logs cut.[16]

A casual reading of Michigan's newspapers makes
clear the importance of weather to the logger, the manufacturer, and the state's economy. Reports from the
woods appeared regularly during the winter, with their
tone routinely alternating between joy and gloom. The
logging season of 1859–60, for example, began auspi-
ciously in December and continued to please all concerned into January. Moderate temperatures and a snow
base of approximately two inches sent lumbermen's spir-
its soaring, but then in early February came warm
weather and "long faces" for the loggers.[17] Good sledding
weather returned only briefly before the season ended
abruptly in mid-March. What lumbermen had hoped
would be a banner year turned out to be just adequate.[18]

Although most loggers operated during the winter
months only, a few attempted to extend operations into
the summer whenever increased demand coupled with a
poor cutting season began to push prices higher. In 1864
Briggs reported to Woodman that Ludington and other
millmen along the western slope between Grand Haven
and Manistee intended to run their camps during the
summer to get out the logs that they had been unable to
remove the previous winter because of excessive snow.[19]
Since dragging timber along heavily wooded or swampy
ground was very difficult, to say nothing of the heat and
insects that plagued the workers, summer logging was
not extensively attempted, nor was it very successful, be-

fore 1870. Many different approaches were tried with varying degrees of success, including skidding, trucking, and the use of pole roads and tramways. One of the most imaginative schemes was attempted by the Luce Company in 1861. That company built a "track," probably for horse-drawn vehicles, to cover a considerable distance between the forest and their mill in the hopes of expanding the logging season into a year-round operation.[20] In 1870 Sylas C. Overpack of Manistee began building logging wheels. A log was attached to the wheels, much as it would be to a travois in the winter, and then pulled by horse or ox. Overpack made his first wheels the size of wagon wheels, but they soon increased to ten or twelve feet in diameter with a capacity to haul three or four large logs at a time. Those "big wheels" reduced the cost of hauling and made summer logging easier for all but the most difficult terrain.[21] Full-scale year-round logging did not become the rule, however, until railroads were built into northern Michigan in the mid-1870s.

The process of cutting a log showed little improvement until about 1870, when the cross-cut saw began to replace the axe as the basic tool of the chopper. The saw increased a woodsman's output by about 10 percent and improved his control over the direction of the tree's fall. As concern increased for maximizing the amount and quality of lumber that could be made from a tree, the sawyer's judgment became especially important, because he was the person who decided how the felled tree would be divided. The logs could be branded on one end with a stamp of the owner's mark before or after sledding to the rollway. Here at the edge of a lake or a river, the logs were piled: sometimes to a height of thirty tiers. When the logs were banked and tallied for number and board feet, the loggers' work was done.[22]

Once cut, the logs had to be moved from the forest to the mill, an operation that remained water bound until the mid-1870s. Crapo called the river drive the most dangerous and difficult part of lumbering.[23] While an owner might manage his own logging, supervision for driving was always put into the hands of a specialist.[24] Driving was a simple, nonmechanical operation that took place as soon as the rivers thawed. The spring freshet swept up the logs that came tumbling into the water as the rollways were broken. Guided by men riding atop, the logs moved downriver with the water's momentum. The problem for the river hogs, as the driving crews were sometimes called, was to keep the logs together and running smoothly. Too much water might overflow the river's banks and carry logs into areas where they would be stranded; too little water meant that the logs could not be run all the way downriver. The greatest hazard of the drive was the jam, which could be caused by logs moving too fast or too slowly, or by some impediment in the channel of the river. A jam not only delayed the drive and endangered the workers, it also prevented navigation of the river and caused flooding behind it. Before dynamite was introduced in the 1880s, men had to break the jam with the most important piece of equipment used on the drive, the peavey.[25] Invented by Joseph Peavey in Stillwater, Maine, in 1858, the tool was a five- to eight-foot pole with a pike at one end and a flexible cant dog, an adjustable arm, attached near the base. Before the peavey, drivers had to use a hand spike or a blunt-ended cant hook that provided much less leverage.[26]

In driving, as in logging, weather remained all important. The winter of 1859–60 had been a disappointment to loggers and manufacturers, and the driving season only compounded their distress. The thaw came rapidly in mid-March, bringing waters too high for driving. Then the scant snowfall of the winter made itself felt in low, slow-moving water. Many logs remained far upstream in April, and lumbermen began to predict dire consequences for the industry unless spring rains were exceptionally heavy. Not until early June was there sufficient rain to bring down most of the logs that had been cut. All in all it was a disappointing season for manufacturers who had been hoping for an exceptionally large supply of logs.[27] Such unpredictability remained the rule rather than the exception during the years of water transport.

Although the process of driving changed little between 1855 and 1870, the volume of logs being handled and the length of the drive increased enormously, as a few random examples demonstrate. Between 1856 and 1864 an estimated 1,700,000,000 feet of logs came down the Tittabawassee River, which would average over 8,000,000 logs a year. In 1860 a local newspaper considered a log run of 90,000,000 feet on all of the tributaries of the Saginaw to be average. Volume on that river system steadily increased to 133,500,000 feet in 1863 and then soared to 457,396,225 feet in 1868. Loggers had moved at least 100 miles up the Tittabawassee by 1870 and probably twice that far up the Muskegon.[28]

A good driving stream had to have a deep, obstacle-free channel and a steady flow of water. For the lumberman, that need usually necessitated cleaning the stream and perhaps building a series of dams to control the water's flow. Sometimes an individual operator would clear a river, as did Thomas Merrill the Pine, G. O. Whittemore the Upper Tawas, and Loud, Priest & Gay the Au Sable, but individual initiative was insufficient or impractical for large-scale projects on streams used by many operators. Cooperative efforts first became necessary on the Muskegon River. By 1857 that stream could no longer handle the increased volume of the drives, and the booming company had to spend $50,000 to straighten parts of the river and build dams. When the river's log-carrying capacity was reached again in 1870, additional improvements became imperative. The Cheboygan Slack Water Company had to construct an extensive series of dams to improve that river.[29]

In response to the growing difficulties of log transportation caused by the number of firms, volume of logs, distance of the drive, and need for river improvements, the legislature of Michigan passed an act authorizing the creation of rafting or booming companies in 1855. Under the provisions of the act interested parties could join together to form companies to run, raft, and sort logs. The wording of the statute, particularly the section dealing with the regulation of floatage, was sufficiently unclear to cause continuing controversy and litigation. Although a state court upheld the legality of booming companies in 1859, the court declared that it was unconstitutional for such a company to handle the logs of an unconsenting party and then charge him for the service. In other words, participation had to be voluntary. The legislature attempted to be more precise in a statute of 1861 that obligated booming companies to leave a navigable channel at all times, but the basic flaws in the old law of 1855 remained. Finally in January of 1864 Governor Austin Blair recommended a new law for booming companies. In less than a month the legislature passed a comprehensive booming act that replaced the voluntary assessment-type associations with companies having full powers to make contracts. That piece of legislation, according to one expert, eliminated the last legal limitations on logging in the state of Michigan; it made possible the coordinated action necessary to bring order from the chaos caused by millions of logs floating down most of the rivers and streams of the lower peninsula. It gave a booming company monopolistic control over log transportation on a specific river.[30]

Booming companies were empowered to own property, drive logs, operate dams, and maintain booming or sorting works on a specific stream. Each company either hired its own crew or contracted for work and set the fees for its services. Whichever choice was made, the men who operated the booming works had to be experts. Once the logs came down the river they had to be sorted for ownership, a process that took place at the booming grounds. Located near the river's mouth, a boom consisted of timbers or logs chained together to form a pen. The logs entered a large holding boom, and as they passed through a narrow "sorting gap" they were separated according to owner's mark and moved along to the small enclosures of each owner, known as "pocket booms." There workmen chained the logs together for running, rafting or towing to the individual mills. Unmarked, or "prize," logs became the property of the booming company.[31]

Cooperative driving and sorting began on the Muskegon River. The Muskegon Lumberman's Association, organized in 1852 and reorganized in 1855, operated as a voluntary association, with assessments proportional to a member's volume of operations. The Association was superseded by the Muskegon Booming Company as soon as the new law was passed in 1864. Manufacturers were the primary investors in the new company, and its first board of directors consisted entirely of local lumbermen. Capitalized at $40,000, the Muskegon Booming Company moved over 96,000,000 feet of logs through large booming grounds and many pocket booms during its first year of operation. Volume rapidly increased, and by 1869 its 250-man work force was sorting over 250,000,000 feet of logs.[32]

Unlike Muskegon's cooperative venture, the first booming company in eastern Michigan was a private business. Organized by Charles Merrill in 1856, the company provided booming services for lumbermen on the Tittabawassee River. It handled 110,000,000 feet of logs the first year and 133,580,000 in 1863, the last year of its operation. By then the volume of logs was becoming too large for Merrill's simple sorting works to handle, and in

1864 the Tittabawassee Boom Company was formed. With a capitalization of $50,000, the boom company was able to build a complex Muskegon-type system that ran for twelve miles and had a capacity that rose from 215,000,000 feet in 1864 to 347,041,250 feet in 1870.[33] The third booming company in the lower peninsula began in the mid-1850s on the Cass River. Reorganized in 1864, it was a relatively small operation, sorting less than 10,000,000 feet in the late 1860s.[34]

The technique of sorting and distributing logs received large-scale testings on the Muskegon and Tittabawassee rivers. Success there encouraged the subsequent formation of booming companies on many other rivers in Michigan. In 1867 the Cheboygan Slack Water Navigation Company was organized, and the following year lumbermen formed the Aus Gres Boom Company to operate on the Thunder Bay River. Because that river was so dangerously swift, the Au Gres Boom Company had to build and maintain many dams to control its flow. By the end of 1870 five more companies had been organized on the Manistee, Little Manistee, White, Grand Rapids, and Rifle rivers. Most of those companies handled less than 50,000,000 feet of logs in 1870, although total volume at the Manistee boom was almost double that amount.[35]

After sorting, logs were run or rafted to the individual mills. In order to be rafted, logs had to be either linked together or placed inside large cribs made of long timber. Several cribs were then linked by chains to form a raft of up to 4,000,000 feet of logs, which was then towed by tugs. Steam tugs were used effectively in moving log rafts at the mouth of the Muskegon and across Saginaw Bay. But tugs proved particularly vulnerable to storms, as a group of manufacturers at Buffalo discovered when they attempted to have logs from Michigan towed to their mills in New York. Rafting on Lake Michigan to Chicago and on Lake Erie to Toledo, Cleveland,

and Buffalo continued sporadically for many years, with varying degrees of success.[36]

Dependence on waterways severely circumscribed the lumber industry in various ways. In the first place, it limited the supply of raw materials. Only pine stands adjacent to streams had any commercial value. Dependence on water transportation also made logging a seasonal operation. Further, it dictated the location of manufacturing, for a mill had to be located where it could both receive its raw resources and market its product by water. This meant the mill had to be placed at or near the mouth of a river, which then became an ever-lengthening supply line. As long as log transportation remained an uncertain and wildly fluctuating variable, lumbermen could not develop rational manufacturing and marketing strategies. A stable lumber industry needed control over volume of raw materials, which was impossible as long as logging was shackled to the weather.

Railroads in Michigan date back to 1836, but they had no important effect on the lumber industry until the 1860s and did not become a supplement or alternative to water as a form of transportation for logs until the mid-1870s. In 1860 Michigan contained only 799 miles of railroad track, and in 1870 only 1,638 miles. During the 1860s the Flint & Pere Marquette and Grand Rapids & Indiana railroads penetrated into the lumbering areas, and for the first time commercial mills began to locate close to their source of supply in the interior counties. The Flint & Pere Marquette began carrying logs in 1872, but the volume of its log business was less than its lumber business. Of equal or greater importance were the railroads specifically built to carry logs. Inspired by an exhibit at the Centennial Exposition, Scott Garrish, a lumberman from western Michigan, built the first steam-powered narrow-gauge logging railroad in Michigan in 1876. He brought logs ten miles by rail to the

Muskegon River from what had been considered inaccessible lands. By the mid-1870s private and common carriers were beginning to open previously unreachable forest tracts, to expand logging into a year-round activity, to eliminate dependence on weather, and, consequently, to reduce the uncertainties of annual output.[37]

The cost of logs delivered at the mill fluctuated from beginning to end of the season and from one season to the next, depending upon both availability and demand, but, in general, prices rose markedly over the years, reaching as high as $7.00 M in 1857. Demand and price dropped off sharply as the effects of the panic of that year began to be felt and then drifted still lower to $2.50 to $5.00 M with the coming of the Civil War. The increased demand for lumber in the early 1860s was not immediately reflected in the value of logs because of large inventories, but from the end of the war, logs steadily appreciated in value, returning to pre-Panic levels by 1870. In addition to increased demand, the rapid exhaustion of the most accessible timber stands helped to boost prices, particularly in the oldest lumbering areas. A summary of prices in the Saginaw Valley in 1870 disclosed that the total cost of a log delivered at the mill was $6.75 M, of which $5.00, or nearly 75 percent, was attributable to transportation. It was estimated that logging costs were $1.00 M and the cost of the standing timber, or stumpage, was $.75. Skidding, driving, booming, and delivery accounted for the remaining $5.00.[38]

Census data summarized in Table 19 support generalizations based upon business records, correspondence, and other contemporary sources. Log prices in 1860 ranged from a low $2.29 M in Kent County to a high of $7.03 M in Detroit. In general, log costs were highest along the eastern shore, from Wayne County to Alpena County. By 1870 the cost of logs showed a substantial increase. Although information is less complete for that year, it appears that prices remained higher for the east

TABLE 19
Log Prices for Selected Michigan Counties, 1860 and 1870

County	Number of Firms		Average Price, M	
	1860	1870	1860	1870
Wayne*	5		7.03	
St. Clair	28	18	4.92	7.97
Huron	6		4.39	
Saginaw	26	61	4.29	6.83
Bay	31		4.17	
Sanilac	9	10	3.83	5.93
Midland	2		3.34	
Tuscola	8		3.25	
Alpena	3		3.24	
Ottawa	5	30	3.20	5.48
Alcona	1		3.00	
Genesee	26	27	2.99	5.23
Allegan	31		2.98	
Muskegon	26		2.92	
Lapeer	34		2.86	
Montcalm	8		2.52	
Osceola	1	1	2.50	5.00
Cheboygan	1		2.50	
Kent	37		2.29	
Emmet		1		5.00
Oceana		11		4.47

*Detroit only

Source: Manuscript Census for the State of Michigan, 1860 and 1870.

coast than for western manufacturers.[39] Not surprisingly, logs were cheaper in the newer, northern, interior counties located closer to the source of supply.

In the years between 1855 and 1870 logging in Michigan was expanded and rationalized. The number of entrepreneurs, camps, and workmen increased, and operations were spread over an ever-larger geographic area. The process of logging was standardized, and the nature of the work became characterized by task differentiation.

CHAPTER 9

Commercial Lumber Manufacturing in Michigan, 1855–1870

Between 1855 and 1870, the sawmills of Michigan increased in number, size, and complexity. Tables 20 and 21 present an industrial profile of the state for 1860 and 1870 that shows the importance of the lumber industry there.[1] As in 1850, Michigan's economy continued to rest on agriculture and the primary and secondary processing of natural resources. The composition of the state's industries, and their relative importance, did not change greatly between 1850 and 1860 (see Table 12, Chapter 6). By the outbreak of the Civil War, lumber still ranked first by a wide margin in number of firms, value added, and number employed. Flour milling, agricultural implements, and iron and copper manufacturing, the next most important industries in the state in 1860, lagged considerably behind lumber in value added by manufacture. By 1870 the lumber industry's percentage of the total labor force remained little changed from 1850, just under 35 percent, but its contribution to output as measured by value added by manufacturing increased to 41 percent of the state's total, from 37 percent in 1850. The percentage of value added by flour milling and agricultural implements decreased, while metal working, the manufacture of machinery, and the production of vehi-

TABLE 20
Selecting Leading Major Industries in Lower Michigan, 1860

Industry	Number of Firms	Percent Total	Value Added	Percent Total	Number of Workers	Percent Total
Lumber	926	27.07	$1,820,971	35.38	6,394	35.38
Flour	317	15.48	1,041,062	4.38	791	4.38
Iron and Copper Manufacture	85	11.32	761,437	10.05	1,816	10.05
Agricultural Implements	108	10.25	689,913	3.51	634	3.51
Vehicles	182	5.56	373,958	4.86	879	4.86
Leather	151	4.15	279,272	3.20	578	3.20
Liquors	60	3.73	250,837	1.03	187	1.03
Boots and Shoes	271	3.60	242,396	6.10	1,102	6.10
Furniture	138	2.42	162,949	3.99	721	3.99
Tin and Sheet Metal	110	2.20	148,196	1.66	300	1.66
Paper	36	1.99	134,036	2.11	382	2.11
Minerals	81	1.77	119,151	1.65	299	1.65
Construction Materials	170	1.74	116,748	6.91	1,248	6.91
Fisheries	121	1.63	109,838	3.43	620	3.43
Cooperage	106	1.56	105,223	3.18	575	3.18
Clothing	66	1.51	101,861	4.92	889	4.92
Blacksmiths	140	1.23	82,929	1.58	286	1.58
Wool	34	1.07	72,142	.99	178	.99
Bakery	35	.85	57,181	.66	120	.66
Gas	4	.50	33,956	.07	12	.07
Tobacco	11	.33	22,153	.33	60	.33
Total	3,152	100.00	$6,726,209	100.00	18,071	100.00

Source: *Manufactures of the United States in 1860.*

TABLE 21
Selected Leading Major Industries in Lower Michigan, 1870

Industry	Number of Firms	Value Added	Percent Total	Number of Workers	Percent Total
Lumber	1,641	$11,390,940	41.14	20,576	34.49
Flour	516	2,606,248	9.41	1,938	3.24
Construction Materials	1,087	1,856,782	6.71	6,182	10.36
Iron and Copper Manufacture	237	1,415,858	5.11	3,881	6.50
Vehicles	624	1,377,367	4.97	3,948	6.61
Furniture	342	895,732	3.23	3,095	5.18
Boots and Shoes	765	735,422	2.66	2,494	4.18
Clothing	310	735,214	2.66	2,810	4.71
Blacksmiths	904	694,443	2.51	1,997	3.34
Tobacco	114	682,288	2.46	1,256	2.10
Minerals	194	633,244	2.29	1,448	2.42
Leather	462	631,405	2.28	1,858	3.11
Tin, Sheet Iron, Brass, Copper	266	583,576	2.11	878	1.47
Paper	76	509,372	1.84	987	1.65
Agricultural Implements	164	491,819	1.78	969	1.62
Liquors	133	483,366	1.75	514	.86
Machinery	105	450,094	1.63	1,311	2.19
Wool	45	343,169	1.24	669	1.12
Fisheries	242	329,244	1.19	1,159	1.94
Gas	13	326,949	1.18	111	.18
Cooperate	291	320,966	1.16	1,139	1.90
Food	107	195,968	.71	429	.71
Totals	8640	$27,689,475	100.00	59,649	100.00

Source: *The Statistics of the Wealth and Industry of the United States, 1870.*

cles all increased in number of firms and output, clear signals of a diversifying economy.

A comparison of number of firms, capital invested, and value of product of the leading lumber-producing states, as tabulated in Table 22, gives perspective to the industry in Michigan. Ohio and Indiana, manufacturers of hardwoods, ranked third and fourth in number of mills in 1870 but stood lower in terms of investment and value of output. Only New York and Pennsylvania exceeded Michigan in all three categories in 1860. Over the next decade, the industry expanded in all six of the states, but the growth was greatest for Michigan, where investment in sawmills more than tripled and output, as measured by value of product, more than quadrupled. Within a brief period, Michigan had become the premier lumber-manufacturing center in the United States, a position it retained until 1900.

Like lumber producers throughout the nation, manufacturers in Michigan could not solve the problem of adjusting supply to demand. This problem resulted in large measure, from the basic organization of the industry, which was marked by a lack of concentration of ownership. The result was that all producers had to operate in an unrationalized market. Excess capacity made it possible to overstock the market almost continually. One of the most easily observable characteristics of the American lumber industry in the nineteenth century was the repetitious pattern of scarcity and high prices followed by overproduction and declining income. Since weather made logging and manufacturing unpredictable, supply was sometimes less than current demand, which would raise the price of lumber. Responding to that stimulus, producers would exert extra efforts to increase their output and gain a share of the higher prices. The inevitable result would be a saturated market and a drop in prices. No single lumberman nor group of lumbermen had sufficient control over the industry to adjust supply to

TABLE 22
The Leading Lumber-Producing States, 1850–1870

State	Number of Firms			Capital Invested			Value of Product		
New York	4,625	3,035	3,510	$8,032,983	$ 7,931,708	$15,110,981	$10,597,595	$13,126,759	$21,238,228
Pennsylvania	2,894	3,078	3,739	6,913,267	10,978,464	24,804,304	10,994,060	7,729,058	28,938,985
Ohio	1,639	1,911	2,230	2,600,361	2,708,153	6,191,676	5,279,883	3,864,452	10,235,180
Indiana	928	1,331	1,861	1,502,811	2,544,538	5,975,946	4,451,114	2,195,351	12,324,755
Maine	732	926	1,099	3,009,240	4,401,482	6,614,875	7,167,762	5,872,573	11,395,747
Michigan	558	986	1,571	1,880,875	7,735,780	26,990,450	9,303,404	2,464,329	31,946,396

Sources: U.S., 35 Cong., 2 sess., *Senate Executive Documents no. 39*, "Abstract of the Statistics of Manufactures According to the Returns of the Seventh Census"; U.S., Bureau of the Census, Eighth Census, 1860, *vol. 3: Manufactures*; U.S., Bureau of the Census, Ninth Census, 1870, *vol. 3: Statistics of the Wealth and Industry of the United States.*

demand. Most felt the need to operate, even at an unprofitable rate.[2]

The cycle of scarcity and glut can be seen quite clearly
in Michigan. Between 1855 and the middle of 1857 the
market for lumber remained strong, making lumbermen
optimistic. Many manufacturers agreed with M. B. Hess
of East Saginaw, who believed that the only factor limit-
ing the sale of lumber was supply.[3] Dealers concurred,
eagerly seeking contracts to buy lumber as prices rose.
Log prices continued to advance as the availability of
logs decreased. By late summer of 1857 G. D. Hill could
not buy logs, whatever the price.[4] The wholesale price of
common lumber at Chicago increased during this time
from around $8.00 per thousand board feet, or M, to
about $13.00 M.[5] Then came the sharp economic down-
turn of 1857. Prices plunged in the autumn, and lumbermen began to feel the chilling effects of the depression.
Manufacturers curtailed production. By the spring of
1858, newspapers were reporting a general cutback of 50
percent of Michigan's sawmills. Yet demand contracted
more sharply, and prices fell to 50 percent or less of the
level reached in mid-1857. Although manufacturers announced their intention of keeping their lumber off the
market until prices improved, few could afford to hold
out. Most needed whatever money they could get to continue operations. Crapo complained to his son that local
manufacturing "sharks" were selling lumber on the
street for "almost any price."[6]

A slight upturn in demand at the end of the season of
1858 coupled with a poor logging winter made lumbermen optimistic that the small supply that would be
available in 1859 could be sold profitably. Prices advanced during the spring, to around $9.00 for common-
grade lumber in the Chicago market, with demand for
the better grades even stronger. Dealers once again became anxious to make contracts with manufacturers as a
hedge against any further increases, and the competition

between Albany and Chicago buyers sent prices higher. With advancing rates, lumbermen began to send to market large quantities of previously manufactured lumber. By the middle of June lumber receipts at Chicago were running one-third ahead of the same time in 1858. In addition, manufacturers increased current output by undertaking summer logging and running the mills twenty-four hours a day. But the anticipated upsurge of demand, especially in the West, failed to materialize in the summer, and by mid-August the great excess of supply over demand sent prices downward one to two dollars. By the end of the season, common-grade lumber, which had sold as high as $10.00 in June, cost wholesalers as little as $6.50 at Chicago. Once again manufacturers were faced with large piles of unsold stock. Total lumber production for the state appears to have been about 50 percent of capacity, but this was still too much. It was a very bad year for the lumber industry in Michigan. Crapo swung from a feeling of optimism that the bottom had been reached in October to extreme pessimism just a month later when he called the manufacture of lumber a "hard, slavish business."[7] By the end of the year he had managed to dispose of less than half of the 12,840,501 feet that he had manufactured over the past three years.[8] Although Crapo claimed that the decline of prices "had no reference to the great principle of supply and demand," a correspondent in Albany saw this as precisely the problem. Business "won't be good for manufacturers again until either some mills close or Western demand improves."[9]

The winter of 1859–60 was ideal for logging, and despite warnings from the business and local press, most lumbermen with any capital resources sent crews into the woods. Only low waters and a bad driving season saved the manufacturers from overproduction in 1860. With supplies reduced, prices held firm before gradually moving upward. By fall demand in both the east and west exceeded supply, and the price of common lumber at Chicago passed $10.00 M. The basic problem for the lumberman was that of excess capacity, yet manufacturers seemed unwilling or unable to control the situation. In spite of several years of over-production and ruinously low prices, men continued to build more mills. The Saginaw *Courier* reported in the winter of 1860 that six new mills were being constructed in the area, with an aggregate capacity of 25,000,000 feet, which would boost existing capacity by 20 percent.[10]

Given the lumbermen's inability to control ever-increasing production, the only hope for a flourishing and profitable industry lay in increased demand, but this did not come in 1861. Volume of sales was low that year, and prices drifted downward in the spring months. At the end of June, lumber receipts at Chicago were under 80,000,000 feet, a decline of almost 50,000,000 feet from 1859. The industry received a further setback with the outbreak of the Civil War. The war "put a quietus" on trade, forcing one manufacturer after another to suspend operations as the bottom dropped out of the market.[11] The depressing effect of the war was brief, however, and 1862 marked the beginning of what H. W. Sage called "eleven fat years."[12] Trade opened briskly and demand continued to rise throughout the spring of 1862 because drought slowed mills and the supply of lumber decreased. Eastern and western buyers and a brisk local trade pushed prices steadily upward until by autumn they were $3.00 to $4.00 M higher than at the beginning of the season. Manufacturers reacted cautiously. Perhaps because of labor shortages, they did not increase output by summer logging and running two shifts at the mill. The result was a rise in prices and, finally, sizable profits. For the first time since 1857 lumbermen in Michigan had reason to be optimistic about the immediate future.[13] Prices soared during 1863 and 1864, with common lumber reaching as high as $23.00 M at Chicago,

Map 5

Organized counties in the lower peninsula in 1872

but in 1865 an excessive cut and good weather resulted in over-production that briefly lowered prices. Between 1865 and 1870 the market fluctuated according to the availability of logs, but in general prices held steady. Every year was a "good year" for the lumber business at Chicago, while the price of common at Saginaw and along the west coast of Michigan averaged $12.00 M. By 1870 the mills throughout the lower peninsula were humming as output continued to expand and the market remained firm. In that year the mills of the Saginaw area, at least were producing at or near their estimated capacities.[14]

TABLE 23
Sawmills in Michigan, 1860–1870

	1860	1864	1870
Total Mills, L.P.	926	1046	1158
Mills in 27 Pine Counties	352	419	710*
% Pine to All Mills	38	40	61

*Figure includes all of Wayne County

Source: Manuscript Census for the State of Michigan, 1860; U.S., Bureau of the Census, Ninth Census, 1870, vol. 3, *The Statistics of the Wealth and Industry of the U.S.*, 679–83.

As lumber manufacturing grew, it spread geographically. A comparison of the locations of sawmills in 1860 and in 1870 not only demonstrates this spread, it also underscores the regional development of the lumber industry (see maps 4 and 5). Sawmills increased most rapidly in Michigan's pine region (see Table 23). In 1860 there were 352 mills located in twenty-seven pine counties. The heaviest concentrations were in the Thumb and Saginaw Bay areas on the east shore and in Allegan, Kent, Ottawa, and Muskegon counties on the west side of the state. There were a few mills in the counties stretching northward along both coasts but little manufacturing development in the unorganized interior counties of the northern half of the peninsula. By 1870 there were 710 mills scattered throughout thirty-eight pine counties, as lumber manufacturing spread northward in the counties bordering Lakes Michigan and Huron. With the exception of Montcalm County, sawmills spread less rapidly into the interior counties, which is not surprising since one of the factors governing plant location remained accessibility to market. The number of mills decreased in St. Clair County as the industry moved into Huron and Sanilac counties in the Thumb but expanded significantly in Saginaw and Bay counties (from forty-eight to 102 mills). Iosco County, which encompassed the mouths of the Pine and Au Sauble rivers, and Alpena County on Thunder Bay were becoming important manufacturing centers. On the western shore the number of mills increased in all the counties from Allegan to Grand Traverse, with Muskegon surpassing Ottawa as the most important lumber-producing county along Lake Michigan. By 1870 the largest concentrations of lumber manufacturing were in Saginaw and Muskegon counties.

Mills increased in size as well as number. According to one expert, a "first-class" mill just before the Civil War could cut about 25,000 feet of lumber in a ten-hour day. In an eight-month milling season, total output would be 5,250,000 feet. A review of the lumber mills in Detroit in 1861 reported capacity for four of the city's largest mills as ranging from 5,000,000 to 10,000,000 feet annually. The largest Michigan mill of the pre-Civil War years was probably that built by Ami Wright, Valorous A. Paine, and Harry Miller at Saginaw City in 1860. It initially had a daily capacity of 55,000 to 75,000 feet, which in yearly terms would have been as much as 15,750,000 feet. By 1870 it was producing nearly 25,000,000 feet annually. Profiles of thirty-one of the largest mills from Flint to Saginaw and north to Presque Isle appeared in three of the early issues of the *Lumberman's Gazette,* and they clearly indicate the increase in capacity by the early 1870s. By that date all but five of the mills had capacities in excess of 25,000 feet per day. The median capacity was 45,000 feet, with the largest firm, Loud, Gay & Company, boasting a daily capacity of 150,000 feet. Potential output of around 100,000 feet a day, or at least 20,000,000 feet a year, was clearly the aim of the largest manufacturers like Sage & McGraw, Eber B. Ward, W. R. Burt & Company, Ami Wright & Company, and Henry H. Crapo. Later research would prove the largest mills of the immediate post-Civil War years, the mills that produced 20,000,000 to 30,000,000 feet per year, to be the most efficient. Further increases in the size of mills produced no additional economies of scale.[15]

The complete manuscript census for Michigan in 1870 is not available, but extant scattered returns indicate that in only one county did one or two large mills dominate the market. That county was Grand Traverse, where Hannah, Lay & Company accounted for fully 68 percent of total output. In Genesee County the two largest manufacturers produced 36 percent of the county's total, while in Saginaw, which had the highest concentration of large-scale firms, the output of the four leading mills accounted for only 25 percent of the total. In St. Clair and Sanilac counties no large firms dominated production.[16]

Improved technology made large increases in production possible. Manufacturers increasingly relied on a variety of relatively sophisticated machines to expand output. While in the years just before and after the Civil War there were no great innovative advances in technology, Michigan's millmen effected improvements to existing equipment. More importantly, they employed additional machines, each for a specific job. It was a time of mechanical specialization.

The most important new piece of equipment to be tested in Michigan in the years between 1855 and 1870 was the band saw, and it was not initially successful. Invented in England in 1808, the band saw was a continuously moving blade that revolved around fixed upper and lower wheels. James J. McCormick introduced the first band saw in the state in 1858, but its unreliability and slowness compared to the circular saw consigned it to the category of impractical curiosities for several more decades. The band saw's thin blade produced a smaller kerf than muley or circular saws. Yet a savings of nearly 10 percent over a circular, the most wasteful saw, did not impress lumbermen who were more concerned with speed than waste of what seemed to be inexhaustible resource. Only when the price of stumpage began to rise sharply in the late 1870s and early 1880s did Michigan's lumber manufacturers adopt the band saw.[17]

In 1870 a large number of small mills still ran only one saw of either the muley or the circular variety, but most of the larger mills used muley, circular, and gang saws in varying combinations. Of the eighty-three mills in the vicinity of Saginaw reviewed by Headly and Lewis in 1869, sixty-one had muleys, seventy-seven employed circulars, and forty-nine had installed gangs. Because of its speed and the quality of its cut, the circular (or buzz) saw became the most widely adopted piece of equipment after its technical problems were solved, displacing the muley in popularity. Manufacturers steadily worked to decrease the thickness of the circular saw's blade, for speed (and output) were proportional to the saw's thinness. By the mid-1860s "challenge" runs in mills had proven that a single circular saw could produce well over 1,000 feet of lumber an hour. Although less slowly adopted than the circular, the gang saw, actually many parallel saws set together, gained acceptance because of its speed and economy. Millmen used either a muley, a circular, or a round gang saw to square the log and then, depending upon the quality of the lumber and the dimensions desired, a circular or flat gang saw to cut the slabs into boards. A circular saw could not be used advantageously on boards of less than one and one-half inches thick, because it tended to split thin pieces of wood.[18]

Finishing the lumber and removing it from the mill remained the slowest part of the operation, but here too machines were adopted to accelerate the process of manufacture. Edgers, double edgers, butting saws, and even planing equipment became standard in the large mills. Over half the mills surveyed in the *Lumberman's Gazette* in 1873 used at least one type of finishing machine, but removing the lumber from the mill remained unmechanized until the introduction of endless carriage feeds later in the decade.[19]

Premature experiments with machinery not yet perfected delayed a general acceptance of the circular saw and then the band saw, but, on the whole, lumber manufacturers in Michigan showed little hesitation in adopting equipment to rationalize production. Improvements in machinery increased output per worker by 100 percent in the decade from 1860 to 1870. By the latter date only one hand was required for every two thousand feet of lumber manufactured.[20]

Millmen just as readily adopted steam as an improved source of power. Although the use of steam required specially trained workmen and constant, careful attention, it was a more reliable source of power than water, and it could extend manufacturing into a year-round operation. In 1860, almost 60 percent of the sawmills in the lumber counties used steam. A high percentage of steam-powered mills characterized those counties with large lumber-manufacturing industries. The ratio of steam- to water-powered sawmills, tabulated in Table 24, indicates a positive correlation between steam power and commercial lumber production. With the exception of Alpena County, which would develop into a major lumber manufacturing center within the decade, and Grand Traverse County, where the largest mill was steam-powered, the counties where water mills pre-dominated in 1860

TABLE 24
Water-Powered and Steam-Powered Sawmills
for Selected Counties, 1860

County	Number Water	Number Steam	Percent Steam	% Capital Invested in Steam
Saginaw	4	24	85.71	96.89
Ottawa	7	22	75.86	88.46
Muskegon	6	21	77.78	95.21
Bay	0	20	100.00	100.00
St. Clair	9	19	67.86	92.41
Allegan	17	16	48.48	63.98
Genesee	12	14	53.85	87.99
Huron	1	12	92.31	99.44
Lapeer	25	11	30.56	46.64
Kent	36	9	20.00	31.33
Sanilac	3	6	66.67	95.36
Wayne[A]	0	5	100.00	100.00
Manistee	2	4	66.67	65.43
Tuscola	4	4	50.00	42.86
Oceana[B]	5	3	37.80	29.51
Newaygo	3	2	40.00	25.32
Cheboygan	0	1	100.00	100.00
Iosco	0	1	100.00	100.00
Midland	1	1	50.00	88.89
Alpena	2	1	33.33	43.18
Grand Traverse	3	1	25.00	64.52
Alcona	1	0	—	—
Leelanau	3	0	—	—
Mecosta	2	0	—	—
Montcalm	8	0	—	—
Osceola	1	0	—	—

[A]Detroit only
[B]Includes Mason County

Source: Manuscript Census for the State of Michigan, 1860.

did not become manufacturing centers. The mills of Kent, Mecosta, and Montcalm counties, for example, continued to produce primarily for limited local markets; these were logging and not milling counties. All of the sawmills of Bay, Cheboygan, and Iosco counties, the most recent areas to experience industrialization, employed steam, while some of the longer-established centers, including Saginaw and Muskegon, still had up to one-third of their mills powered by water. In terms of capital invested, the difference is even greater. Steam

mills absorbed over 82 percent of the capital invested in
lumber manufacturing in those counties. The relatively
greater cost of a steam-powered mill partially accounts
for that difference, but, more importantly, the largest
mills tended to use steam as their motive power.

The shift to steam continued during the decade of the
1860s. All of the counties listed in Table 25 show at least
a modest increase in the percentage of steam-powered
sawmills between 1860 and 1870. Of the thirteen counties, water-powered sawmills outnumbered their steam
counterparts only in Grand Traverse and Leelanau counties. In terms of capital invested and actual production,
steam mills dominated the lumber industry in Michigan
by 1870. In Saginaw, the largest lumber producing
county in the state, steam mills absorbed 99 percent of
the capital invested in lumber manufacturing and accounted for 90 percent of the county's total output of
304,171,849 feet. Even in Grand Traverse County where
only 27 percent of the mills were steam powered in 1870,
steam mills produced over 78 percent of the county's total of 13,105,000 feet in that year.[21]

TABLE 25
Water-Powered and Steam-Powered Sawmills
for Selected Counties, 1870

County	Number Water	Number Steam	Percent Steam	% Capital Invested in Steam
Saginaw	6	58	90	99
Muskegon	11	45	80	98
Genesee	9	29	76	89
Ottawa	4	27	87	99
Huron	0	16	100	100
St. Clair	6	16	72	97
Sanilac	7	14	87	99
Mason	4	7	87	99
Oceana	5	6	54	50
Midland	0	3	100	100
Leelanau	4	3	42	40
Grand Traverse	8	3	27	44
Emmet	1	1	50	62

Source: Manuscript Census for the State of Michigan, 1870.

High-volume lumber manufacturing required a large capital investment in mill buildings, complex equipment, steam engines and boilers or race and dams, holding booms, docks, and other support facilities, often including stores and housing. The aggregate sum invested in Michigan's lumber industry over the decade rose dramatically. Despite the difficult years of the late 1850s, new mills continued to be built, and in 1860 there was $4,906,480 invested in lumber manufacturing in the pine counties, a 376 percent increase from the

TABLE 26
Aggregate Capital Invested in Lumber Manufacturing
for Selected Counties, 1860 AND 1870

	1860	1870	% Change
Muskegon	$635,150	$2,810,900	443
Saginaw	607,000	4,199,600	692
Wayne[1]	425,000	1,207,850	284
Bay	416,200	2,542,500	611
St. Clair	410,050	586,000	143
Huron	355,000	936,000	264
Manistee	332,600	1,256,000	378
Genesee	324,780	1,147,100	353
Ottawa	281,700	486,900	173
Allegan	213,500	553,000	1,780
Kent	173,950	559,200	321
Grand Traverse	115,000	112,500	-27.5
Oceana[2]	152,500	1,159,900	761
Lapeer	93,700	296,200	316
Sanilac	75,580	730,600	986
Montcalm	54,000	344,000	637
Alpena	44,000	855,500	1,940
Newaygo	39,500	221,300	560
Tuscola	35,000	11,3410	324
Iosco	20,000	841,000	4,025
Alcona	20,000	356,000	1,780
Midland	9,000	110,000	1,222
Leelanau	4,000	27,700	693
Cheboygan	2,300	345,500	15,022

[1]Detroit only in 1860
[2]Includes Mason County

Source: Manuscript Census for the State of Michigan, 1860; U.S., Bureau of the Census, Ninth Census, 1870, vol. 3, *The Statistics of the Wealth and Industry of the U.S.*, 679–83.

$1,304,675 total in 1850. By 1870 this regional lumber industry had a total capital investment of $22,277,567. As much as any other statistic, the 454 percent increase in capital investment over the decade reflects the maturation of the industry.[22] A breakdown by county is presented in Table 26. Only Grand Traverse County showed a decrease. That was because Hannah, Lay and Company was credited with an investment of only $50,000, a decrease of fully 50 percent from the census records of 1860. In 1860 there was little manufacturing north of Saginaw on the east coast and, with the exception of Grand Traverse, lumbering extended only to Manistee on the western shore. Aside from Genesee, the interior counties lagged in lumber manufacturing. In terms of capital investment, Detroit, the Thumb, Saginaw, Ottawa, and Muskegon ranked as the leading centers of the industry. By 1870 Saginaw ranked first and Bay third, making Saginaw Bay the premier lumber area. Capital flowed more rapidly into the counties along the northeastern shore than into the northwest counties for two reasons: first, because of the high quality and easy accessibility of the timber; and second, because the marketing strategy of many lumbermen put a premium on the eastern half of the state.

Tables 27 and 28 provide a summary of manufacturing units in terms of capital invested. The lack of data for 1870 makes a full comparison impossible, but the trend toward ever-larger mills in very clear. In 1850 there were only eleven mills in the pine counties with a capital investment of at least $20,000 (see Table 15, Chapter 6). By 1860 there were seventy-seven, with six capitalized at a minimum of $100,000. Since the 1860 returns are complete, it is interesting to review the pattern of investment for some of the counties. Alpena and Cheboygan do not yet reflect the great lumbering booms that were to come in the following decade, but the expansion of the industry into Bay County shows clearly. The pattern of invest-

TABLE 27
Capital Invested in Manufacturing for Selected Counties, 1860

County	Under $5,000	$5,000 to $9,999	$10,000 to $19,999	$20,000 to $29,999	$30,000 to $39,999	$40,000 to $49,999	$50,000 to $99,999	$100,000 +
Manistee	1	0	1	1	0	0	1	2
Wayne*	0	0	0	1	0	1	2	1
Muskegon	4	3	7	6	2	3	1	1
Genesee	14	8	0	1	1	0	1	1
Grand Traverse	2	0	0	0	0	0	1	1
Saginaw	3	7	7	4	1	1	5	0
Huron	2	3	1	1	2	0	4	0
St. Clair	8	4	10	2	1	1	2	0
Bay	2	4	6	2	4	0	1	0
Ottawa	12	4	9	3	1	1	0	0
Oceana	1	1	1	4	1	0	0	0
Allegan	18	9	3	2	1	0	0	0
Kent	38	3	3	1	0	0	0	0
Sanilac	3	2	3	1	0	0	0	0
Alcona	0	0	0	1	0	0	0	0
Iosco	0	0	0	1	0	0	0	0
Montcalm	4	1	3	0	0	0	0	0
Mecosta	0	0	2	0	0	0	0	0
Lapeer	30	5	1	0	0	0	0	0
Newago	2	2	1	0	0	0	0	0
Alpena	1	1	1	0	0	0	0	0
Tuscola	5	3	0	0	0	0	0	0
Midland	1	1	0	0	0	0	0	0
Leelanau	3	0	0	0	0	0	0	0
Cheboygan	1	0	0	0	0	0	0	0
Osceola	1	0	0	0	0	0	0	0
Totals	156	61	59	31	14	7	18	6

*Detroit only

Source: Manuscript Census for the State of Michigan, 1860.

TABLE 28
Capital Invested in Manufacturing for Selected Counties, 1870

County	Under $5,000	$5,000 to $9,999	$10,000 to $19,999	$20,000 to $29,999	$30,000 to $39,999	$40,000 to $49,999	$50,000 to $99,999	$100,000 to $200,000	$300,000 +
Saginaw	12	5	6	6	4	4	15	10	2
Muskegon	9	7	6	5	4	3	10	11	1
Mason	2	1	0	0	1	0	0	3	1
Genesee	18	9	4	0	3	0	1	2	1
Sanilac	6	4	1	1	0	0	1	2	1
Huron	2	1	2	1	3	0	4	3	0
Oceana	3	4	0	2	0	0	0	2	0
St. Clair	12	0	1	1	2	3	3	0	0
Oceana	11	3	8	3	1	3	2	0	0
Grand Traverse	6	2	1	0	1	0	1	0	0
Midland	0	0	1	1	0	1	0	0	0
Leelanau	6	0	1	0	0	0	0	0	0
Osceola	0	0	1	0	0	0	0	0	0
Totals							37	33	6

Source: Manuscript Census for the State of Michigan, 1870.

ment in Bay, Huron, and Manistee suggests lumber activity on a very large scale. This is particularly clear when compare to the level of capital investment in Kent, Lapeer, Newaygo, or Tuscola counties, where small, local mills predominated. The commercial lumber manufacturing concentrations at Muskegon and Saginaw indicated that these counties would soon replace the older lumbering centers of Ottawa and St. Clair counties.

Many small, low-capital mills remained in Michigan in 1870. Indeed, the number rose in the thirteen counties listed in Table 28 over the decade from 1860 to 1880, demonstrating the persistence of easy entry into the industry. But the number of highly capitalized sawmills also increased rapidly over the decade. In 1870 there were 137 mills showing a capital investment of at least $20,000 in the thirteen counties, more than a 100 percent increase over the sixty listed for the same counties in 1860. Scale of investment also continued to expand. Mills capitalized at $100,000 or more were not uncommon in 1870, with a few claiming investments in excess of $300,000. Although these large firms were scattered throughout the pine counties, two industrial centers clearly emerge: Saginaw and Muskegon. The number of medium and highly capitalized entries for those two counties suggests their great importance for distribution as well as for manufacturing.

In addition to higher fixed costs, commercial lumber manufacturing on an increased scale required working capital to pay for larger quantities of raw materials and an expanding labor force. For the largest mills, such as Ami Wright & Company or H. H. Crapo, annual operating expenses ran between $200,000 and $300,000 by 1870.[23] Lumbermen, like other businessmen, often experienced difficulties with cash flow. The long cycle of lumbering from logging preparations in the fall to sales the following summer meant that a manufacturer was able to turn his capital over only once a year. Many experienced financial difficulties.[24] The great difficulty in doing business in Michigan, Crapo complained to his associates back east, was the lack of available capital. "There is no money in circulation," he wrote in 1860, "no Banker to afford aid to the businessman . . . and no neighbor or retired capitalists of whom he can borrow money in any emergency . . . ."[25] Crapo knew the problem firsthand. Without the financial assistance of Arnold, the partnership of Crapo, Arnold, and Prescott could not have withstood the depression years.[26]

Manufacturers did not normally need outside assistance, as self-financing remained a standard procedure. If credit were needed, it usually came from eastern or Chicago sources. Despite a thorough investigation of the records remaining for Hannah, Lay & Company, Wolfe could not determine the total capital investment in it, but he did conclude that with the exception of short-term notes, the partners used no outside financing.[27] This must have been the arrangement employed by the large multi-partner or joint-stock firms with wealthy members or the companies that moved into Michigan after highly successful operations elsewhere. Eddy, Avery & Murphy or Sage & McGraw would be examples of the latter, while Imlay, Smith, Keley & Company or Smith, Tompkins & Company are examples of firms owned by eastern businessmen. Such men had the personal resources or private contacts to finance operations. During the mid- and late-1860s, those "fat years" as Sage called them, expansion through self-generated capital was common. Institutional financial intermediaries played only a small role in Michigan's lumber industry.

Sources of outside capital broadened slightly between 1855 and 1870. After about 1860 commission dealers in Chicago became an important source of financial support for Michigan lumbermen. These specialized agents supplied the manufacturer with working capital, particularly during the winter months, as an advance against the next season's consignments. According to George W. Hotchkiss, historian of the Great Lakes-Chicago lumber trade, the financial backing of the commission dealers was "almost a prerequisite" for lumbermen for the remainder of the nineteenth century.[28] Hotchkiss does not comment upon wholesalers' advances for capital improvements, but there is reason to believe that such support was given to manufacturers, since the increased production possible with an improved physical plant would have benefitted both lumberman and middleman.

While costs increased steadily, in good times lumber manufacturing proved a lucrative business. H. F. Purmont of Flint summarized his expenses for Crapo in early 1856. It cost him $2.50 M to stock his mill and $1.50 M to mill the logs, for a production total of $4.00. Without apparent difficulty he sold his lumber green at the mill for $12.00, leaving an extremely handsome profit.[29] It is not surprising, therefore, that Michigan's lumber industry of the mid-1850s attracted so many to its ranks. The statement of accounts Crapo prepared for his partners in late 1859, however, has a different tone, reflecting the severe effect of the Panic. Cost of supply, manufacturing, and selling at two yards came to $7.05 M, but if the salary of $3,000 per year and the 6.5 percent commission Crapo credited to himself were excluded, production expenses were $5.89 M. Total costs for the period amounted to $90,967.98, while sales in the same months equalled only $56,161.77.[30] More than half the lumber manufactured remained unsold. The data available for the immediate postwar years attest to a healthier tone for the industry. Expenses were up but so were volume and prices. Costs of supplies and manufacture at Mears's mills at Pentwater in 1866–1867 amounted to $8.00 M.[31] Mears's costs of production were standard for west coast mills in the late 1860s, according to a summary of average expenses for Ottawa County submitted to Congress in 1870 by Thomas W. Ferry. In

that year it cost the lumbermen $4.75 for logs delivered
at the mill and $3.50 for manufacturing, or a total of
$8.25. Costs of production were slightly higher for the
Saginaw Valley. The report stated that total expenses
equalled $10.75, $6.75 for logs and $.400 for sawing.[32]
Those figures are remarkably accurate for A. W. Wright
& Company, where procurement and manufacturing
costs were $10.87 in 1870. With local wholesale prices
ranging from $12.00 for common grade to $35.00 for
clear lumber, this company with an output of
24,000,000 feet had a very good year. At minimum the
company sales would have exceeded operating expenses
by $27,000, which would have been a return on invest-
ment of 17 percent.[33]

The decade of the 1860s confirmed the optimism of
Michigan's earliest lumber entrepreneurs. Manufacturing was expanding northward and into the interior.
Plants were becoming larger, and there was increasing
reliance on specialized machinery to increase output.
Ease of entry meant that no firm, or small group of
firms, could control the market, and the great upsurge in
demand after about 1862, bringing prosperity to the industry, encouraged additional investment and expansion.

CHAPTER 10

Commercial Marketing in the Pre-Railroad Era, 1855–1870

By 1855 a basic distribution network for Michigan pine had been established that would last for twenty-five or thirty years. In addition to supplying the home market, lumber from the lower peninsula traveled by water in three directions: east via Albany; southeast through Ohio's lake ports; and west on Lake Michigan to cities from Chicago to Milwaukee. Over the next several decades the pattern remained virtually unchanged, although the size of the market area continued to expand. Most lumbermen paid less attention to distribution than to manufacturing, responding to situations rather than anticipating them, yet marketing strategies did alter and become more elaborate during the last fifteen years of the pre-railroad era. The most significant aspects of marketing during those years were the increasing integration of milling and selling and the growing importance of the specialized commission agent and the wholesaler. The railroad moved into Michigan's pine country in the 1860s but initially did not change the marketing of lumber, which remained essentially a bulk commodity for water transport.

Although it is impossible to apportion precisely the amount of lumber sent from Michigan to various markets, it it not difficult to demonstrate the importance of that product in the major lumber centers from Albany to Chicago. Between 1855 and 1870 the marketing network along which lumber from Michigan passed became longer and more heavily traveled. Demand increased at the major consuming and trans-shipment centers, and the volume of lumber shipped from the lower peninsula expanded. By 1870 Michigan pine held a larger percentage of all of the eastern markets than it had in 1860, and Michigan lumbermen were the largest suppliers at Buffalo, Cleveland, Sandusky, Toledo, and Chicago.

Much of the state's output did not go beyond its own borders, however, for Michigan had a large home market. The population of the Lower Peninsula increased from 704,596 in 1860 to 1,139,468 by 1870 and so did its need for lumber to build houses, towns, and farm buildings. Many small mills produced almost exclusively for this local trade, and its importance for the major producers should not be overlooked. In his study of Muskegon, James Glasgow emphasizes the significance of the home market. Muskegon, like the other towns of Michigan, was made of wood—from plank streets and sidewalks to frame houses and stores.[1] As the records of Crapo, Mears, and Hannah, Lay & Company demonstrate, the local market was indeed important. Crapo worked diligently to sell his lumber to farmers south of Flint and was particularly happy to deal in volume with a large building company in Detroit.[2]

Of all the major lumber markets in America in the mid-nineteenth century, Chicago ranked an overwhelming first, easily surpassing Albany in the late 1850s. Its geographic location between the pineries and a vast treeless expanse in the process of settlement insured that preeminence, for as Wilson Compton has determined, rates of lumber consumption are highest for areas in early stages of development.[3] Lumber arrived by water from Michigan and, later, Wisconsin for transshipment west by rail. The statistics of the city's lumber trade clearly indicate the growing demands of a local and hinterland market as well. Between 1865 and 1870 lumber receipts at Chicago more than doubled, rising from 501,592,406 feet to 1,018,998,685 feet. Just over half this total was shipped from the city: 269,496,579 feet in 1865 and 583,490,634 feet in 1870. To judge from estimates made by the city's board of trade, Michigan was the source of approximately 60 percent of the lumber received at Chicago. For 1870 this would have meant a volume slightly in excess of 600,000,000 feet.[4]

Some lumber from the lower peninsula continued to move west across Lake Michigan to the port cities of Wisconsin, particularly Kenosha and Milwaukee, which remained minor but steady customers. In 1860 lumber receipts at Milwaukee totaled 34,639,26 feet, with just over 50 percent, 16,717,000 feet, from Michigan. Even after the Civil War, Detroit's commercial newspaper included Milwaukee in its report on lumber markets. Despite the growth of an important lumber industry in Wisconsin, Michigan pine could remain competitive, for it was closer to the cities on the lake than were the Wisconsin pineries. By water, the distance between Muskegon and Milwaukee is shorter than from Green Bay to Milwaukee. Lumber imports to Milwaukee in 1870 amounted to 73,000,000 feet.[5]

Vast quantities of Michigan pine moved east as well as west. The pattern of trade with Ohio was clearly established by the time of the Civil War; after the war the volume of trade increased as the railroad expanded the size of the market area. Lumber moved by water across Lake Erie to the port cities of Toledo, Sandusky, and Cleveland, all of which were important wholesale centers for Michigan lumbermen. Lumber receipts at Toledo in 1869 amounted to just over 100,000,000 feet. What was not consumed there was shipped by canal or railroad to Dayton, Cincinnati, and the rural area of southwestern Ohio and southeastern Indiana. From about 1860

Cincinnati became an important market for Michigan pine, as it became cheaper than that brought down the Ohio River from Pennsylvania. Sandusky was the smallest of the Ohio lumber port cities, receiving less than 60,000,000 feet in 1869, while Cleveland's lumber market was the largest in the state. Of the 142,445,770 feet shipped to Cleveland in 1867, just over 30,000,000 remained for local distribution. The remainder went east and south by canal and railroad. In the late 1860s demand at Cleveland soared, reaching 225,278,000 feet by 1869. Pine from Michigan dominated the Ohio markets.[6]

Between 1855 and 1870 the source of supply for the lumber markets east of Lake Erie changed. As the quantity and quality of timber from Maine, New York, and Pennsylvania declined, eastern buyers became increasingly interested in pine lumber from Canada and from Michigan, the latter of which quickly gained an international reputation. Even before the Civil War some manufacturers in Michigan, operating on their own or through agents, sent their lumber to all the major eastern cities from Philadelphia to Boston, but most sold through the major wholesale centers of Buffalo and Albany. Located at the eastern end of Lake Erie and the western terminus of the Erie Canal, Buffalo rapidly became a leading distribution center as well as a point of transshipment. In 1858 it received 67,059,173 feet of lumber by lake, approximately one-third of which came from Michigan. Of this amount, only 5,018,116 feet was sold locally; the remainder was sent to Albany and Troy. With the exception of 1861 and 1863, volume of trade increased annually, reaching 224,935,748 feet in 1869. No exact figures are available, but commercial reports for the city estimated that at least 50 percent of the imported lumber came from Michigan either directly or via the Ohio ports. By 1869, about 25 percent of the lumber arriving at Buffalo stayed there, with the remainder being shipped farther east along the Erie Canal to Albany.

Albany also received lumber from Michigan by way of Oswego. It does not seem unreasonable to assume that of the 495,287,400 feet shipped into Albany in 1869, a minimum of 25 to 30 percent came from Michigan. Although the volume of lumber shipped east was not as great as that going west, eastern markets were a vital part of the Michigan lumberman's distribution network.[7]

As the lumber industry matured in Michigan and the distribution area expanded, marketing strategies became more diverse. For many years, lumbermen showed a general disinclination to advertise in local, commercial, or trade papers. At most they might allow editors and dealers to visit their plants in hopes of making a good impression, but advertisements, even in the trade journals, did not begin to appear on a regular basis until the 1880s. Contacts with buyers or agents remained on the personal basis of conversation or correspondence. On that level, lumbermen became increasingly sophisticated, adopting a wider variety of marketing strategies than they had employed earlier.[8]

Cargo sales persisted throughout the period. It appears that small-scale manufacturers continued to rely on this method, particularly in the Michigan and Lake Michigan markets, since this was one of the few ways that small-quantity sales could be made. For the large-volume dealer, however, this method of distribution had many limitations. The greatest problem with blind cargo sales was the instability of the market. Too often manufacturers found themselves trying to sell cargoes in an overstocked area.[9] As millmen turned away from blind cargo sales in the wholesale market, they made increasing use of specialized agents. Commission agents had always been used for the sale of lumber shipped to the east, but they became more important as the volume of trade increased. Indeed, Michigan millmen came to rely on commission merchants in all marketing areas after 1855. Crapo and George D. Hill, a St. Clair County lumberman, for example, found agents more than willing to sell their lumber, and both used those dealers to expand their market, even within the state of Michigan. By the end of the Civil War, commission agents at Detroit and Saginaw, and to a lesser extent at Grand Haven and Muskegon, had become important in the marketing system. Many manufacturers must have had frustrating and disappointing experiences with agents located at a distance, such as at Albany, and became receptive to Michigan-based dealers with whom they could have direct contact. Between 1855 and 1870 the specialized lumber agent became an important part of the Chicago market. Agreements called for a commission fee of either a specified sum per thousand board feet (M) or a percentage of the sale, usually 10 percent.[10]

One of the most important developments in distribution in the years before 1870 was the growth of wholesale houses. These specialized merchants who were active in the short-term financing of many manufacturers, could often purchase in very large quantity. Buyers for wholesalers traveled through Michigan before 1855, but they became more numerous and important in the following decade and a half. Some wholesalers, such as David Whitney, Jr., of Detroit, located in the major manufacturing and distribution centers of the state, but most wholesale houses were outside the state. These firms either had buyers residing more or less permanently in Michigan or sent buyers through the state on a regular basis. As the market improved after the Civil War, the manufacturers found themselves increasingly courted by wholesalers, who displayed great eagerness to establish continuing relationships with the millmen. Many manufacturers were receptive to this arrangement since it saved them from the day-to-day instability of the market, commission fees, and the sorting and grading costs of distribution. Once the lumber left the mill by ship or rail, the manufacturer's worries ended. Wholesale houses remained an important part of the marketing structure in Michigan until the late nineteenth century, when many manufacturers began to supply retail yards directly.[11]

Not all lumbermen relied on middlemen, however. The number of companies combining manufacturing and marketing increased in the years between 1855 and 1870. Impetus for the integration of those two functions came from two directions. Some manufacturers moved forward into marketing when they saw an area of strong demand. That was particularly the case with local mill outlets or yards. Some of the wholesale-retail outlets were quite small, but others, like those in Detroit, did a large volume of business. It appears, however, that the impulse for integration usually came from those with a primary interest in marketing. The sources available for the period indicate a higher rate for backward than forward integration. Backward movement was particularly common among eastern dealers anxious to insure a steady supply of lumber to their wholesale houses or retail yards in the face of a declining intraregional supply. A rapid review of the Dun & Bradstreet credit reports for Michigan's leading lumbering counties clearly illustrates that trend. Dealers, usually well capitalized, built large mills, which were designed to supply their own needs almost exclusively. The Buffalo firm of Cunningham, Robinson, Haines & Company is representative. In 1869 the company built a "splendid" mill at Osseneke in Alpena County and had all of its lumber shipped to the company's yard at Buffalo.[12]

While lumber manufacturers had a variety of means that they could employ in marketing their product, most chose to limit those options because their interest lay more in manufacturing than in distribution. But there were some who saw the importance of development market strategies to insure their success in the industry. Crapo was such a man. From his correspondence and journals emerges a detailed picture of the opportunities and problems facing the lumber manufacturer in the middle of the nineteenth century. His perception of and responses to a change market tell us a good deal about the growing importance of the distribution function. Like his contemporaries, Crapo sold by grade. Best quality and number one grade were almost always shipped east, while the lesser grades from second through common were sent to Ohio or Chicago or kept for local trade. That pattern prevailed until the mid-1880s, when the finest quality pine had been exhausted and eastern markets had to accept third- and fourth-quality pine.[13]

Crapo maintained personal control of both the manufacturing and distribution functions of his business. He understood the importance of marketing to insure the scale of operations made necessary by the amount of capital invested, and he employed various strategies to sell his product to buyers from many different locations. He opened branch yards in Flint and the nearby towns of Holly and Fentonville, hoping to capture a larger share of the local trade and to make use of the railroad at the latter two places to expand his territory into the interior. His best grades went to Fentonville (and later Holly) for transshipment, while the coarser lumber remained in the yards for local sales. He used commission agents, particularly in the east, but his problems with them and in that market convinced him that he could do better by maintaining complete personal supervision. Time and again he complained to his son about the unreliability of his agents, delays in shipping, high transportation costs, punitive inspections systems, "lumber shark" intermediaries, and, most of all, the uncertainty of the market. By 1860 he was convinced that while the East was a natural outlet for manufacturing along the eastern shore of the lower peninsula, given his interior location it was better to keep sales within his own control and supervision, where there would be greater certainty.[14] Expanding his market to Chicago and into Ohio required a never-ending search for buyers. Crapo made at least one trip a year to the various markets: Detroit, Chicago, Cincinnati, Toledo, Cleveland, Buffalo, and Albany. By such visits, steady correspondence, and personal inspection of all shipments, Crapo was able to attract and maintain a growing number of buyers, particularly at Detroit and in Indiana and Ohio. By the time he became governor of Michigan in 1864, he had developed a dependable distribution network.[15]

Crapo's story is not unique. Mears was another lumberman who assessed his market in terms of the locations of his mills and available transportation facilities and then worked to develop a trade within that area.[16] The concern with marketing that had been minimal at the middle of the nineteenth century increased after 1870 as millmen came to understand its importance to an industry characterized by rising costs and increased capital investment and output. Marketing strategies that insured a steady volume of trade became all important; lumbermen had to seize the initiative.

Under optimum conditions, which is to say in response to steady demand, manufacturers moved the freshly cut green lumber, usually by hand or by cart, directly from the mill to the dock for loading. Manufacturers located upstream from the shipping centers had to bring their lumber down by raft or flatboat, which not only added to the expense, but reduced its value if the lumber became soaked and dirty during shipment.[17] Little thought was given to seasoning the wood. Only if supply exceeded demand would lumber be piled, providing an opportunity for air drying. Kilns were first tried in America in the 1860s, but they did not gain acceptance from manufacturers in Michigan for at least a decade. They became a regular part of the manufacturing process only when millmen came to realize that dry timber increased its value sufficiently to warrant an additional step.[18] Any sorting by grade was done at the dock, but much was simply sent mill-run. Occasionally an inspection was completed before loading, but grading remained unstandardized until 1881. The responsibility for grading, sorting, and inspecting was usually assumed by the agent or wholesaler rather than the manufacturer.

One of the major problems a lumbermen faced concerned the timing of shipments to market. If he sent his cargoes early in the season and prices later rose, he lost money; but if he waited, he had to pay higher shipping rates in late summer and there was the possibility of falling prices from oversupply. Most lumber was shipped either very early in the season, which usually indicated that it had been manufactured the previous season, or during the middle of the summer, when there was little competition with the grain trade for vessels. Much lumber was carried west to Chicago from eastern Michigan by vessels that were picking up grain in Chicago for eastern markets.[19] Rates fluctuated from season to season as well as during a season. The charge for carrying a thousand feet of lumber from Saginaw to Chicago dropped from around $3.50 in 1856 and 1857 to $1.75 in 1860. Rates began to rise again in 1862, and by 1869 they had returned to their 1856–57 level. Rates also increased on shipments east, reaching approximately $5.00 per thousand feet in 1869 for loads from Saginaw to Buffalo. The charge for shipments across Lake Michigan was $2.50– $2.75 M for the same year.[20]

Some manufacturers, including Mears, Hannah, Lay & Company, and Eber B. Ward, owned their own ships, but others made use of the ever-growing fleet of sail and steam vessels that were especially adapted for carrying lumber. Schooners were the first carriers, and over the years their capacity was increased until they could accommodate piles of lumber nearly twenty feet high on their decks. Propellers, steam-powered ships driven by a screw propeller, were introduced on the lakes in the

1840s. These "unhandsome steamers" had open holds to maximize their space for cargo.[21] As ships became scarce and rates rose during the Civil War, a few lumbermen began experimenting with alternative methods of shipping. Rafting and towing were both tried on the Great Lakes in 1862 and quickly adopted. Skeptics doubted that lumber piled in cribs would travel well, but the 2,000,000 feet sent from Thunder Bay to Chicago by that method in August of 1862 arrived in good condition. Experiences on Lake Erie were just as positive. As more powerful propellers were built, they could handle longer chains of barges and rafts. In the early 1860s a load of 800,000 feet was considered large, but by the end of the decade, cargoes in excess of 2,000,000 feet per tug were not uncommon. Several tugs would often combine to pull five or more barges or rafts, whose total length would exceed a quarter of a mile.[22]

Because water transportation was of vital importance to the lumber industry, manufacturers in Michigan were concerned with the condition of the ports. The lower peninsula possessed a number of potentially great natural harbors, but they were too shallow to permit passage of heavily laden ships. Lumbermen anxious to avoid the expenses, delays, and losses incurred in lightering lumber out into the rougher waters of Lake Michigan or Lake Huron sought private, state, and federal assistance to deepen the harbors and river mouths and remove sandbars.

TABLE 29
Federal Appropriations for River and Harbor Improvements
in Michigan, 1866–1870

Grand Haven	$ 96,866.15	Manistee	$105,000
Black Lake	116,000.00	White	196,550
Saginaw	38,500.00	Muskegon	79,000
Au Sable	87,950.00	Pentwater	107,820
Grand	40,000.00	Pere Marquette	111,185

Source: U.S., 49th Cong., 2d sess., Misc. Doc. 91, *Laws of the United States Relating to the Improvement of Rivers and Harbors from August 11, 1790 to March 3, 1887*, pp. 131–59.

Individuals, including Charles Mears at the Pentwater and Pere Marquette harbors and Noah H. Ferry at White River, sometimes undertook improvements, but the scale of work usually required cooperative effort. The most noticeable example of cooperation was the formation of the Muskegon Harbor Company by the city's lumbermen in 1863. The company invested $40,000 to remove the sandbars that sometimes closed the harbor and to deepen the channel. Such endeavors, however, could accomplish relatively little. Government assistance began as early as 1852, but large-scale federal projects date from 1866. In the five-year period from 1866 through 1870, Congress appropriated $978,771.15 for ten harbors in the northern part of the lower peninsula (see Table 29). Individual grants ranged from under $2,000 to $75,000. In addition, lumbermen benefitted from the $662,680 the federal government spent to improve the St. Clair Flats at the mouth of the St. Clair River. State appropriations for river and harbor improvements were less generous. The largest state-sponsored project, to improve navigation at the mouth of the Muskegon River, was completed in 1860. It appears that the state legislature preferred to authorize a special tax in specific counties for river and harbor improvements rather than appropriate money from state funds.[23]

According to one expert, as late as 1880 less than 10 percent of the lumber manufactured in the Saginaw Valley was shipped to market by rail. In his classic study of Michigan's early railroads, Paul W. Ivey determined that the roads presented little challenge to an established water route but were usually used to carry lumber into and out of previously inaccessible areas.[24] His findings dramatize the very modest role the railroad played in the state's lumber industry until late in the nineteenth century. Michigan contained only 799 miles of track in 1860. Despite great enthusiasm and planning by lumbermen and other businessmen, less than 900 miles were

laid over the next ten years. By 1870 there were only
1,698 miles or railroad in the entire state. Before 1855
railroad building had been confined to east-west routes
across the southern quarter of the lower peninsula, but
after that date railway lines were begun into the pine
counties. The most important route was the Flint & Pere
Marquette, organized in 1857. In 1863 just over thirty-
three miles between Flint and East Saginaw were in operation, and the line did not reach its western terminus
at Ludington until 1874. The Grand Rapids & Indiana,
organized in 1856, was the first north-south line to penetrate the northern counties. It reached the pine areas in
1868, and mills rapidly sprang up along its route. Several
other railroads and connecting lines important to lumbermen were built between 1855 and 1870. In 1858 the
Detroit & Milwaukee passed through Fentonville, giving
the area of Flint a connection with Detroit, its nearest
major manufacturing center. In 1863–64 Crapo spear-
headed the construction of the Flint & Holly Railroad, a
fifteen-mile line that connected with the Detroit & Milwaukee. The state legislature authorized local aid to railroads in 1863, and by 1870 fifty-five additional
corporations had been chartered, although actual construction lagged far behind planning.[25]

Lumbermen enthusiastically embraced the building of
railroads into the pine-producing counties, not only to
open new forest areas but also to expand their area of
distribution, to reduce costs, and to increase marketing
flexibility. Railroad investors sought the great tonnage of
lumber. The railroad opened new areas and provided an
alternative form of transportation, but its importance to
the industry was not fully appreciated until the 1880s,
when direct carload sales became an important marketing strategy. Until that time less expensive water transportation to the major lumber centers prevailed. In
1869, for example, 96 percent of the lumber received at
Chicago came by water. The lumber that did come by

rail was hardwood from southern Michigan and Indiana; pine continued to arrive by vessel.[26] The Grand Rapids & Indiana and the Pere Marquette railroads did not immediately alter the structure of the lumber industry; in fact, their initial impact was minimal. They were important, however, because they broadened the geographical base of the industry. Ultimately they proved that proximity to water was not essential. Mills could be located in the interior and could ship directly to markets far distant from major lake, river, or canal routes.

CHAPTER 11

Laborers and Businessmen, 1837–1870

An expanding industry required an ever-increasing labor force. The scant evidence that exists uniformly suggests that the industry suffered a chronic shortage of labor during the period under study. This was true throughout the state, but especially along the northward-moving frontier and in areas experiencing rapid manufacturing growth. In 1854 the *Saginaw Times* reported that 500 additional workmen would have to be hired that year because of the increased number of mills.[1] The shortage was most acute in the years before 1855 and in the Civil War years, when manpower was at a premium. During the latter years, the lumbermen at Pentwater in Oceana County resorted to hiring Indian workers to keep their mills in operation.[2] The cyclical nature of the industry meant that extraordinary demands were placed on a small local labor pool during peak seasons. From the earliest days, therefore, loggers and manufacturers aggressively sought workers by use of handbills, advertisements in newspapers, and active personal recruitment.[3]

Local agricultural workers provided the most convenient source of labor, and many sawmills and logging camps were manned by farmers and sons of farmers drawn from a relatively close radius. These men were especially important for logging operations, because the

195

demand for unskilled hands fluctuated radically. In many cases, however, local rural sources could not supply all the workers needed. Lumbermen then had to bring in laborers from other parts of the state, the surrounding Great Lakes region, and the East. Charles Mears, for example, contracted with a large number of men and some married couples at Chicago to work in his various mills and camps in western Michigan, while Henry H. Crapo sometimes employed men from the East, but was careful to choose only those who seemed capable of adjusting to frontier life. There is no way to know the number of workers coming from the East or the West, but scholars agree that most of the skilled labor came from the East. Although this migration began before 1855, the depletion of the eastern forests by that date facilitated the transfer of laborers already trained in woods and mill work.[4]

It is relatively easy to draw a composite of a workman in Michigan's woods or mills during the year of commercialization: young, male, and native-born. Lumbering was a male-dominated industry that place a premium on strength, stamina, and coordination. Nevertheless, women and children were employed in camps and mills in modest numbers. Sometimes the female workers were the wives or daughters of the owner or manager, but often they were employees. In 1855 Delos Blodgett brought two unattached women into his camp in Newaygo County, making them the first female settlers in the county and the first known female employees in a Michigan lumber camp. Usually, however, women were not hired individually, but with their husbands. Women usually worked as cooks in the camps and boarding houses, while youths were employed as cooks' assistants or choreboys in the woods and common hands in the mills. In 1860 census enumerators listed a total of ninety-five women but no youths employed in the twenty-six pine counties. According to the 1870 census, the number of females employees had decreased to sixty-three, but there were 757 male youths under the age of fifteen working in the industry. The reasons for this increase in child labor are unclear. Perhaps the census takers were careless in 1860, or it is possible that employers could use young, inexperienced help in their more mechanized mill operations.[5]

Native-born Americans dominated Michigan's lumber industry. A nonscientific survey of men who spent some time in logging or milling in Michigan in the 1840s and 1850s showed that the overwhelming majority were native-born Americans from the northeast. The small remainder came from northern Europe, particularly the British Isles and Germany. Over the next fifteen years the number of immigrants working in the industry increased, but native-born Americans continued to predominate until the early 1870s. In his study of labor in the lakes states lumber industry, George Engberg calculated that more than 51 percent of the workers were native-born in 1869. Of the foreign-born, Canadians constituted the largest group, about 24 percent of the total labor force. Next came the Germans and then immigrants from the British Isles. Scandinavians, who later became legends in the industry, accounted for less than 3 percent. The movement of Canadians into the industry began in the 1850s and accelerated in the next two decades as timber grew scarce in the eastern provinces and wages rose in Michigan. The percentage of English settlers who entered the lumber industry was proportionally smaller than that of the Germans and Irish, which suggests that the English tended to be more highly skilled than other immigrants. Scandinavians did not begin to settle in Michigan in substantial number until the late 1860s, but their communities rapidly increased after the date.[6]

In spite of the chronic shortage of labor, wages were low because the percentage of skilled workers in the lumber industry was quite small. In addition, the large number of casual, unskilled, and unmarried laborers made lumbering a very mobile and unstable occupation. It is striking how many of the men who appear in county histories had been employed for brief periods in one or the other branch of the industry, particularly in logging. Lumbering appears to have been one of the most common ways for young men to gain experience and capital for subsequent occupations. Again without any attempt at statistical analysis, it appears that nonpermanent labor was greater in the years of commercialization than it was in the later decades. In other words, there was a greater interoccupational flow of workers before 1855. The most noticeable connection was between logging and agriculture. Since the seasonal demands of the two occupations complemented each other so well, it was convenient and profitable for a worker to spend part of the year in each. Such an arrangement was ideal for a farmer who could work his land from plating through harvest and then earn cash wages for logging during the winter months. Conversely a "professional" logger might supplement his earnings through agricultural day labor during the summer and fall. Seasonal employment opportunities in lumber manufacturing also complemented those in logging, which led to a growing intraoccupational movement of labor by the mid 1850s.[7]

Owners did not have to deal with the problems of workers' mobility as long as there was a sufficient supply of local, day laborers. Crapo wrote his son in New Bedford, Massachusetts, in 1860 that he wanted to know the "probability" of permanence with skilled workers, but "common mill hands are of little consequence in that respect as I merely want their bone and muscle and when they do not earn their wages I discharge them."[8] Vertical integration maximized an owner's control over workers, because he could rotate his hands between the woods and the sawmill, and in most contract arrangements the employee agreed to take on whatever tasks were assigned.[9] The very nature of the industry, however, made displacement and a certain amount of unemployment inevitable. One student of the American logging industry has estimated that manufacturing and logging required about the same number of workers at the peak of their respective seasons but that at their low points manufacturing retained about one-third more men than did the logging camps. Logging released fully two-thirds of its employees during the off-season, only a portion of whom could possibly find jobs in lumber manufacturing.[10]

TABLE 30

Number Employed in Sawmills for Selected Counties, 1850–1870

| | Total Number Employed | | |
	1850	1860	1870
Ottawa	442	316	477
St. Clair	335	463	429
Michilimackinac (and 21 unorganized counties)	218	245	—
Wayne[a]	187	189	743
Saginaw	95	457	2,477
Thumb (Tuscola, Sanilac, Huron)	91	433	1,055
Allegan	64	246	832
Genesee	53	157	869
Lapeer	46	104	342
Muskegon	—	571	1,713
Bay	—	353	1,404
Oceana[b]	—	301	538
Manistee	—	275	872
Grand Traverse	—	93	117
Newaygo	—	78	136
Midland	—	25	148
Iosco	—	20	432
Cheboygan	—	6	225
Alcona	—	6	83
Mecosta	—	6	13
Alpena	—	—	606

[a]Detroit only in 1850 and 1860
[b]Includes Mason County

Source: Manuscript Census for the State of Michigan, 1850; Manuscript Census for the State of Michigan, 1860; U.S., Bureau of the Census, Ninth Census, 1870, vol. 3, *The Statistics of the Wealth and Industry of the U.S.* (Washington, 1872), 679– 83.

The size of the work force in Michigan's lumber industry before 1850 is not possible to determine, but after
that date it was one of the categories reported in the
federal census. Margaret Walsh has amply proven that
such figures are often inaccurate and must be used with
great caution, but they remain the best source available
to document labor trends in sawmilling.[11] No data exist
on logging as separate from manufacturing, but it is
likely that the number of men employed in each branch
of the industry was roughly equal in peak seasons. From
1,669 in 1850, the size of the labor force in the mills of
the pine counties rose to just over 4,000 in 1860 and to
nearly 15,000 by 1870. Table 30 presents a breakdown of
employment by county for 1850, 1860, and 1870.

The aggregate figures by county confirm the previous
generalizations on geographic spread. In the decade between 1850 and 1860, commercial-scale manufacturing
moved into the Thumb and the Saginaw Valley. The
counties of Saginaw, Bay, and Midland had over 800 men
employed in sawmilling by that date. On the western
side of the peninsula the major lumber manufacturing
centers in 1860 were located in the coastal counties of
Ottawa, Muskegon, Oceana, and Manistee and had a
labor force of over 1,400. Lumbering activity had moved
as far north as Grand Traverse. The number of workers
in the mills of the interior counties, such as Allegan and
Lapeer, also increased. Number employed showed only a
moderate gain in St. Clair County, the earliest-
developed lumber county, and virtually no change in Detroit. By 1870 the industry had spread up the
northeastern shore to Alpena and Cheboygan counties.
Grand Traverse and Newaygo counties reflect relatively
little industrial expansion, and St. Clair County showed
a slight decrease in worker, since lumbering had reached
its peak there in 1860. Saginaw and the Bay counties on
the east and the Ottawa-Manistee region in the west
were the largest manufacturing centers, employing 4,000
and 3,600 men respectively.

Not only did aggregate employment per county increase, the size of the work force per unit also expanded. The number of firms in the lumber counties employing five or fewer hands went from 55 percent in 1850 to about 45 percent in 1860 to perhaps 28 percent in 1870 (the manuscript census is incomplete for the latter date). Over those years the number of sawmills in the pine counties employing six through fifteen workers showed only a modest increase, from about 26 percent to 29 percent, but the number of units with more than fifteen employees grew from approximately 19 percent in 1850 to 26 percent in 1860 and to 44 percent in 1870. The greatest increase in the decade of the 1860s came in mills with a work force of twenty to fifty, where the change was from 14 percent to 29 percent of the total. There were twenty-five mills by 1870 that employed more than fifty hands.[12]

Logging camps as well as mills increased in size. The earliest camps often consisted of just two buildings, one for the workers and the other for the animals, but by 1870 even a small camp like Joseph Procter's, a contract logger with an eight-man crew, had at least four single-storied buildings: a bunk house, a cook house, a barn, and a blacksmith shop. Willis C. Ward remembered that his father's camp on the Tobacco River had two additional buildings, an office and a carpenter's shop. But even a large camp must have looked very small in its clearing, surrounded as it would have been by massive, old conifers.[13]

Although camps increased in size, their comforts did not. Living conditions were "rather primitive," according to one contemporary.[14] The men lived in log cabins that had earthen floors and slept on hemlock boughs in bunks that circled the room. An open fireplace in the center of the room provided heat and light. Later bunkhouses sometimes had a single window located at one end of the structure. The dining halls were equally spartan, serving very plain, simple fare. Most logger's basic diet consisted of pork, beans, bread, and tea. Few if any camps provided the level of provisions routinely supplied by Hannah, Lay & Company, to its loggers, which included fish, meats, fruits, vegetables, butter, and soap. Since loggers, it has been estimated, burned between 6,000 and 9,000 calories a day, quantity of food was no doubt more important than quality.[15]

Some manufacturers and jobbers owned farms from which they could supply their own camps, but others preferred to buy from local merchants and farmers. Fresh meat and vegetables were often scarce, although occasional hunting forays were undertaken to bolster the basic menu. This was particularly true in bad weather when it was difficult to bring supplies to a camp. James Fraser, for example, had to undertaken to bolster the basic menu. This was particularly true in bad weather when it was difficult to bring supplies to a camp. James Fraser, for example, had to undertake a treacherous journey to sled food across the Saginaw River in a storm to his men at Kawkawlin.[16]

Loggers lived a dangerous life. As one journal said, "Going into the pineries is like going to war."[17] Yet there was little recreation or diversion from danger and monotony. According to one camp poet, the only entertainment came from "jokes and songs to pass dull time away."[18] The chicken and oyster dinner given by George Tennant at his camp on the Cass River when the local newspaper editor visited must have been a rare treat.[19] Daily life was strictly regulated from 4 a.m. to bedtime at 9 p.m. The rules David Ward attempted to enforce in his camps were typical: no card playing, no drinking, and no entry into the dining hall except at meal times. The camp owner or a foreman assumed responsibility for supervision of the men and their work.[20]

Life was only somewhat better for mill hands in isolated regions. Those workers usually lived in boarding houses owned by the manufacturer. Unlike loggers, whose room and board were included in their wages, mill workers were usually charged a board bill that was subtracted from their pay before they received it. Mears, for example, charged Jacob Loaf $1.50 a week for board when he came in from the woods to work at the Duck Lake mill in 1851.[21] In the more settled towns and villages, manufacturers usually did not provide living accommodations for their employees.

The risks of lumbering were high for both owner and worker. If the entrepreneur invested his time and capital with no guarantee of return, it is no exaggeration to say that the worker risked life and limb. Contemporary newspapers regularly carried lists of occupational accidents that occurred in woods and mills. Boiler explosions, maimings of machine operators, and crushings by trees or draft animals headed the list of most common disasters. Together the accidents earned lumbering a reputation as "the most hazardous of the major occupations in the Lake States."[22] Although mishaps were usually blamed on the carelessness of the worker, there is no doubt that the lack of safety procedures and unsafe equipment, such as guards on machinery, contributed to the high accident rate. A worker, or his survivors, received little if any compensation for injuries suffered on the job. At most, the company might make a small settlement. Later, beginning around 1880, voluntary programs provided some assistance to the wounded. Laborers purchased tickets for special woodsmen's hospitals, as they were called, where the injured could go for treatment. Begun at Bay City, the practice spread throughout the Great Lakes area in the following decades.[23]

Despite the dangers and the long hours (about an eleven-hour daily average in the woods and eleven and one-half to twelve hours in the mills in 1870), workers as a group appeared to be contented. There is little information on labor unrest before the early 1870s, but it is clear that the few strikes occurring in these years were spontaneous, localized actions. Crapo made no notations in his diary about restive workers before his entry of June 29, 1864: "My men strike!!!"[24] The issues and outcome of the action are unknown, but the strike lasted only a week and does not appear to have spread beyond Crapo's mills. A strike at Saginaw in 1865 failed because the workers were not organized and could readily be replaced. Another strike there in 1870 for a ten-hour day met with no greater success. The first attempt to organize labor in the Saginaw Valley came in 1872, but there was no major labor agitation for at least another decade.[25] Based on his research of the industry, Vernon H. Jensen concluded that five factors account for the lack of labor problems: (1) strength of individualism; (2) seasonability of the work; (3) isolation of workers in small groups; (4) employers' control of towns; and (5) independence of farmers who worked in the industry only to supplement their income.[26]

Manufacturers (or their mill superintendents) kept close control of their workers. In the woods, life was carefully regimented, as it was to only a slightly lesser degree in the mills. Crapo personally supervised his manufacturing operation, often noting in his diaries and correspondence the problems with labor. He found the men to be "thickheaded," untrustworthy, undependable, and unstable. James Whittemore of Tawas Bay, who also personally supervised his mill, called his men "disagreeable" with a "laziness . . . both chronic and epidemic." Mears's diaries similarly record his close supervision of men and mills.[27] Not surprisingly, manufacturers were disinclined to listen to any worker's dissatisfaction with hours, conditions, or wages. Most agreed with Henry Sage, a leading manufacturer of the Saginaw Valley, that their only obligation was to provide jobs. Wage rates reflect this philosophy. Since millmen could not maintain prices by balancing output with demand, they sought to reduce costs by controlling wages. If prices declined, so did wages; but wages tended to rise if labor became scarce, or if lumber prices rose. Wage rates, therefore, reflected both the lumber and labor markets.[28]

Woodsmen, later known as lumberjacks, received lower wages than mill hands because room and board was a part of their working agreements. Wage rates for members of a logging crew varied with their degree of specialization, from unskilled to blacksmith and cook. Since sawyers and swampers were the most numerous, their wages can be considered typical. The few business records for the pre-1870 period that have survived, particularly the journals and ledgers of Crapo, Mears, and Hannah, Lay & Company, as well as census records, provide some clues to wage levels in logging. It appears that until about 1840 loggers' wages were as inflated as lumber prices. In Newaygo County, for example, Augustus Pennoyer was paying woodsmen with some experience $25.00 per month in the late 1830s. By 1846 wages for logging in the Muskegon area had dropped to around $13.00, only slightly more than half what they had been five or six years earlier.[29]

The federal census of 1850 listed logging as a separate enterprise in only two counties, with a total labor force of 171. According to the census, there were eighty-eight men employed in twelve lumbering camps to St. Clair County. Wages in the camps ranged from a low of $10.00 to a high of $28.66, with average monthly earnings per worker equalling $13.46. The manuscript data for Ottawa County differs. Here eighty-three men in eighteen camps received a total of $2,126 a month, an average of $25.61.[30] This disparity in the census returns places a premium on evidence fro the few business records that are available. Papers in the Mears Collection at the University of Michigan, show that Mears consistently paid monthly wages ranging from $10.00 to $16.00 at his White River camps in the years 1849–52.

Only his managers received $25.00 a month. Since Mears usually represented the low end of prices and wages, it is helpful to compare his labor costs with those of Hannah, Lay and Company at Grant Traverse. For the winter of 1854–55, that company hired a maximum of 107 loggers on a monthly basis and paid them an average of $16.66. Salaries ranged from $15.00 for unskilled laborers to $40.00 for a foreman. The average monthly wage clearly indicates that the bulk of the company's employees were unskilled workers who commanded minimum wages. These examples substantially support the census reports for St. Clair County and contribute to the conclusion that wage rates were slowly rising through the 1850s. The abnormally high wages reported for Ottawa County in the 1850 census cannot be satisfactorily explained. The small size of the operations, however, suggest that these may have been largely family ventures that did not reflect a more competitive commercial arrangement. The *Saginaw Enterprise* noted that loggers in the Saginaw Valley were receiving an average wage of $17.00 for the 1854–55 season, which corresponds to the prevailing rates of Hannah, Lay and Company on the Western shore.[31]

Wages dropped during the depression years 1858–1861. Crapo, for example, considered labor unusually cheap in 1860.[32] At Big Sauble, Mears paid his men an average of $12.00 during the winter of 1861–62, with $10.00 and $16.00 the lower and upper limits. Influenced by a scarcity of labor and the strong demand of the war years, wages rapidly increased in the early 1860s. Although Mears complained in 1865 that he could not afford to pay more than $20.00 a month for the most skilled woodsman, his labor contracts at Duck Lake in 1863–66 ranged from $20.00 to $34.00 a month, with $26.00 the most common figure. Assuming a work month of twenty-six days, his average wage was $1.00 a day, which appears to be in line with rates elsewhere in the state during the mid-1860s. William Vance recorded a wage range of $1.25 to $20.00 a day on the Tittabawassee River in 1865–66, while Hannah, Lay & Company paid wages of $.70 to $2.00 a day at Grand Traverse.[33]

Compensation for mill labor is somewhat easier to document. Foremen, engineers, and head sawyers, who stood closest to the saw and determined the way a log would be cut to maximize the feet of upper quality lumber obtained from it, received the highest pay. Filers, setters, and tail sawyers earned somewhat more than pilers, handlers, edgers, and unskilled laborers. In large mills filers and setters took care of the saws, but in a small mill the head sawyer also assumed those responsibilities. The tail sawyer was necessary only to help guide the log or slab.

If John Estabrook, a tail sawyer, is at all representative, wages in the mills of Michigan were low during the mid-1840s. Working in a St. Clair County mill, Estabrook earned only $12.00 a month in 1845. According to the manuscript census, wages increased in the second half of that decade, for by 1850 the average lumber worker in the pine counties received $22.70 a month. Based on a work month of twenty-six days, the average daily rate was $.87. the average monthly wage in 1850, as listed in Table 31, was lowest in Genesee, an interior county with less developed commercial manufacturing, and highest in Detroit, the leading lumber center in the state at mid-century. The variation by county, which is not very great, may be at least partially explained by the size of the local labor pool.[34]

There are problems in comparing data when business records became more available in the 1850s. Some owners calculated their workers' wages on a daily basis, while others used a monthly rate. George Engberg, an authority on labor in the Great Lakes lumber industry, has estimated that unskilled mill hands earned $.60 to

TABLE 31
Average Monthly Wage for Sawmill Employees
for Selected Counties, 1850–1870

	1850	1860	1870
Wayne*	$26.97	$32.28	$ NA
Ottawa	25.00	22.46	46.76
Michilimackinac	25.00	—	—
Saginaw	21.00	26.00	55.47
Thumb (Huron, Sanilac, Tuscola)a	20.00	26.25	41.23
Genesee	19.74	25.37	34.41
Grand Traverse	—	24.04	35.21
Midland	—	19.20	46.04
Muskegon	—	17.45	50.73
Oceanab	—	12.03	41.26

*Detroit only
aDoes not include Tuscola County in 1870
bIncludes Mason County

Source: Manuscript Censuses for the State of Michigan, 1850, 1860, and 1870.

$.80 a day in 1850 and $1.00 a day by 1855. Those with special skills, such as sawyers, could expect to earn 50 to 300 percent more.[35] On the basis of the limited data available, Engberg's conclusions are reasonable. In 1853, for example, Z. W. Bunce, owner of a medium-sized sawmill in St. Clair County, paid his unskilled labor $14.00 to $16.00 per month and his sawyer $34.41. Wages in several areas were even higher. In the Saginaw Valley they rose from about $1.00 a day in 1850 to as much as $2.50 by 1855. According to the ledger of the Woods Company in Lexington, the only known records of a Saginaw area mill operating before 1855, mill hands earned from $1.00 to $1.75 a day in the mid-1850s.[36]

From the evidence available, it does not appear that wages declined significantly in the depression; rather in some cases wages improved. The daily rate for common labor in 1860 in the Saginaw area, according to one scholar, was $1.25, an increase of $.125 over the decade. On the western shore, Mears's rates held fairly steady at $.60 to $1.25 a day.[37] Calculations from the manuscript census of 1860, tabulated in Table 31, in large measure support these generalizations. With the exception of

Oceana County, which is clearly out of line, average monthly wages did not very greatly among the counties in 1860. Assuming a work month of twenty-six days, the daily rate ranged from $.67 in Muskegon County to $1.01 in the Thumb and $1.24 in Detroit. The average daily wage for the ten counties was $.87, unchanged from a decade earlier.

The price of labor increased in the following years as the pool of workers diminished. For example, by 1862 unskilled labor commanded $1.25-$2.50 a day at Saginaw. To forestall further increases, manufactures in Bay County met in 1865 and agreed to a scale of $1.50 for unskilled workers to $3.00 for head sawyers. Mears's records indicate a similar trend. Wages for common laborers increased little, but the upper rates for skilled labor advanced as much as 50 percent. Mears listed his wage rates at his Middlesex mill at $1.00-$4.00 a day in 1867. Daily wages in excess of $3.00 were not uncommon by the middle of the decade, but the greatest number of employees were unskilled and earned considerably less. by 1870 the spread was around $1.50 to $4.50.[38] Census information on wages in 1870 confirms the considerable increase in wages over the preceding decade. Wages in 1870 were lowest in Genesee County, at a daily rate of $1.32, and highest in Saginaw County, at $2.13 a day, with an average of $1.69 a day. These wage rates reflect both the availability of labor and the level of industrialization. In Grand Traverse, for example, one large firm dominated the county, and the effect of this worked to keep wages down, while competition for labor among many firms in Saginaw and Muskegon counties permitted workers to command a somewhat higher wage.

Cash wages and regular paydays appear to have been relatively uncommon in Michigan's lumber industry until late in the nineteenth century. Generally, workers received a combination of goods and cash, with settlement usually occurring once a year. Lumbermen found that

paying hands at the end of the season increased labor
stability while at the same time reducing the need for
operating capital. In an industry where capital was tied
up for long periods of time, that arrangement was especially attractive, as Crapo discovered. In the early years
of the industry and in the more remote areas, little cash
ever exchanged hands. Many employers operated a small
company store or chest. From it their workers could obtain food, clothing, toiletries, medicines, or even cash
advances that would be charged against gross earnings.
By the end of the season the worker often must have been
disappointed to see how high his personal expenses had
run. Alfred Tanner, for instance, received from Bunce
only $38.38 in cash after his store bill had been deducted
from his wages in 1853, while Francis Gaugen actually
owed his employer, Mears, $3.32 at the end of the 1849–
50 logging season.[39] Company stores were still important
in the 1860s. Carrie Mears recalled that her father,
Charles, eventually issued passbooks for his store and settled accounts with his employees annually. Hannah, Lay
& Company used the same system, selling store passbooks to their crews for twenty-five cents. Many other
lumbermen issued either checks or vouchers that could
be cashed before the end of the season only at a discount,
or orders at stores where the employer commanded
credit. George Hotchkiss gives A. V. Mann & Company
of western Michigan credit for first instituting regular
paydays, but this was not a general practice as late as
1885.[40]

According to the census of 1850, the owners of the 558
sawmills in Michigan paid their 2,730 employees a total
of $740,076 in wages, or an annual average of $271.09
per workers.[41] In comparison to the industry, the mill
hand in Michigan fared well, receiving 8 percent more
than the $249.38 national average. In terms of earnings
of workers in other industries in the state, Table 32 shows
that those in the lumber industry earned significantly

less than skilled millwrights or even the average workers in a flour or grist mill. Wages of workers in the forest industries were quite comparable, however, to those earned in extracting and processing minerals or in secondary wood-processing industries such as coopering and were higher than the wages earned by the makers of sashes and blinds and other construction materials.

If the average number of workers per establishment and the value added per worker are computed for lumber and flour, the state's two largest industries in 1850, the role of labor becomes readily apparent. Sawmills employed an average of 4.89 men, while flour or grist mills averaged only 2.34 per firm. Yet the value added per worker in flour milling was $1,021.39, nearly double the $450.89 added per worker in the state's sawmills. Lumber manufacturing was less mechanized than flour milling; it required a larger, predominantly unskilled labor force and had a low value added per worker.

In 1860 owners of the 926 lumber mills in Michigan paid their 6,394 workers $1,708,796, or an annual average wage of $267.25. In 1870, 20,576 hands received a total of $6,597,110 from 1,641 employers, or an annual average wage of $320.62. Table 32 compares these rates with average wages for laborers in other industries. In 1860 and 1870 the average laborer in the lumber industry was paid less than flour millers, skilled furniture workers, or metal workers. His wages were comparable to those paid by other primary and secondary processors of natural resources, who employed largely unskilled labor. Fisherman and coopers were consistently paid less money than workers in the lumber industry. According to government calculations, the average wage for sawmill employees nationally was $311.00, which would make Michigan's rate quite competitive.[42]

The continuing importance of labor in the lumber industry can be seen quite clearly when comparisons of employment per firm and value added per worker are

TABLE 32
Annual Average Wage for Selected Industries
in Michigan, 1850–1870

	1850	1860	1870
Machinists and millwrights	449.13	—	541.31
Brass and copper, tin and sheet iron	375.97	351.45	315.50
Flour and grist mills	323.79	338.44	333.59
Iron and copper foundries	316.91	261.07	508.79
Furniture	295.91	301.61	276.78
Fishing	276.94	135.77	118.48
Coopering	273.84	235.48	285.42
Minerals, extracting and processing	273.23	286.78	355.52
Lumber, planed and sawed	271.09	267.25	320.62
Bricks and other construction materials	245.51	288.15	324.13

Source: U.S., Bureau of the Census, *Abstract of the Statistics of Manufacturers, 1850;* U.S., Bureau of the Census, *Manufactures of the United States in 1860;* U.S., Bureau of the Census, Ninth Census, 1870, vol. 3, *The Statistics of the Wealth and Industry of the United States.*

made. Value added per worker in lumbering increased from $284.79 in 1860 to $553.60 in 1870. Yet in comparison to flour milling, where value added per worker reached $1,344.87 in 1870, the lumber industry continued to be more labor intensive. The number of workers per unit increased from 6.90 in 1860 to 12.54 in 1870, while flour milling required only 2.50 hands in 1860 and 3.76 in 1870. Lumbering remained an industry characterized by high labor input and low output per worker, compared to more highly mechanized manufacturing, like flour milling.

Who were the men who owned the sawmills and managed this large labor force? Information about entrepreneurs, which is only slightly easier to come by than that for their workers, suggest that the men who invested their time, energy, and capital in the pineries of Michigan were similar to each other in many respects. Sufficient information for study of 294 lumber manufacturers who operated in Michigan before 1870 has been found.[43]

Of the 133 men who entered the lumber business before 1856, the overwhelming majority were native-born, as Table 33 clearly demonstrates. A full 90 percent were

TABLE 33
Place of Birth for Lumber Manufacturers
Entering the Industry Before 1856

New England		Other Regions	
Massachusetts	16	Michigan	4
Vermont	14	Ohio	3
Maine	11		7
New Hampshire	6		
Connecticut	6	Foreign born	
	53	Scotland	6
		Ireland	2
Middle Atlantic		Germany	2
New York	49	Canada	1
Pennsylvania	8		11
New Jersey	2		
	59	NA	3
		Total	133

born in America, but just 3 percent were natives of
Michigan. By far the largest number came from New
York, although the total number born in New England
nearly equalled that for the Middle Atlantic States. Of
the foreign-born, nine came from Canada and the British Isles. Only two of the 130 lumbermen were born in a
non-English-speaking country. This pattern of nativity is
important because it emphasizes the lateral migration to
Michigan. The narrow geographic range of the westward movement facilitated the diffusion of technology
and the transfer of capital.

Information on the father's occupation was available
for only sixty-one of the 133 lumbermen of the early period. Twenty-nine were sons of farmers. Ten were sons of
lumbermen, while another nine had fathers who combined lumbering with either farming or merchandising.
Thus, nineteen had a family connection with the lumber
industry. The remaining thirteen came from merchant,
professional, or artisan families. It appears that few men
in the sample came from well-to-do or socially prominent families. Curtis Emerson and Albert Lay were
probably quite unrepresentative in terms of family back-

ground. Emerson was the son of a wealthy Vermont merchant and banker, while Lay's father was a successful lawyer and Congressman from New York.[44]

Study of the lumberman's educational background yielded a modest surprise in the number who received more than a rudimentary education. Of the seventy-four about whom information is available, thirty-five attended common schools at least briefly, while thirty-nine received additional vocational, professional, or academic training. One served an apprenticeship as a blacksmith, one was trained in medicine, and a third in law. The remaining thirty-six attended seminaries, academies, business colleges, colleges, and universities.

Lumbermen in Michigan before 1856 brought many occupational experiences to their work (see Table 34).

TABLE 34
Previous Occupational Experience, for Lumber Manufacturers Entering the Industry Before 1856

Lumbering	47	Real Estate	4
Mercantile	24	Transportation	3
Farming	12	Metalworking	2
Professional*	8	Military	2
Construction	7	Other	3
Manufacturing	5	Total	117

*Includes education, law, medicine, religion.

Forty-seven of the 117 about whom information is known had earlier experience in some aspect of the lumber industry. Of the remaining seventy, the majority (thirty-six) had been employed in agriculture or storekeeping, both occupations providing business and technical skills important in lumbering. In addition, merchants and farmers often had direct contacts with lumbering: farmers both used and supplied sawmills, and merchants sometimes served as middlemen for the manufacturer.

Of the 130 men whose age at entering the lumber industry could be ascertained, nine became lumbering entrepreneurs in Michigan before the age of twenty-one, and fourteen after the age of forty. The overwhelming number, however, began their businesses while in their twenties and thirties. There were exceptions, but the majority of men under twenty-one entered either into a family mill or began their careers in logging. John Canfield, for example, became a bookkeeper for his father at eighteen and a full partner in his mill the next year. The oldest men entering the industry before 1856 were not successful lumbermen moving westward; rather, they were successful merchants in Michigan who decided to add lumbering to their economic activities. Alvah Sweetzer was a teacher and merchant before he entered into a partnership in logging and milling with James Sanborn at the age of forty-five, while Evert B. Dyckman, the eldest subject, added a sawmill to his mercantile business when he was fifty-three years old.[45]

Eighty of the 133 lumbermen were partners in a business; the other fifty-three operated as sole proprietors. There were no members of corporations in the group. Without more complete information, it is impossible to know the extent and variety of lumbermen's other business activities. It is interesting to note, however, that of the thirty-three men for whom information was available, seventeen had mercantile interests and seven owned grist mills. For these men, at least, lumbering appears to have been only one part of their active business interests. Sweetzer and Sanborn, the Gilbert brothers, and many others gave up their mercantile and real estate businesses to concentrate on lumber manufacturing as a large-scale commercial venture that demanded all their time, talent, and resources.[46]

The data for manufacturers entering the industry in Michigan during the years between 1856 and 1870, particularly in comparison with those for the earlier period, reveals some interesting similarities with the earlier lumbermen and some clues to the changing nature of entre-

TABLE 35
Place of Birth for Lumber Manufacturers
Entering the Industry Between 1856 and 1870

New England		Foreign Born	
Maine	16	Canada	14
Massachusetts	11	Ireland	5
Vermont	8	Scotland	4
New Hampshire	6	England	3
Connecticut	5	Netherlands	2
	46	Norway	1
		Sweden	1
		Germany	1
Middle Atlantic		Unspecified	1
New York	60		32
Pennsylvania	6		
New Jersey	3		
	69		
Other Regions			
Ohio	8		
Michigan	5		
Indiana	1		
	14	Total	161

preneurship. As Table 35 shows, Michigan's lumbermen were still overwhelmingly native-born. Over 80 percent of the 161 manufacturers who entered the industry after 1855 for whom information was found were born in the United States. The largest number of manufacturers still came from New York. Only thirty-two men, or less than 20 percent, were foreign-born, and just 3.2 percent were non-English speaking. The number of Canadians increased markedly compared with the pre-1855 period, but the other categories showed less change. This pattern of nativity demonstrates the continuance of a lateral migration confined to quite narrow geographical limits, a pattern that corresponded closely to that of labor.

The family background and educational training of entrepreneurs entering the lumber industry in Michigan between 1855 and 1870 also changed little from the previous years. The available biographical material suggests that few lumbermen came from wealthy or socially prominent families. There was no information on father's occupation for sixty-two of the lumbermen, but of the remaining ninety-nine, the greatest number, forty eight (48.5 percent), were sons of farmers. Twenty-seven (27.3 percent) fathers had been in lumbering, and twenty-one (21.2 percent) were merchants, professional men, or artisans. Three of the lumbermen were orphans. These figures, viewed as percentages, are little different from those of the group in the pre-1855 period. Nor did the percentage who enjoyed various levels of educational training change markedly. Forty-seven of the sample of ninety (52.2 percent) for whom information is available attended common schools, while the remaining forty-three (47.8 percent) received additional vocational, professional, or academic training. Slightly more than half of those, twenty-two, attended academies, while sixteen went to colleges or business colleges, and five read law or medicine or served apprenticeships.

TABLE 36
**Previous Occupational Experience for Lumber Manufacturers
Entering the Industry Between 1856 and 1870**

Lumbering	80	Professional*	5
Mercantile	17	Office Work	4
Farming	15	Real Estate	3
Construction	9	Other	4
Manufacturing	7	Total	144

*Includes education, law, medicine, religion.

As Table 36 indicates, eighty of 144 men (55.5 percent) who entered lumber manufacturing in Michigan by 1870 had previous experience in some phase of the industry. This increase from 40.2 percent in the previous period demonstrates the transfer of labor and entrepreneurs from other lumber regions as well as the growing pool of lumbermen within the state. Of the eighty manufacturers with previous experience in the lumber industry, twenty-five had owned sawmills outside the state, while nineteen had been loggers. Sixteen had been marketers of lumber, and twenty had been employed in the woods and mills, often in an office or supervisory capacity. The remainder of the entrepreneurs came from various occupations, particularly mercantile, agricultural, and construction, all of which can be considered traditional paths of entry into lumber manufacturing.

One striking change in the entrepreneurial profile of the later group of men was age at entry into lumber manufacturing. Of 155 men, only five (3.2 percent) became manufacturers before they were twenty-one. Forty-six entered the industry while they were in their twenties, and fifty were in their thirties. Fifty-four did not become entrepreneurs in Michigan until they were past forty. The youngest entrepreneurs usually went into a family business, while many of the men over forty were either millmen moving west to new timberstands or successful lumber dealers, usually from outside the state, who were entering manufacturing to supply their yards. A few of the older lumbermen, like Crapo, came with no experience, but Sage and McGraw, who had owned a large mill in Canada, were more typical of this period.

A second striking shift in the years after 1855 was in the form of ownership of the manufacturing units. Proprietorships decreased, while partnerships increased. Of 157 millmen for whom information was available, 113, or 72 percent, were members of a partnership. The remainder were proprietors of their own operations. In light of the increased capital requirements and expanding scale of production, this trend is not surprising. A corollary to this change was the increase in number of multiple-partner firms. Three or four partners were usual, but for H. A. Braddock & Company of Portsmouth the Dun and Bradstreet reporter listed nine partners—three living in Michigan and six in the East.[47] Such an organizational form was likely to be found in firms that were adding manufacturing to marketing, transferring operations to new locations, or both. Joint stock and corporate arrangements were only just beginning. The Forest Valley Salt and Lumber Company of Saginaw and the Port Sheldon Company in Ottawa County were two the early joint-stock companies. Both were begun in the late 1860s and lasted only a few years before failing or being restructured. The Pere Marquette Lumber Company, which was formed in 1870, appears to have been the only corporation of the period. It was organized as the successor to James Ludington's proprietorship, with Ludington furnishing all the capital for the five other shareholders, who were to pay off their $375,000 indebtedness to him in annual installments. The corporate form of business became increasingly popular in succeeding years as capital requirements rose and the tie between ownership and management was often broken.[48]

A few of the men who became manufacturers before 1870 gained great wealth or importance, like Charles Mears, Henry H. Crapo, Martin Ryerson, or Thomas Ferry, but most achieved more moderate success. The great "lumber barons" who assumed huge fortunes, built imposing Victorian houses, and often contributed generously to local and state projects appeared in the years after 1870. Nor were woodsmen before 1870 the colorful and daring characters of later legend. Yet these men, whether workers or owners, developed a great industry based on a vast forest wilderness.

Conclusion

The period from 1837 to 1870 marked the rise of a great commercial lumber industry in Michigan. Large-scale mills producing for a regional and then a national market took their place beside and then supplanted the small, scattered one- and two-man custom mills. Sawmilling was transformed from an aid to settlement to a major export enterprise. The transition was rapid, for by 1850 lumber was the largest, most important industry in the state. Yet it was strangely unobtrusive. Few contemporaries appear to have been aware of the dynamics or implications of the growth of lumbering. Perhaps its broad base muted or weakened their awareness of changes in scale.

The lumber industry played a key role in the development of Michigan. It opened new areas to economic development and settlement, created urban centers, and attracted men and capital. In the early years of the state, timber was cheap and cost of entry into the industry low, enabling men of very modest means to embark on lumbering careers. As pinelands shifted from government ownership into private hands and the size and complexity of manufacturing units increased, cost of entry rose. Yet through the 1860s lumbering remained an open industry of mixed large and small mills where no single firm, or group of firms, dominated production.

Acquisition of both fixed and working capital was a problem common to most lumbermen, as it was to all frontier manufacturers. Financial support came almost exclusively from private sources—family, acquaintances, or eastern capitalists. Financial intermediaries were not important in the years before 1870. Men who began lumbering with modest means in the early years of the state were often able to finance their own operations and expansion out of income; those who entered the industry after 1860 needed sufficient capital or credit to undertake large-scale manufacturing. Credit was particularly important in the lumber industry, with its long cycle of production, which permitted only annual turnover of capital. Local merchants and, by the late 1850s, specialized wholesalers provided many lumbermen with supplies or cash needed to see them through the long season.

All phases of the lumber industry operated on a seasonal basis until the last quarter of the nineteenth century. Cutting took place in the winter when logs could be moved by sleds over snow-covered roads, and spring freshets brought the logs to the mill. Sawmills operated from spring into autumn, and marketing was limited to the navigational season. Although lower Michigan possessed an ideal climate for the industry, the unpredictability of the weather too often reduced preseason calculations of production. In addition to constraints imposed by nature, dependence on water transport for both logs and lumber established the limits of logging and marketing areas. Fortunately, the lower peninsula had a fine river system of 16,000 miles and many excellent harbors. In the early years of the industry, therefore, there were fewer constraints on logging than on marketing, but by the mid-1860s lack of ample transportation facilities was felt throughout the industry. Not surprisingly, lumbermen supported railroad construction, which could open new resource and market areas and reduce the unpredictability of supply by lessening dependence on the weather.

Despite the limitations inherent in the industry before the railroad, a spirit of expansion—expressed in plant size, equipment, and output—was apparent from territorial days, as was the willingness to experiment with and adopt new technology. Such optimism coupled with ease of entry made lumber manufacturing a very competitive—and uncertain—undertaking. That was particularly true during the years 1858 to 1861, when contracting markets brought ruin to many manufacturers. With renewed prosperity, the movement of settlers westward onto the treeless plains, and the exhaustion of high-quality eastern timber, the outlook for the industry brightened.

Commercial lumber manufacturing was a well-established, fully developed industry in Michigan in 1870. By that date it dominated both the economy of the state and the major lumber markets of the nation. Optimism, even exuberance, characterized the spirit of the industry as it entered the final three decades of the nineteenth century and what would be the golden age of lumber in the Wolverine State.

Notes

INTRODUCTION

1. U.S., Census office, *Manufactures of the United States in 1860; Compiled from the Original Returns of the Eighth Census* (Washington, 1865), 733–42.

2. William Gerald Rector, *Log Transportation in the Lake States Lumber Industry, 1840–1918: The Movement of Logs and Its Relationship to Land Settlement, Waterway Development, Railroad Construction, Lumber Production and Prices* (Glendale, Cal., 1953), 44–45; Milton O. Nelson, "The Lumber Industry of America," *Review of Reviews* 36 (1907), 564.

3. Margaret Walsh, *The Manufacturing Frontier: Pioneer Industry in Antebellum Wisconsin, 1830–1860* (Madison, 1972), v.

4. See Table 13, and Tables 20 and 21.

5. For example, see Joseph Zaremba, *Economics of the American Lumber Industry* (New York, 1963), 7; Thomas R. Cox, *Mills and Markets: A History of the Pacific Lumber Industry to 1900* (Seattle, 1974), xi.

6. See Table 28.

CHAPTER 1

1. Quoted in Ellen Churchill Semple, *Influences of Geographic Environment* (New York, 1911), 11.

2. Michigan State University, Graduate School of Business Administration, Division of Research, *Michigan Statistical Abstract*, 9th ed. (Lansing, 1972), 227; "Public Lands of the United States," *Merchant's Magazine and Commercial Review* 57 (1867), 281; Willis Frederick Dunbar, *Michigan: A History of the Wolverine State* (Grand Rapids, Michigan, 1970), 24; James Elliott Defebaugh, *History of the Lumber Industry of America*, 2 vols. (Chicago, 1906–07), I, 284, 358.

3. A. H. Eichmeier, "Climate of Michigan," in Charles M. Davis, ed., *Readings in the Geography of Michigan* (Ann Arbor, 1964), 41–42; George Newman Fuller, *Economic and Social Beginnings of Michigan: A Study of the Settlement of the Lower Peninsula During the Territorial Period, 1805–1837* (Lansing, 1916), 6, 12; Dieter Brunnachweiler, "Precipitation Regime in the Lower Peninsula of Michigan," in Davis, ed., *Readings in the Geography of Michigan*, 49–52; Dewey A. Seeley, "Factors Controlling Climate," in Davis, ed., *Readings in the Geography of Michigan*, 40.

4. For a brief history of Michigan's geological development, see Helen M. Martin, "The First Four Billion Years," in Davis, ed., *Readings in the Geography of Michigan*, 7–27; Arthur Field, "Road Patterns of the Southern Peninsula of Michigan," *Papers of the Michigan Academy of Science, Arts and Letters* 15 (1930), 307; Charles M. Davis, "The Hydrographic Regions of Michigan," *Papers of the Michigan Academy of Science, Arts and Letters* 16 (1931), 212; Earl J. Senninger, Jr., *Atlas*

of Michigan, 2d ed. (Flint, Michigan [1963]), 1.

5. George S. McIntire and Russell McKee, "100 Years of Michigan Forests," in Davis, ed., *Readings in the Geography of Michigan*, 97; Senninger, Jr., *Atlas of Michigan*, 4; Arthur Martin Weimer, "An Economic History of Alma, Michigan" (Ph.D. diss., University of Chicago, 1934), 14; Fuller, *Economic and Social Beginnings of Michigan*, 23; Olin W. Blackett, ed., "Water Resources of Michigan," in Davis, ed., *Readings in the Geography of Michigan*, 75–76; Michigan Economic Development Department, "Michigan's Water Resources for Industry," in Davis, ed., *Readings in the Geography of Michigan*, 71.

6. Fuller, *Economic and Social Beginnings of Michigan*, 23–25; Blackett, ed., "Water Resources of Michigan," in Davis, ed., *Readings in the Geography of Michigan*, 80; Truman B. Fox, *History of Saginaw County, From the Year 1819 down to the Present Time. Compiled from Authentic Records and Other Sources. Also, A Business Directory of Each of the Three Principal Towns of the County* (East Saginaw, 1858), 12–14; William Gerald Rector, *Log Transportation in the Lakes States Lumber Industry, 1840–1918. The Movement of Its Logs and Its Relationship to Land Settlement, Waterway Development, Railroad Construction, Lumber Production and Prices* (Glendale, Cal., 1953), 48.

7. Clifford Allen, ed., *Michigan Log Marks* (East Lansing, 1941), 41.

8. Fuller, *Economic and Social Beginnings of Michigan*, 25; Blackett, ed., "Water Resources of Michigan," in Davis, ed., *Readings in the Geography of Michigan*, 81.

9. *History of Muskegon County, Michigan, with Illustrations and Biographical Sketches of Some of its Prominent Men and Pioneers* (Chicago, 1882), 17; Allen, ed., *Michigan Log Marks*, 63.

10. Fuller, *Economic and Social Beginnings of Michi-*

gan, 32–33; Dunbar, *Michigan,* 22; Allen, ed., *Michigan Log Marks,* 52.

11. B. E. Quick, "A Comparative Study of the Distribution of the Climax Association in Southern Michigan," *Papers of the Michigan Academy of Science, Arts and Letters* 3 (1924), 215; R. D. Burroughs, "Land Our Basic Resource," in Davis, ed., *Readings in the Geography of Michigan,* 4; Davis, ed., *Readings in the Geography of Michigan,* 55; Fuller, *Economic and Social Beginnings of Michigan,* 14, 17.

12. Field, "Road Patterns of the Southern Peninsula of Michigan," 309; Charles S. Wheeler, "The Early Flora and Fauna of Michigan," *Michigan Pioneer and Historical Society Historical Collections* 32 (1902), 354; Charles Herbert Otis, *Michigan Trees: A Handbook of the Native and Most Important Introduced Species,* 8th ed., rev. (Ann Arbor, 1926), passim; Quick, "A Comparative Study of the Distribution of the Climax Association in Southern Michigan," 215–16, 219–20; Charles M. Davis, "The High Plains of Michigan," *Michigan Papers in Geography* 6 (1936), 312; H. F. Bergman, "The Composition of Climax Plant Formations in Minnesota," *Papers of the Michigan Academy of Science, Arts and Letters* 3 (1923), 51; Defebaugh, *History of the Lumber Industry,* I, 284; Norman F. Smith, "Michigan Trees Worth Knowing," in Davis, ed., *Readings in the Geography of Michigan,* 89–90.

13. N. T. Mirov, *The Genus Pinus* (New York, 1967), 175; U.S. Dept. of the Interior, Bureau of the Census, *Tenth Census of the United States, 1880,* maps accompanying vol. 9, *Forest Trees of North America,* map 15; George W. Hotchkiss, *History of the Lumber and Forest Industry of the Northwest* (Chicago, 1898), 30; Otis, *Michigan Trees,* 7; Fuller, *Economic and Social Beginnings of Michigan* 37; E. P. Whiteside, J. F. Schneider and R. L. Cook, "The Soils of Michigan," in Davis, ed., *Readings in the Geography of Michigan,* 63; Jethro Otto

Veatch, "Soil Maps as a Basis for Mapping Original Forest Cover," *Papers of the Michigan Academy of Science, Arts and Letters* 15 (1931), 272; Leslie A. Kenoyer, "Forest Distribution in Southwestern Michigan as Interpreted from the Original Survey, 1826–1832," *Michigan Papers in Geography* 4 (1924), 109.

14. Mirov, *The Genus Pinus*, 3–4, 10, 313; Otis, *Michigan Trees*, 17–33. The three indigenous pine species are *Pinus Strobus* L., *Pinus Resinosa Ait*, and *Pinus Banksiana Lamb*. The six generas are *Latrix* (tamarack), *Picea* (spruce), *Abies* (fir), *Tsuga* (hemlock), *thuga* (cedar) and *Juniperus* (cedar).

15. Mirov, *The Genus Pinus*, 175, 391–392, 397, 435, 440; Otis, *Michigan Trees*, 7; *Tenth Census of the United States, 1880*, vol. 9, *Forest Trees of North America*, 187; Gifford Pinchot and Henry S. Graves, *The White Pine: A Study* (New York, 1896), 6–7.

16. *Tenth Census of the United States, 1880*, vol. 9, *Forest Trees of North America*, 187; Otis, *Michigan Trees*, 7; *Lumberman's Gazette* (Bay City, Michigan), April, 1873.

Comparative wood weights by pound per cubic foot:

Cork	15
White pine	25
Yellow pine	38
Birch	45
Hickory	52
Ebony	62

17. Joseph Russell Smith and M. Ogden Phillips, *Industrial and Commercial Geography*, 3d ed. (New York, 1946), 339; Milton O. Nelson, "The Lumber Industry of America," *Review of Reviews* 36 (Nov. 1907), 564.

18. Rolland H. Maybee, *Michigan's White Pine Era, 1840–1900* (Lansing, 1960), 11, 13.

19. Ibid; Bureau of the Census, *Tenth Census of the United States*, vol. 9, *Forest Trees of North America*, 187; Kenoyer, "Forest Distribution in Southwestern

Michigan as Interpreted from the Original Survey, 1826–1832," 109; Hotchkiss, *History of the Lumber and Forest Industry of the Northwest*, 29, 33; *History of Muskegon County, Michigan*, 18; William Lee Jenks, *St. Clair County, Michigan: Its History and Its People*, 2 vols. (Chicago, 1912), I, 362; Defebaugh, *History of the Lumber Industry*, I, 308; Carl A. Leech, "Lumbering Days," *Michigan History Magazine* 18 (Spring 1934), 135; Alexander Winchell, *The Grand Traverse Region: A Report on the Geological and Industrial Resources of the Counties of Antrim, Grand Traverse, Benzie and Leelaman in the Lower Peninsula of Michigan* (Ann Arbor, 1866), 31–32.

20. H. Robinsons, *Economic Geography* (London, 1968), 181; *Tenth Census of the United States, 1880*, vol. 9, *Forest Trees of North America*, 553; Hotchkiss, *History of the Lumber and Forest Industry*, 143; Victor S. Clark, *History of the Manufactures in the United States, 1607–1860* (Washington, 1916), 75.

21. *The Pinelands and Lumber Trade of Michigan, Exhibiting the Extent, Quality and Advantages, Compiled from Official and Authentic Sources* (Detroit, 1856), 3.

22. Weiner, "An Economic History of Alma, Michigan," 14; Dennis G. Cooper and Floyd A. Stilgenbauer, "The Urban Geography of Saginaw, Michigan," *Michigan Papers in Geography* 5 (1935), 301; Robinson, *Economic Geography*, 181; Smith and Phillips, *Industrial and Commercial Geography*, 48; H. R. Garrett, *A Geography of Manufacturing* (London, 1969), 22–23.

23. Robinson, *Economic Geography* 8, 25–26; Smith and Phillips, *Industrial and Commercial Geography*, 48.

24. Charles Richard Tuttle, *General History of the State of Michigan: with Biographical Sketches* (Detroit, 1874), 120; Calvin Goodrich, *The First Michigan Frontier* (Ann Arbor, 1940), 121–122, 143; James V. Campbell, *Outlines of the Political History of Michigan* (Detroit, 1876), 234; Henry M. Utley and Byron M. Cut-

cheon, *Michigan as a Province, Territory and State, the Twenty-sixth Member of the Federal Union*, 4 vols. ([New York], 1906), I, 347.

25. W. O. Hedrick, "A Sketch of Some Institutional Beginnings in Michigan," *Michigan History Magazine* 5 (January 1921), 198; George B. Catlin, "Early Settlement in Eastern Michigan," *Michigan History Magazine* 26 (Summer 1942), 321; U.S., Dept. of the Interior, Bureau of the Census, *A Compendium of the Ninth Census, 1870* (Washington, 1872), 58; Milo M. Quaife and Sidney Glazer, *Michigan: From Primitive Wilderness to Industrial Commonwealth* (New York, 1948), 150; Dunbar, *Michigan*, 250.

26. Hotchkiss, *History of the Lumber and Forest Industry*, 37, 64, 90; Fuller, *Economic and Social Beginnings of Michigan*, 26; Jenks, *St. Clair County*, I, 365; Leo C. Lillie, *Historic Grand Haven and Ottawa County* (Grand Haven, Mich., 1931), 192; *Lumberman's Gazette*, Jan. 18, 1882; *History of Bay County, Michigan, with Illustrations and Biographical Sketches of Some of Its Prominent Men and Pioneers* (Chicago, 1883), 25; Campbell, *Outlines of the Political History of Michigan*, 234; George N. Fuller, "Settlement of Southern Michigan, 1805–1837," *Michigan History Magazine* 19 (Spring-Summer 1935), 180.

27. William Vipond Pooley, *The Settlement of Illinois from 1830 to 1850* (Madison, 1908), 476, 479, 544, 551; Bessie Louise Pierce, *A History of Chicago*, 3 vols. (New York, 1937–1957), I, 133–34, 413; John Moses and Joseph Kirkland, *History of Chicago, Illinois: Aboriginal to Metropolitan*, 2 vols. (Chicago, 1895), I, 107; Isaac Guyer, *History of Chicago: Its Commercial and Manufacturing Interests and Industry* (Chicago, 1862), 123; Hotchkiss, *History of the Lumber and Forest Industry*, 44, 168, 193, 667; _____, *Industrial Chicago: The Lumber Interests* (Chicago, 1894), 26, 38; *Northwestern Lumberman*, June 14, 1890; *Compendium of the Ninth Census, 1870*, 38, 44, 46, 66, 68; *History of Muskegon*

County, Michigan, 21; Lillie, *Historic Grand Haven and Ottawa County,* 192; St. Mary's Falls Ship Canal Co., *560,000 Acres Pine Lands, in the State of Michigan, with Lumber Statistics and other Valuable Information Concerning the Pine Lands of the St. Mary's Falls Ship Canal Company* (Detroit, 1857), 11; unidentified clipping, Jan. 3, 1857, Yates Scrapbook, Albert Yates Papers (Michigan Historical Collections, Bentley Historical Library, University of Michigan); Henry H. Crapo, notebook, Jan. 4, 1856, Henry H. Crapo Papers (Michigan Historical Collections, Bentley Historical Library, University of Michigan); William B. Mershon, "Historical Notes," *Michigan History Magazine* 14 (Spring 1930), 178; George S. Kaime, "Where Our Lumber Comes From," *The Western Monthly* 3 (1870), 189.

28. James Cooke Mills, *History of Saginaw County, Michigan,* 2 vols. (Saginaw, 1918), I, 402; Hotchkiss, *History of the Lumber and Forest Industry,* 48, 62, 361–362; *Lumberman's Gazette,* Feb. 8, 1882; James Abbott to Horace Bunce, Nov. 6, 1845, and unidentified author to Henry W. Taylor, Aug. 22, 1842, William Lee Jenks Papers; (Burton Historical Collection, Detroit Public Library); George Angus Belding, "Thunder in the Forest," *Michigan History Magazine* 33 (March 1949), 35; Richard G. Wood, *A History of Lumbering in Maine, 1820–1861* (Orono, Maine, 1935), 226–27; Irene M. Hargreaves and Harold M. Foehl, *The Story of Logging the White Pine in the Saginaw Valley* (Bay City, Michigan, 1964), 4; *Northwestern Lumberman,* May 31, 1890; Ormond S. Danford, "The Social and Economic Effects of Lumbering on Michigan, 1835–1890," *Michigan History Magazine* 26 (Summer 1942), 349; H. Perry Smith, ed., *History of the City of Buffalo and Erie County,* 2 vols. (Syracuse, 1884), I, 418, II, 199–200; James Elliott Defebaugh, *History of the Lumber Industry,* II, 55, 408–10.

29. *Merchants' Magazine* 19 (1848), 40.

CHAPTER 2

1. *U.S. Statutes at Large*, II (Boston, 1845), 73–78; ibid., III (Boston, 1846), 566–67; ibid., IV (Boston, 1853), 593; ibid., V (Boston, 1856), 453–58; ibid., X (Boston, 1855), 574; ibid., XII (Boston, 1863), 392–93.

2. U.S., 46 Cong., 2 sess., House Executive Doc. no. 46, *Report of Public Lands Commission*, 22; John Ise, *The United States Forest Policy*, (New Haven, 1920), 19; Ralph W. Hidy, Frank Ernest Hill, Allan Nevins, *Timber and Men: The Weyerhaeuser Story* (New York, 1963), 123; Edward S. Meany, Jr., "The History of the Lumber Industry in the Pacific Northwest to 1917" (Ph.D. diss., Harvard University, 1935), 168; Charles E. Belknap, *The Yesterdays of Grand Rapids* (Grand Rapids, 1922), 127.

3. James Willard Hurst, *Law and Economic Growth: The Legal History of the Lumber Industry in Wisconsin, 1836–1915* (Cambridge, Mass., 1964), 10. The first chapter in this book is especially useful for an understanding of nineteenth-century American thought and the formation of public land policy. Henry Nash Smith, *Virgin Land: The American West as Myth and Symbol* (New York, 1950) provides a provocative analysis of the agrarian cost of social thinking that created the American myth of the garden. Mary E. Young, "Congress Looks West: Liberal Ideology and Public Land Policy in the Nineteenth Century," in David M. Ellis, ed., *The Frontier in American Development: Essays in Honor of Paul Wallace Gates* (Ithaca, 1969), 74–112; U.S. Bureau of Corporations, *The Lumber Industry*, 3 vols. (Washington, 1913–14, I, xvii–svii, 182–83, 219; John Ise, *The United States Forest Policy*, 56.

4. *U.S. Statutes at Large*, XXVII (Washington, 1893), 348; *Report of the Public Lands Commission*; U.S., 43 Cong., 2 sess., vol. 6, *Interior*, no. 1, part 5, *Report of the Commissioner of the General Land Office*, 6–7; Ben-

jamin Horace Hibbard, *A History of the Public Land Policies*, reprint (Madison, 1965), 459. For the effects of timber legislation on the American lumber industry, see Paul Gates, "The Homestead Law in an Incongruous Land System," reprinted in Vernon Carstensen, ed., *The Public Lands* (Madison: University of Wisconsin Press, 1968), 338–40.

5. For detailed studies of the relationship of timber, development, and contemporary values, see Susan L. Flader, *The Great Lakes Forest: An Environmental and Social History* (Minneapolis: University of Minnesota Press, 1983), esp. Charles Twining, "The Lumbering Frontier," James Willard Hurst, "The Institutional Environment of the Logging Era in Wisconsin," and Raleigh Barlowe, "Changing Land Use and Policies: The Lake States."

6. Fred W. Foster, "Farmsteads and Land Types in Emmet County, Michigan," *Papers of the Michigan Academy of Science, Arts and Letters* 27 (1942), 356; George Newman Fuller, *Economic and Social Beginnings of Michigan: A Study of the Lower Peninsula During the Territorial Period, 1805–1837* (Lansing, 1916), 39–42; Hibbard, *A History of the Public Land Policies*, 457–58; *History of Muskegon County, Michigan With Illustrations and Biographical Sketches of Some of Its Prominent Men and Pioneers* (Chicago, 1882), 17; William Lee Jenks, *St. Clair County, Michigan: Its History and Its People*, 2 vols. (Chicago, 1912), I, 362; Oran W. Rowland, *A History of Van Buren County, Michigan: A Narrative Account of its People, and its Principal Interests*, 2 vols. (Chicago, 1912), I, 433–34; *The Lumber Industry*, I, 183, 270; Charles M. Davis, "Lumbering in the High Plains," in Charles M. Davis, ed., *Readings in the Geography of Michigan* (Ann Arbor, 1964), 87; Mary F. Robinson, "Rix Robinson, Fur Trader," *Michigan History Magazine* 6 (1922), 285. David D. Oliver, *Centennial History of Alpena County, Michigan: The Survey,*

*Settlement and Growth of Alpena County, From 1837 to
1876* (Alpena, 1903), 24; George M. Blackburn and
Sherman L. Ricards, "The Timber Industry in Manistee
County, Michigan," *Journal of Forest History* 18 (1974),
16–17; Lucile Kane, "Federal Protection of Public Timber in the Upper Great Lakes States," in Vernon R. Carstensen, ed., *The Public Lands: Studies in the History of
the Public Domain* (Madison, 1963), 440–41; *Lumberman's Gazette* (Bay City), Feb. 4, Mar. 18, 1885; James
Glasgow, "Muskegon, Michigan: The Evolution of a
Lake Port" (Ph.D. diss., University of Chicago, 1939),
14; Ise, *The United States Forest Policy, 41.*

7. *The Merchant's Magazine, and Commercial Re-
view* 24 (1851), 71–72, 57 (1867), 272–86; *History of
Muskegon County*, 32; Kane, "Federal Protection of
Public Timber in the Upper Great Lakes States," 439–40;
Ise, *the United States Forest Policy*, 40; Blackburn and
Ricards, "The Timber Industry in Manistee County," 17;
George W. Hotchkiss, *History of the Lumber and For-
est Industry of the Northwest* (Chicago, 1898), 246;
Weekly Observer (Fentonville), June 2, 1854.

8. A proposal to sell stumpage rather than land was
unsuccessfully suggested by the Public Lands Commission, although not until 1879. *Report of the Public
Lands Commission*, 33; Hurst, *Law and Economic
Growth*, 27–28.

9. Hibbard, *A History of the Public Land Policies*,
459; *Niles' National Register* 75 (1849), 209; *Western
Emigrant* (Ann Arbor), Aug. 4, 1830; Dallas Lee Jones,
"The Survey and Sale of the Public Lands in Michigan"
(M.A. thesis, Cornell University, 1952), 37.

10. The author surveyed land records for 147 townships in forty-nine counties of Michigan's lower peninsula for the years 1818–1870. These townships were
selected on the basis of vegetation maps and the movement of the lumber industry within the state. Land
transfers to known lumbermen and speculators were re-

corded and tabulated. Through this method the author was able to determine how 320 buyers acquired 304,811.85 acres of timberland. U.S., Dept. of the Interior, Bureau of Land Management, Eastern Division, Tract Books, Michigan N and E and Michigan N and W, vols. 1–17, 19–33, 35–36.

11. *Report of the Commissioner of the General Land Office*, 6; Henry W. Sage, a leading Saginaw businessman, dated the price increase from 1873; Anita Shafer Goodstein, *Biography of a Businessman: Henry W. Sage, 1814–1897* (Ithaca, 1962), 136; Tract Books, Michigan N and W, vol. 23; *The Lumber Industry*, I, 256–57.

12. Jones, "The Survey and Sale of the Public Lands in Michigan," 103–23; Harry L. Spooner, "The First White Pathfinders of Newaygo County, Michigan" (unpub. ms., Library of Michigan), 8–9, 30–31; *History of Ottawa County Michigan, with Illustrations and Biographical Sketches of Its Prominent Men and Pioneers* (Chicago, 1882), 24; *History of Muskegon County, Michigan*, 24; George W. Hotchkiss, *History of the Lumber and Forest Industry of the Northwest*, 219.

13. Charles B. Mears, diaries, July 28, 1859, Charles B. Mears Papers (Michigan Historical Collections, Bentley Historical Library, University of Michigan); Charles B. Mears to Thomas H. Wood, May 31, 1859, Charles B. Mears Papers (Chicago Historical Society).

14. Jones, "The Survey and Sale of the Public Lands in Michigan," 127–29. Use of the Pre-emption Act to secure timberlands was typical in all forest areas of the country. Ise, *The United States Forest Policy*, 48.

15. Jones, "The Survey and Sale of the Public Lands in Michigan," 99, 101. See also above fn. 9. The Graduation Act was in effect from 1854 to 1862.

16. Data drawn from U.S., Public Land Commission, *The Public Domain: With Statistics* (Washington, 1884), 351–55. For an example of arrest for logging Homestead

land, see diary of James Olin Whittemore, Apr. 28, 1866, Clarke Historical Library, Central Michigan University.

17. The eight townships are T13N, R1E; T14N, R1–4E; T15N, R3–RE; T16N, R4E.

18. Roy M. Robbins, *Our Landed Heritage: The Public Domain, 1776–1936* (Princeton, 1942), 240; U.S., 58 Cong., 3 sess., Senate Docs., No. 189, *Final Report of the Public Lands Commission* 8; *The Lumber Industry*, I, 182–83; Ise, *The United States Forest Policy*, 48.

19. Henry Howland Crapo to William H. Crapo, January 25, 1868, quoted in Martin D. Lewis, *Lumberman from Flint: The Michigan Career of Henry H. Crapo, 1855–69* (Detroit, 1958), 58.

20. *U.S. Statutes at Large*, V, 497; Ibid., X, 3–4; Hibbard, *A History of the Public Land Policies*, 126.

21. Hibbard, *A History of the Public Land Policy*, 125; U.S., 40 Cong., 2 sess., General Land Office Commissioner to Rep. George Julian, July 13, 1868, App., 424.

22. *Detroit Daily Advertiser*, Jan. 1, Oct. 22, 1859, Apr. 2, July 2, 1860.

23. See above fn. 10; Jones, "The Survey and Sale of the Public Lands in Michigan," 146–47.

24. David Ward, *The Autobiography of David Ward* (New York, 1912), 117.

25. Kate Ball Powers, Flora Ball Hopkins and Lucy Ball, comps., *Autobiography of John Ball* (Grand Rapids, 1925), 177; Ward, *Autobiography*, 100; Mears, Diaries, June 6, 1856, Mears Papers (Michigan Historical Collections, Bentley Historical Library, University of Michigan).

26. Paul Wallace Gates, *The Wisconsin Pinelands of Cornell University: A Study in Land Policy and Absentee Ownership* (Madison, 1943), 30–31, 57–58.

27. Goodstein, *Biography of a Businessman*, 138.

28. Ibid., 181–82.

29. Jones, "The Survey and Sale of the Public Lands in Michigan," 83–84; Alec R. Gilpin, *The Territory of Michigan, 1805–1837* (Lansing 970), 132; *History of Bay County, Michigan, with Illustrations and Biographical Sketches of Some of its Prominent Men and Pioneers* (Chicago, 1883), 17–18; Powers, Hopkins and Ball, comps., *Autobiography of John Ball*, 133; Robbins, *Our Landed Heritage*, 61–62; Malcolm J. Rohrbough, *The Land Office Business: The Settlement and Administration of American Public Lands, 1789–1837* (New York, 1968), 234, 241; Joe L. Norris, "The Country Merchant and the Industrial Magnate," *Michigan History Magazine* 40 (1956), 331.

30. Rohrbough, *The Land Office Business*, 246–47; Douglas H. Gordon and George S. May, eds., "The Michigan Land Rush in 1836," *Michigan History Magazine* 43 (1959), 7.

31. John M. Gordon, "Michigan Journal, 1836," *Michigan History Magazine* 43 (1959), 13–14, 292.

32. Powers, Hopkins and Ball, comps., *Autobiography of John Ball*, 102, 140–41, 143.

33. I. P. Christiancy, "Recollections of the Early History of the City and County of Monroe," *Michigan Pioneer and Historical Society Historical Collections* 6 (1883), 368.

34. *History of Kent County, Michigan* (Chicago, 1881), 224; G. A. Morgan, "The Township of Allegan— Its Topography, Products, Early Settlement, and History," *Michigan Pioneer and Historical Society Historical Collections* 3 (1881), 279.

35. Jones, "The Survey and Sale of the Public Lands in Michigan," 102–03; Robbins, *Our Landed Heritage*, 92; Rolland H. Maybee, *Michigan's White Pine Era, 1840–1900* (Lansing, 1960), 14.

36. Ira Davenport to W. G. Butler, July 20, 1849, Davenport Collection (Cornell University), cited in

Jones, "The Survey and Sale of the Public Lands in Michigan," 149.

37. *Lumberman's Gazette*, Sept. 1873; Ward, *Autobiography*, 87.

38. Hotchkiss, *History of the Lumber and Forest Industry of the Northwest*, 170; Charles Chandler, "Life and Labors of Hon. Thomas D. Gilbert," *Michigan Pioneer and Historical Society Historical Collections* 27 (1896), 236.

39. Crapo, Journals, May 22, Oct. 31, 1863, Crapo Papers, Michigan Historical Collections, Bentley Library, University of Michigan; Ward, *Autobiography*, 62; "The Michigan Lumber Interest, As told in Sketches of Some of Its Leading Men, II: Ami W. Wright," *Magazine of Western History* 5 (1886), 126; Goodstein, *Biography of a Businessman*, 159; Irene D. Neu, *Erastus Corning, Merchant and Financier, 1794–1872* (Ithaca, 1960), 158; Mears, Diaries, Mar. 22, 1856, Oct. 6, 1858, Feb. 23, Mar. 15, 1859, Mears Papers (Michigan Historical Collections, Bentley Historical Library, University of Michigan); Thaddeus D. Seeley, *History of Oakland County, Michigan*, 2 vols. (Chicago, 1912), II, 499.

40. Harold G. Foran, "Modified System of Cruising," University of *Washington Forest Club Annual* 4 (1916), 34; Wilson Compton, *The Organization of the Lumber Industry: With Special Reference to the Influences Determining the Prices of Lumber in the United States* (Chicago, 1916), 108; *Northwestern Lumberman* (Chicago), July 16, 1892; *Forest History* 2 (1958), 4; Examination Reports of S. S. Hastings and Albert S. French, Michigan Pine Lands Association Papers (Burton Historical Collection of the Detroit Public Library); William J. Mead Timber Survey and Tally Burke, 1867–68, Amasa Brown Watson Papers, Clarke Historical Library, Central Michigan University.

41. Goodstein, *Biography of a Businessman*, 159.

42. Ward, *Autobiography*, 34, 61–62, 76; *Mecosta*

County Pioneer (Big Rapids), Apr. 17, 1862; Goodstein, *Biography of a Businessman,* 139; Powers, Hopkins, and Ball, comps., *Autobiography of John Ball,* 133; George Barker Engberg, "Labor in the Lake States Lumber Industry, 1830–1930" (Ph.D. diss., University of Minnesota, 1949), 307; Clifford Allen, ed., *Michigan Log Marks* (East Lansing, 1941), 30; Paul Wallace Gates, *The Wisconsin Pine lands of Cornell University: A Study in Land Policy and Absentee Ownership* (Madison, 1943), 92.

43. Unknown landlooker to Cyrus Woodman, Jan. 15, 1866, Michigan Pine Land Association Papers; Charles J. Wolfe, "Hannah, Lay and Company: A Study in Michigan's Lumber Industry" (M.A. thesis, Wayne State University, 1938), 44–45; St. Mary's Falls Ship Canal Company, *560,000 Acres Pine Lands, in the state of Michigan, with Lumber Statistics and Other Valuable Information Concerning the Pine Lands of the St. Mary's Falls Ship Canal Company* (Detroit, 1857), back insert.

44. Marion Clawson, *The Land System of the United States: An Introduction to the History and Practice of Land Use and Land Tenure* (Lincoln, 1968), 60; Harold Titus, "The Land Nobody Wanted," in Charles M. Davis, *Readings in the Geography of Michigan* (Ann Arbor, 1964), 272.

45. Wolfe, "Hannah, Lay and Company," 51.

46. *History of Kent County, Michigan,* 100, 285; Jones, "The Survey and Sale of the Public Lands in Michigan," 88; George N. Fuller, ed., *Messages of the Governors of Michigan,* 3 vols. (Lansing, 1925–26), II, 39–41.

47. The state had received 500,000 acres of land for internal improvements in 1841, but this was largely taken up by settlers during the decade of the 1840s. *U.S. Statutes at Large,* V, 453–58; *The Revised Statutes of the State of Michigan,* 1846, 244; Powers, Hopkins and Ball,

163, 166; *History of Kent County, Michigan*, 285.

48. Fuller, *Messages of the Governors*, II, 261; *Acts of the Legislature of the State of Michigan, Passed at the Annual Session of 1850, with an Appendix* (Lansing, 1850), 322–23; "The Michigan Swamp Land Controversy Settled at Last," *Northwestern Lumberman*, Jan. 2, 1892; Jones, "The Survey and Sale of the Public Lands in Michigan," 95–96; Truman B. Fox, *History of Saginaw County, From the Year 1819 down to the Present Time. Compiled from Authentic Records and other Sources; Traditionary Accounts, Legends, Anecdotes, & C. With Valuable Statistics, and notes of its Resources and General Information Concerning its Advantages. Also, A Business Directory of Each of the three Principal Towns of the County* (East Saginaw, 1858), 10–11; *Mecosta County Pioneer*, Mar. 12, 1863; *Acts of the Legislature of the State of Michigan, Passed at the Annual Session of 1857, with an Appendix* (Lansing, 1857); 234–36; Titus, "The Land Nobody Wanted," 272; "Commission of the Land Office Report," *Detroit Daily Advertiser*, Jan. 20, 27, 1860. A clear example of the interest in cheap timberlands through swampland purchase can be found in the correspondence of W. J. Mead, Watson Papers.

49. U.S. Public Land Commission, *The Public Domain*, 228; William A. Spill, "University of Michigan: Beginnings—III," *Michigan History Magazine* 13 (1929), 232–33; *Michigan Compiled Laws Annotated* (St. Paul, 1967), vol. 15, 322, 301, p. 884; Willis Frederick Dunbar, *Michigan: A History of the Wolverine State* (Grand Rapids, 1970), 396; *Detroit Daily Advertiser*, May 7, 1841; *Acts of the Legislature of the State of Michigan, Passed at the Annual Session of 1837* (Detroit, 1837), 209–11; *The Revised Statutes of the State of Michigan, Passed and Approved May 18, 1846* (Detroit, 1846), 29; *Acts of the Legislature of the State of Michigan, Passed at the Regular Session of 1863, with an Appendix* (Lan-

sing, 1863), 165; Hotchkiss, *History of the Lumber and Forest Industry of the Northwest*, 52.

50. *Acts of the Legislature of Michigan, 1863*, 201–04; *Acts of the Legislature of the State of Michigan, Passed at the Annual Session of 1869, with an Appendix* (Lansing, 1869), 51.

51. Lloyd M. Atwood, "Cheyboygan as a Nineteenth Century Lumber Area" (M.A. thesis, Wayne State University, 1947), 25; *History of Kent County, Michigan*, 280–281; Spooner, "The First White Pathfinders of Newaygo County, Michigan," 50, 58; _____, *Lumbering in Newaygo County* (White Cloud, Michigan, n.d.), 3; *Messages of the Governors*, II, 245–46.

52. Jenks, *History of St. Clair County*, I, 84; *Mecosta County Pioneer* (Big Rapids), July 9, 1868.

53. Wolfe, "Hannah, Lay and Company," 49, 51. For other examples of purchase through tax sales, see Watson Papers, and Amos Gould Collection, Box 12, Clarke Historical Library, Central Michigan University.

54. U.S. Public Land Commission, *The Public Domain*, 269–72; *Lumberman's Gazette*, Feb., 1873; Edmund A. Calkins, "Railroads of Michigan Since 1850," *Michigan History Magazine* 13 (1929), 8–9; Hibbard, *History of the Public Land Policy*, 245.

55. Paul Wesley Ivey, *The Pere Marquette Railroad Company* (Lansing, 1919), 217, 219, 221.

56. *Northwestern Lumberman*, Dec. 9, 1876; Byron S. Reetz, "A History of a Lumbered County" (M.A. thesis, Michigan State University, 1951), 18.

57. *U.S. Statutes at Large*, X, 35–36; ibid., XIII (Boston, 1866), 519–20; ibid., XIV (Boston, 1868), 80–81.

58. St. Mary's Falls Ship Canal Company, *560,000 Acres Pine Lands in the State of Michigan, with Lumber Statistics and other Valuable Information Concerning the Pine Lands of the St. Mary's Falls Ship Canal Company* (Detroit, 1857), 3–4, 15, front map. According to this company pamphlet, 480,730 acres were located in

27 counties in the lower peninsula. Maps of the company's holdings were arranged geographically and indicated lumber settlements and mill sites in addition to the location of canal lands. See St. Mary's Falls Ship Canal Company, maps 3 and 4, Charles B. Mears Papers (Burton Historical Collection, Detroit Public Library); George S. Frost to Erastus Fairbanks, Oct. 9, 1856, Erastus and T. Fairbanks Letters (Michigan Historical Collections, Bentley Historical Library, University of Michigan). For a discussion of the mineral lands of the company, see Irene D. Neu, "The Mineral Lands of the St. Mary's Falls Ship Canal Company," in David M. Ellis, ed., *The Frontier in American Development*, 162–91.

59. St. Mary's Falls Ship Canal company, *560,000 Acres Pine Lands*, back insert; Larry Gara, *Westernized Yankee: The Story of Cyrus Woodman* (Madison, 1956), 155–59, 172–74; Neu, *Erastus Corning*, 154–59; *Detroit Daily Advertiser*, Apr. 1, July 12, 1862; Erastus Fairbanks to R. M. Richardson, July 1, 1864, E. and T. Fairbanks Letters.

60. Unidentified clipping, Jan. 3, 1857, Yates Scrapbook, Albert Yates Papers (Michigan Historical Collections, Bentley Historical Library, University of Michigan); *The Pinelands and Lumber Trade of Michigan, Exhibiting the Extent, Quality and Advantages, Compiled from Official and Authentic Sources* (Detroit, 1856), 13; *Pine Lands in Michigan. 150,000 Acres For Sale by W. H. Craig Real Estate Broker, No. 39 Woodward Avenue, Detroit, Michigan* (Detroit, 1864), 1; St. Mary's Falls Ship Canal Company, *560,000 Acres Pine Lands*, back insert.

61. H. H. Crapo to W. Crapo, July 7, 1860, notebooks, undated entry, 1856, Crapo Papers.

62. *Lumberman's Gazette*, Aug., 1873; Goodstein, *Biography of a Businessman*, 136, 138.

63. Charles C. Trowbridge, 1836–37 land receipts,

C. C. Trowbridge Papers (Burton Historical Collection, Detroit Public Library); Powers, Hopkins and Ball, comps., *Autobiography of John Ball*, 172; Ward, *Autobiography*, 101; *Port Huron Observer*, Aug. 23, 1845; *The Pinelands and Lumber Trade of Michigan*, 13; Goodstein, *Biography of a Businessman*, 143; Wolfe, "Hannah, Lay and Company," 49, 50–51; *History of Berrien and Van Buren Counties, Michigan With Illustrations and Biographical Sketches of Its Prominent Men and Pioneers* (Philadelphia, 1880), 233; Crapo, Notebooks, Jan. 6 and undated entry, 1856, Crapo Papers; Unknown landlooker to Cyrus Woodman, Jan. 15, 1866, "statement of Sales of Lands of the Michigan Pine Land Association from September 2, 1863 to December 31, 1864, Michigan Pine Land Association Papers; Deed of St. Mary's Falls Ship Canal Company to Charles Mears, Oct. 1, 1863, Mears Papers (Burton Historical Collection, Detroit Public Library); James Abbott to Horace Bunce, Dec. 14, 1851, Jenks Collection (Burton Historical Collection, Detroit Public Library).

64. *The Lumber Industry*, I, 84, 184; Spooner, *Lumbering in Newaygo County*, 8; St. Mary's Falls Ship Canal Company, *560,000 Acres Pine Lands*, back insert; Rodney Hart to father, Feb. 27, Oct. 25, Nov. 6, 1872, Hart Family Papers (Michigan Historical Collections, Bentley Historical Library, University of Michigan); *Representative Men of Michigan*, II, 36; *Fenton Independent*, Sept. 22, 1868; Contract between H. H. Hunnewell and Holcombe and Evans, 1869, Michigan Pine Lands Association Papers; Goodstein, *Biography of a Businessman*, 143; Carrie Mears, "Description of Mears Village," typescript, Mears Papers (Michigan Historical Collections, Bentley Historical Library, University of Michigan); Wolfe, "Hannah, Lay and Company," 52; Atwood, "Cheyboygan as a Nineteenth Century Lumber Area," 26.

65. Compton, *The Organization of the Lumber Industry*, 50, 64–66, 71; *Lumberman's Gazette*, May 27, 1885; *Northwestern Lumberman*, Nov. 28, 1891.

CHAPTER 3

1. George Newman Fuller, *Economic and Social Beginnings of Michigan: A Study of the Settlement of the Lower Peninsula During the Territorial Period, 1805–1837* (Lansing, 1916), vi; James V. Campbell, *Outline of the Political History of Michigan* (Detroit, 1876), 112; Charles Richard Tuttle, *General History of the State of Michigan: With Biographical Sketches* (Detroit, 1874), 128.

2. George W. Hotchkiss, *History of the Lumber and Forest Industry of the Northwest* (Chicago, 1898), 34; Calvin Goodrich, *The First Michigan Frontier* (Ann Arbor, 1940), 220; William Lee Jenks, *St. Clair County, Michigan: Its History and Its People*, 2 vols. (Chicago, 1912), I, 362; Carl Addison Leach, "Paul Bunyan's Land and the First Sawmills of Michigan," *Michigan History Magazine* 20 (1936), 73.

3. Nelson V. Russell, *The British Regime in the Old Northwest, 1760–1790* (Northfield, Minn., 1939), 103.

4. Little is known about the firm of Meldrum and Parks, but it was engaged in supplying ships timbers and in fur trading and probably had an outpost at Mackinac as well as a store in Detroit and milling facilities in St. Clair County. Jenks, *St. Clair County*, I, 364–65; Fuller, *Economic and Social Beginnings*, 116–117; F. Clever Bald, *Detroit's First American Decade, 1796–1805* (Ann Arbor, 1948), 26, 73, 86, 133.

5. _____ Catlin to Israel Catlin, Feb. 16, 1830, William Lee Jenks Collection (Burton Historical Collections of the Detroit Public Library); Fuller, "Early Set-

tlement in Southern Michigan, 1805–1837," *Michigan History Magazine* 19 (1935), 183.

6. Hotchkiss, *History of the Lumber and Forest Industry*, 33; Fuller, *Economic and Social Beginnings*, 116–117

7. Milo M. Quaife and Sidney Glazer, *Michigan: From Primitive Wilderness to Industrial Commonwealth* (New York, 1948), 127; Joe L. Norris, "The County Merchant and the Industrial Magnate," *Michigan History Magazine* (1956), 332; Alec R. Gilpin, *The Territory of Michigan, 1803–1837* (Lansing, 1970), 70, 74; U.S., 22 Cong., 1 sess., House of Representative Documents, no. 263, *Abstract of the Returns of the Fifth Census*, 42; George B. Catlin, "Early Settlement in Eastern Michigan," *Michigan History Magazine* 26 (1942), 321; George N. Fuller, "Settlement of Southern Michigan, 1805–1837," *Michigan History Magazine*, 182–83, 188; *Compendium of the Enumeration of the Inhabitants and Statistics of the United States, as Obtained at the Department of State, From the Returns of Sixth Census, By Counties and Principal Towns*, Washington, 1841, p. 94.

8. *Northwestern Lumberman* (Chicago), Sept. 26, 1891.

9. *History of Bay County, Michigan, with Illustrations and Biographical Sketches of Some of its Prominent Men and Pioneers* (Chicago, 1883), 15; Hotchkiss, *History of the Lumber and Forest Industry*, 94.

10. The literature on Michigan's territorial period emphasizes the importance of both the isolated mills and the few lumbering towns. See, for example, Hotchkiss, *History of the Lumber and Forest Industry*, 37; Tuttle, *General History of the State of Michigan*, 222–223; Thaddeus Seeley, *History of Oakland County, Michigan*, 2 vols. (Chicago, 1912), I, 455; Charles F. Hoffman, "Winter Scenes in Early Michigan," *Michigan History Magazine* 9 (1925), 229; Fuller, "Settlement of Southern Michigan, 1805–1837," *Michigan History Magazine*,

183; Carl Addison Leach, "Sharon Hollow: Story of an Early Muley Sawmill of Michigan," *Michigan History Magazine* 17 (1936), 378–83; Henry Little, "Grand Rapids History," *Michigan Pioneer and Historical Society Historical Collections* 4 (1881), 289.

11. Victor S. Clark, *History of Manufactures in the United States, 1607–1680* (Washington, 1916), 187; Seeley, *History of Oakland County*, I, 320; Gilpin, *The Territory of Michigan*, 134–35; W. B. Hartzog, "General Joseph Brown," *Michigan History Magazine* 5 (1921), 564; Dana P. Smith, "The Old Mottville Bridge," *Michigan History Magazine* 10 (1926), 400; Franklin Ellis, *History of Shiawassee and Clinton Counties, Michigan, with Illustrations and Biographical Sketches of Their Prominent Men and Pioneers* (Philadelphia, 1880), 288–89.

12. Seeley, *History of Oakland County*, I, 75, 189–90, 287; Gilpin, *The Territory of Michigan*, 134; Hotchkiss, *History of the Lumber and Forest Industry*, 36–37; Fuller, "Settlement of Southern Michigan, 1805–1837," *Michigan History Magazine*, 184–85. The resident manager was probably Elias Streeter, a native of New York State and an associate of Ely, who had had previous experience in the lumber industry. Streeter continued lumbering in Allegan County after the dissolution of the company. *History of Allegan and Barry Counties, Michigan, with Illustrations and Biographical Sketches of Their Prominent Men and Pioneers* (Philadelphia, 1880), 151.

13. *History of Allegan and Barry Counties*, 148; G. A. Morgan, "The Township of Allegan—Its Topography, Products, Early Settlement, and History," *Michigan Pioneer and Historical Society Historical Collections* 3 (1881), 270–93.

14. List of Debts of Howard & Wadham, Jan. 21, 1835, Jenks Collection; Jenks, *St. Clair County*, I, 123–24, 235, 243–44; Silas Farmer, *The History of Detroit*

and Michigan, 2d ed., 2 vols. (Detroit, 1889), II, 1035; *Michigan Biographies,* 2 vols. (Lansing, 1924), I, 418; William B. Mershon, "Elk in Michigan," *Michigan History Magazine* 16 (1932), 42.

15. Inventory of estate of F. P. Browning, Oct. 16, 1834, Jenks Collection; Jenks, *St. Clair County,* I, 143, 366, 368; *Representative Men of Michigan,* I, 126; Leach, "Paul Bunyan's Land and the First Sawmills of Michigan," *Michigan History Magazine,* 73.

16. Hotchkiss, *History of the Lumber and Forest Industry,* 37. Like other early settlers, lumbermen often exhibited a certain frontier disdain for the necessity of buying land. Joseph Smith, for example, supplied his mill from 1832 to 1835 with timber from government land. *Representative Men of Michigan,* II, 58–59; Black River Steam Mill Company, Journal, May 20, Nov. 13, 1833, Account Book, Feb. 25, 1832. Jenks Collection; *History of Allegan and Barry Counties,* 175; *History of Kent County, Michigan* (Chicago, 1881), 224; Jenks, *St. Clair County,* I, 369.

17. This had been the common pattern of entry since colonial days. Clark, *History of Manufactures in the United States,* 151.

18. Estimated costs for early, small sawmills range from $200 to $1,000. Clark, *History of Manufactures,* 177; *Penny Magazine* (Boston), 11 (1842), 134. Reliable capitalization figures for sawmills in territorial Michigan do not exist, but figures for a later period confirm low cost of entry levels. In 1850 half the mills of Kalamazoo County, chosen as an example because it was not a large, commercialized lumbering county, were capitalized at $1,000 or less. Manuscript Census for the State of Michigan, 1880, Kalamazoo County.

19. Fuller, *Economic and Social Beginnings,* 28; Hotchkiss, *History of the Lumber and Forest Industry,* 95–96; *Northwestern Lumberman,* May 31, 1890; George B. Catlin, "About Detroit 100 Years Ago," *Michigan History Magazine* 15 (1931), 685.

20. Black River Steam Mill Co., Journal, May 20, Aug. 22, Sept. 13, 1833, Jenks Collection; Robinson, "Rix Robinson, Fur Trader," *Michigan History Magazine* (1922), 286. The calculations on board feet per log are based on Clark's International Log Rule, a widely adopted formula of the nineteenth century.

21. Black River Steam Mill Co., Journal, Nov. 13, 1833, Feb. 22, 1834, Jenks Collection.

22. John M. Gordon, "Michigan Journal, 1836," *Michigan History Magazine* 43 (1959), 292; R. B. Nye, "The Lure of the West a Century Ago," *Michigan History Magazine* 29 (1945), 206.

23. Leo C. Lillie, *Historic Grand Haven and Ottawa County* (Grand Haven, 1931), 124–31; *History of Kent County*, 224; *History of Ottawa County, Michigan, with Illustrations and Biographical Sketches of Some of Its Prominent Men and Pioneers* (Chicago, 1882), 24, 39; Hotchkiss, *History of the Lumber and Forest Industry*, 656–66; *Fuller*, "Settlement of Southern Michigan, 1805–1837," *Michigan History Magazine*, 209–210.

24. George H. Hazelton, "Reminiscences of Seventeen Years Residence in Michigan, 1836–1853," *Michigan Pioneer and Historical Society Historical Collections* 21 (1892), 383.

25. *History of Ottawa County*, 103; *History of Bay County*, 39; Hotchkiss, *History of the Lumber and Forest Industry*, 47, 51; George C. Hotchkiss, *Industrial Chicago: The Lumber Interests* (Chicago, 1894), 206; *Northwestern Lumberman*, May 31, 1890.

26. A. B. Markham, "Early History of the Township of Plymouth," *Michigan Pioneer and Historical Society Historical Collections* 2 (1880), 557.

27. Hotchkiss, *History of the Lumber and Forest Industry*, 51; *Michigan Emigrant* (Ann Arbor), Dec. 12, 1833; *Northwestern Lumberman*, No. 12, 1892.

28. *History of Bay County*, 39; James Cooke Mills, *History of Saginaw County, Michigan*, 2 vols. (Saginaw, 1918), I, 168; Black River Steam Mill Journal, 1883–

1884, Jenks Collection; Seeley, *History of Oakland County*, I, 290; Jenks, *St. Clair County*, I, 313; George R. Fox, "The Ark in Michigan," *Michigan History Magazine* 42 (1958), 78. Little information is available about the grading of lumber in this period, but apparently grading was of little concern and done on an individual basis. The Black River Steam Mill Company graded its lumber as "common," "best of sound," and "clear."

29. Hotchkiss, *History of the Lumber and Forest Industry*, 43, 45, 666.

30. *History of Bay County*, 39; Seeley, *History of Oakland County*, I, 391.

31. Clark, *History of Manufactures*, 176; Robert F. Fries, *Empire in Pine: The Story of Lumbering in Wisconsin* (Madison, 1951), 60; Will Holmes, "Early American Sawmills," Eleutherian Mills-Hagley Foundation Research Report, 1960, pp. 2–4; *Lumberman's Gazette* (Bay City), Oct. 15, 1879; Goodrich, *The First Michigan Frontier*, 220–21; Leach, "Paul Bunyan's Land and the First Sawmills of Michigan," *Michigan History Magazine* 75.

32. *Lumberman's Gazette*, Oct. 15, 1879.

33. Clark, *History of Manufactures*, 175, 176; Mills, *History of Saginaw County*, I, 128; Hotchkiss, *History of the Lumber and Forest Industry*, 48, Franklin Everett, *Memorials of the Grand River Valley* (Chicago, 1878), 3; Holmes, "Early American Sawmills," 9–11; "American Saw-Mills," *The Penny Magazine*, 134; interview with Robert A. Howard, Curator of Engineering, Hagley Museum, August 28, 1974; *Operation of a Model*. Eleutherian Mills-Hagley Foundation film of January 1971. The fullest description of an early sawmill in Michigan can be found in Leach, "Sharon Hollow . . . ," *Michigan History Magazine*, passim.

34. Hotchkiss, *History of the Lumber and Forest Industry*, 43, *History of Kent County*, 231; Holmes, "Early American Sawmills," 10–11.

35. *Lumberman's Gazette*, Oct. 15, 1879.

36. *Lumberman's Gazette*, Oct. 15, 1870; Holmes, "Early American Sawmills," 11–12.

37. U.S., 25th Cong., 3d sess., 1839, House of Representative Doc. 21, *Steam Engines*, 346–48; Hotchkiss, *History of the Lumber and Forest Industry*, 38–39, 64, 94, 104; Leach, "Paul Bunyan's Land and the First Sawmills of Michigan," *Michigan History Magazine*, 75–76; Jenks, *St. Clair County*, I, 369; Catlin, "About Detroit 100 Years Ago," *Michigan History Magazine*. 685.

38. Hotchkiss, *History of the Lumber and Forest Industry*, 48; Seeley, *History of Oakland County*, I, 450; Charles F. Hoffman, "Winter Scenes in Early Michigan," *Michigan History Magazine* 9 (1925), 87.

39. See the Black River Steam Mill Co., Journal, 1833, Jenks Collection.

40. For example, see Everett, *Memorials of the Grand River Valley*, 81; *History of Berrien and Van Buren Counties, Michigan, with Illustrations and Biographical Sketches of its Prominent Men and Pioneers* (Philadelphia, 1880), 340.

41. Gordon, "Michigan Journal, 1836" *Michigan History Magazine*, 440, Zephaniah Bunce, Ledger, Nov. 1835–Jan. 1836, Jenks Collection; *History of Berrien and Van Buren Counties*, 129.

42. For a summary of the categories and methodology employed in studying Michigan's lumber entrepreneurs, see footnote 43, chpt.

43. Jenks, *St. Clair County*, I, 114–15, 364.

44. Black River Steam Mill Co., Journal, 1833–34, Jenks Collection; Peltier & Doran to William Woodbridge, Oct. 30, 1834, Woodbridge Collection (Burton Historical Collection, Detroit Public Library).

45. Hotchkiss, *History of the Lumber and Forest Industry*, 666; _____, *Industrial Chicago*, 21–22, 201.

46. Richard G. Wood, *A History of Lumbering in Maine, 1820–1861* (Orono, Me. 1935), 142; Fries, *Em-*

pire in Pine, 65; Hotchkiss, *History of the Lumber and Forest Industry*, 52.

47. F. P. Browning to [David Oakes], Dec. 10, 1833, David Oakes Collection (Burton Historical Collection, Detroit Public Library); *History of Allegan and Barry Counties*, 77; Hotchkiss, *History of the Lumber and Forest Industry*, 51.

CHAPTER 4

1. The coexistence of all stages of industrial production was characteristic of the mid-nineteenth century frontier in the Midwest. See Margaret Walsh, *The Manufacturing Frontier: Pioneer Industry in Antebellum Wisconsin, 1830–1860* (Madison, 1972), x–xi.

2. See also map 2, p. 7.

3. William G. Rector, *Log Transportation in the Lakes States Lumber Industry, 1840–1918. The Movement of Logs and Its Relationship to Land Settlement, Waterway Development, Railroad Construction, Lumber Production and Prices* (Glendale, Cal., 1953), 54; St. Mary's Falls Ship Canal Co., *560,000 Acres Pine Lands, in the State of Michigan, with Lumber Statistics and other Valuable Information Concerning the Pine Lands of the St. Mary's Falls Ship Canal Company* (Detroit, 1857), 10; *Census and Statistics of the State of Michigan, May 1854*, (Lansing, 1854).

4. The federal census bureau began gathering information on the lumber industry as early as 1810, but the summaries remained very incomplete until the 1850 census. Figures on quantity produced by state did not begin until 1870. U.S. Bureau of the Census, *Historical Statistics of the United States: Colonial Times to 1957* (Washington, 1960), 306; for a full discussion of the manuscript censuses "Products of Industry" for 1850 and 1860 and an assessment of their reliability, see Walsh,

The Manufacturing Frontier, appendix A, 221–29, and
—————, "The Census as an Accurate Source of Information: The Value of Mid-Nineteenth Century Manufacturing Returns," *Historical Methods Newsletter* 3
(1970), 3–13.

5. U.S., 35th Cong., 2 sess., Senate Exec. Doc. no. 39
*Abstract of the Statistics of Manufactures, According to
the Returns of the Seventh Census.* See also Table 22, p.
215.

6. Census records that are organized by township and
county place restrictions on a complete regional analysis,
but with some care the data can be adjusted to reflect a
regional character.

7. Gunnar Alexandersson, *Geography of Manufacturing* (Englewood Cliffs, N.J., 1967), 8–9, and Allen R.
Pred, *The Spatial Dynamics of U.S. Urban-Industrial
Growth; Interpretive and Theoretical Essays* (Cambridge, 1966), 161, emphasize the importance of the energy factor in the location of early manufactories, but
the necessity for placing sawmills along water routes reduced energy's importance as an independent variable.
Small mills in Gratiot County produced lumber solely
for local consumption; timber taken for wider markets
was processed in Saginaw. Arthur M. Weimer, "An Economic History of Alma, Michigan: (Ph.D. diss., University of Chicago, 1934), 58. Rector, *Log Transportation in
the Lakes States Lumber Industry,* 193; Victor S. Clark,
History of Manufactures in the United States, 1607–1860
(Washington, 1916), 315–16; 445–46, 467; Rolland H.
Maybee, *Michigan's White Pine Era, 1840–1900* (Lansing, 1960), 44.

8. William Lee Jenks, *St. Clair County, Michigan: Its
History and Its People,* 2 vols. (Chicago, 1912), I, 114–
15; Zephaniah Bunce folder, William Lee Jenks Manuscript Collection (Burton Historical Collection, Detroit
Public Library); Silas Farmer, *The History of Detroit
and Michigan,* 2d ed., 2 vols. (Detroit, 1889), I, 38, 135,

486; *The Merchant's Magazine, and Commercial Review* 20 (1849), 278–84.

9. *The Merchant's Magazine, and Commercial Review* 20 (1849), 278–84; Manuscript Census for the State of Michigan, 1850, Wayne County. The information on Detroit in the 1854 census of the state is too incomplete to be of any use.

10. George W. Hotchkiss, *History of the Lumber and Forest Industry of the Northwest* (Chicago, 1898), 52.

11. *Port Huron Observer*, Dec. 23, 1848.

12. *Port Huron Observer*, Jan. 1, Dec. 23, 1848; *Compendium of the Enumeration of the Inhabitants and Statistics of the United States, 1840*; Manuscript Census for the State of Michigan, 1850, St. Clair County; *Lake Huron Observer*, Jan. 20, 1845.

13. For this reason lumbering activity along the lower Cass River in Tuscola county is considered with the Saginaw Region.

14. Oliver Raymond, "Port Sanilac Settlers," *Michigan History Magazine* 33 (1949), 168–69 dates the first sawmill in Sanilac County from 1848, but this date of entry is too late. The Manuscript Census for the State of Michigan, 1850, Sanilac, Tuscola, and Huron County, lists thirteen sawmills. *Census and Statistics of the State of Michigan Sanilac County*, 1854.

15. *Northwestern Lumberman* (Chicago), May 31, 1890; Hotchkiss, *History of the Lumber and Forest Industry*, 43; Manuscript Census for the State of Michigan, 1850, Lapeer County; *Census and Statistics of the State of Michigan, 1854*.

16. *Genesee Whig*, April 22, June 24, 1854; "Historical Notes," *Michigan History Magazine* 14 (1930), 702; Manuscript Census for the State of Michigan, Genesee County, 1850; *Census and Statistics of the State of Michigan, Genesee County, 1854*.

17. James C. Mills, *History of Saginaw County, Michigan*, 2 vols. (Saginaw, 1918), I. 142, II, 322; Tru-

man B. Fox, *History of Saginaw County, From the Year 1819 down to the Present Time. Compiled from Authentic Records and Other Sources: Traditionary Accounts, Legends, Anecdotes, & C. with Valuable Statistics, and Notes of its Resources and General Information Concerning its Resources and General Information Concerning its Advantages: Also, a Business Directory of Each of the Three Principal Towns of the County* (East Saginaw, 1858), 44; William H. Sweet, "Brief History of Saginaw County," *Michigan Pioneer and Historical Society Historical Collections* 28 (1900), 28; *Longworth's American Almanac, New-York Register, and City Directory of the Sixty-first Year of American Independence* (New York, 1836), 432; *History of Bay County, Michigan, with Illustrations and Biographical Sketches of Some of Its Prominent Men and Pioneers* (Chicago, 1883), 18–22, 41; Augustus H. Gansser, ed., and comp., *History of Bay County, Michigan, and Representative Citizens* (Chicago, 1905), 89–90.

18. Hotchkiss, *History of the Lumber and Forest Industry*, 98; Fox, *History of Saginaw County*, 31; *Lumberman's Gazette* (Bay City), Jan. 18, 1882; *Northwestern Lumberman*, Feb. 13, 1892, Sept. 23, 1893; Mills, *History of Saginaw County*, I, 396; *History of Bay County*, 41, 46; George W. Hotchkiss, *Industrial Chicago: The Lumber Interests* (Chicago, 1894), 326; quoted in Carl A. Leach, "Paul Bunyan's Land and the First Sawmills of Michigan," *Michigan History Magazine* 20 (1936), 82.

19. Manuscript Census for the State of Michigan, 1850, Saginaw County.

20. Hotchkiss, *History of the Lumber and Forest Industry*, 95; *Lumberman's Gazette*, July 12, 1882; *Northwestern Lumberman*, May 31, 1890, Oct. 3, 1891; Henry H. Crapo, Diaries, 1855, Henry H. Crapo Papers (Michigan Historical Collections, Bentley Historical Library, University of Michigan); Mills, *History of Sag-*

inaw County, I, 182–83, 400, 402. As early as 1837 E. W. Perry brought lumber from his Tuscola mill down the Cass River to Saginaw. Sources differ on the number of sawmills in operation in the Saginaw Valley and their aggregate production, but the variance is minor.

21. Hotchkiss, *History of the Lumber and Forest Industry*, 156, 160; David D. Oliver, *Centennial History of Alpena County, Michigan* (Alpena, 1903), 23–24, 26, 28; Arthur S. White, "Early Days Around Alpena," *Michigan History Magazine* 9 (1925), 357; Bernhard E. Fernow, "American Lumber," in Chauncey M. Depew, ed., *One Hundred Years of American Commerce*, 2 vols. (New York, 1895), I, 197; Manuscript Census for the State of Michigan, 1850, Michilmackinac County. White dates the Oliver mill from 1851, but it was already in operation at the time of the 1850 census. In that year it produced 300,000 feet.

22. Lloyd M. Atwood, "Cheboygan as a Nineteenth Century Lumber Area" (M.A. thesis, Wayne State University, 1947), 3–4, 7–10, 53–54, 142–43; Manuscript Census for the State of Michigan, 1850, Michilmackinac County.

23. See *History of Berrien and Van Buren Counties, Michigan, with Illustrations and Biographical Sketches of Its Prominent Men and Pioneers* (Philadelphia, 1880); *History of Allegan and Barry County, Michigan, with Illustrations and Biographical Sketches of Their Prominent Men and Pioneers* (Philadelphia, 1880), 239, 289, 326–27, 330, 353; Hotchkiss, *History of the Lumber and Forest Industry*, 1931, 45. See also, chapter 3 above, p. 61.

24. *Compendium of the Inhabitants and Statistics of the United States, 1840;* Manuscript Census for the State of Michigan, 1850, Allegan County; *Census and Statistics of the State of Michigan, Allegan County, 1854.*

25. James H. Lanman, *History of Michigan, Civil and Topographical, in a Compendium Form; with a*

View of the Surrounding Lakes (New York, 1839), 121.

26. Franklin Everett, *Memorials of the Grand River Valley* (Chicago, 1878), 76–77; Hotchkiss, *History of the Lumber and Forest Industry*, 169, 193; *Grand Rapids Enquirer*, Aug. 26, 1842; Leo C. Lillie, 169; *Historic Grand Haven and Ottawa County* (Grand Haven, 1931), 238–39; *History of Kent County, Michigan* (Chicago, 1881), 804–08; *History of Ottawa County, Michigan, with Illustrations and Biographical Sketches of Some of Its Prominent Men and Pioneers* (Chicago, 1882), 42; *Census and Statistics of the State of Michigan, 1854*. Total production in 1854:

Kent County	13,650,000	(incomplete return)
Ottawa County	6,450,000	(total for Ottawa less Muskegon and White River townships)

27. *Grand Rapids Enquirer*, Mar. 8, 1842; Hotchkiss, *History of the Lumber and Forest Industry*, 169; Manuscript Census for the State of Michigan, 1850, Kent County and Ottawa County; *Census and Statistics of Michigan, 1854*.

28. *Lumberman's Gazette*, Mar. 28, 1883; James Glasgow, "Muskegon, Michigan: The Evolution of a Lake Port" (Ph.D. diss., University of Chicago, 1939), 8–9, 28.

29. *History of Muskegon County, Michigan, with Illustrations and Biographical Sketches of Some of Its Prominent Men and Pioneers* (Chicago, 1882), 24–25, 28, 32; Hotchkiss, *History of the Lumber and Forest Industry*, 219; George W. Hotchkiss, *Industrial Chicago: The Lumber Interests* (Chicago, 1894), 31; Glasgow, "Muskegon, Michigan," 9–10, 12–14; *Michigan Pioneer and Historical Society Historical Collections* 1 (1874–75), 288–89; Lillie, *Historical Grand Haven and Ottawa County*, 1–5, 162.

30. *History of Muskegon County*, 25; Manuscript Census for the State of Michigan, 1850, Ottawa County;

Census and Statistics of the State of Michigan, 1854.

31. Harry L. Spooner, *Lumbering in Newaygo County* (White Cloud, Mich., n.d.), 1; _____, "The First White Pathfinders of Newaygo County, Michigan," unpublished mss., Library of Michigan, Lansing, Michigan, 46, 60.

32. Spooner, "The First White Pathfinders," 8–9, 11, 31, 37–40, 42; _____, Letter to the Editor, *Michigan History Magazine* 20 (1937), 259; *Lumberman's Gazette*, Mar. 28, 1883.

33. Spooner, "The First White Pathfinders," 58, 73; Manuscript Census for the State of Michigan, 1850, Ottawa County; *Census and Statistics of the State of Michigan, 1854*; Amasa Brown Watson Papers, Clarke Historical Library, Central Michigan University.

34. *History of Muskegon County*, 29–30; Louis M. Hartwick and W. H. Tuller, *Oceana County Pioneers and Businessman of Today* (Pentwater, Mich., 1890), 148, 240; Hotchkiss, *History of the Lumber and Forest Industry*, 246; Manuscript Census for the State of Michigan, 1850. Biographical material on Charles Mears can be found in the Charles Mears Collection of the Chicago Historical Society; Hotchkiss, *History of the Lumber and Forest Industry*, 259–61; _____, *Industrial Chicago*, 208–11; Carrie Mears, "Charles Mears, Lumberman," *Michigan History Magazine* 30 (1946), 535–45.

35. Hotchkiss, *History of the Lumber and Forest Industry*, 244–45; Frances Caswell Hanna, *Sand, Sawdust and Saw Logs: Lumber Days in Ludington* (Ludington, 1955), 4–7; Manuscript Census for the State of Michigan, 1850, Ottawa County; Charles Mears to Thomas H. Woods, May 31, 1852; Mears Papers (Chicago Historical Society). Mears planned to control the area by either buying lands personally or selecting settlers who would buy the land, build mills, and improve the harbor at Pere Marquette.

36. Manuscript Census for the State of Michigan, 1850, Ottawa, St. Clair, Saginaw counties.

37. Hotchkiss, *History of the Lumber and Forest Industry*, 261–62; George M. Blackburn and Sherman L. Ricards, "The Timber Industry in Manistee County, Michigan," *Journal of Forest History* 18 (1974), 16; *Manistee News-Advocate* reprint in "History in Michigan Newspapers," *Michigan History Magazine* 26 (1942), 93–94; Manuscript Census for the State of Michigan, 1850, Michilmackinac County; *Census and Statistics of the State of Michigan, 1854.*

38. Hotchkiss, *History of the Lumber and Forest Industry*, 285; John H. Wheeler, comp., *History of Wexford County, Michigan: Embracing a Concise View of Its Early Settlements, Industrial Development and Present Conditions* (n.p., 1903), 221–22; Charles J. Wolfe, "Hannah, Lay and Company: A Study in Michigan's Lumber Industry" (M.A. thesis, Wayne State University, 1938), 21–24; *Census and Statistics of the State of Michigan, 1854.*

CHAPTER 5

1. "Lumbering, or the Manner of Conveying Timber to Market," *The Penny Magazine* (Boston), Sept. 30, 1837; p. 374, describes some aspects of logging in the early period.

2. *Portrait and Biographical Record of Muskegon and Ottawa Counties, Michigan* (Chicago, 2893), 357.

3. *Michigan Biographies*, 2 vols. (Lansing, 1924), I, 95; "The Michigan Lumber Interest, As Told in Sketches of some of the Leading Men: II, Ami W. Wright," *Magazine of Western History*, 5 (Nov. 1886), 128.

4. *American Lumberman* (Chicago), July 15, 1905; *American Lumbermen: The Personal History and Public and Business Achievements of One Hundred Eminent Lumbermen of the United States*, 3 vols. (Chicago, 1905–06), II, 209–12; *Portrait and Biographical Album of Osceola County, Containing Portraits and Biographi-*

cal Sketches of Prominent and Representative Citizens of the County (Chicago, 1884), 331–33; George W. Hotchkiss, *History of the Lumber and Forest Industry of the Northwest* (Chicago, 1898), 177–79. Blodgett became a partner in a sawmill and grist mill in 1858, but this was a local mill intended as part of his town development enterprise at Hersey.

5. Memorandum of Agreement of November 1855, between Alex Dunfield and Bunce & Sons, William Lee Jenks Manuscript Collection (Burton Historical Collection, Detroit Public Library); Receipt to Sweetser & Sanborn [n.d.], George D. Hill Papers (Michigan Historical Collections, Bentley Historical Library, University of Michigan).

6. For an inventory of logger's equipment, see receipt by Robert Hawkes, September 8, 1855, Charles Mears Collection (Chicago Historical Society).

7. Henry H. Crapo, Notebooks, Jan. 3, 1856, Henry H. Crapo Papers (Michigan Historical Collections, Bentley Historical Library, University of Michigan). Veteran Lumberman John Pierson warned Crapo to advance contract loggers with supplies rather than money, which might be squandered.

8. Manuscript Census for the State of Michigan, 1850, Ottawa and St. Clair counties.

9. Crapo, Notebooks, undated notations, 1855–1856, Crapo Papers.

10. Henry L. Spooner, "Letter to the Editor," *Michigan History Magazine* 20 (1936), 259–60; *Portrait and Biographical Album of Newaygo County, Michigan* (Chicago, 1884), 423–25; *History of Muskegon County, Michigan, with Illustrations and Biographical Sketches of Some of Its Prominent Men and Pioneers* (Chicago, 1882), 51.

11. Hotchkiss, *History of the Lumber and Forest Industry*, 51, 223; _____, *Industrial Chicago: The Lumber Interests* (Chicago, 1894), 220. By the time

Throop left the lumber business for politics in 1854 he was a wealthy man. He subsequently engaged in the dockage business before moving to California, where he endowed Throop Polytechnic University, now California Institute of Technology. Otis A. Singletary, *American Colleges and Universities*, 10th ed. (Washington, 1968), 193.

12. For brief summaries of logging as a seasonal activity, see William Gerald Rector, *Log Transportation in the Lakes States Lumber Industry, 1840–1918. The Movement of Its Logs and Its Relationship to Land Settlement, Waterway Development, Railroad Construction, Lumber Production and Prices* (Glendale, Cal., 1953), 25, 34–45; George Barker Engberg, "Labor in the Lake States Lumber Industry, 1830–1930" (Ph.D. diss., Univeristy of Minnesota, 1949), 261–62.

13. Rector, *Transportation in the Lakes States Lumber Industry*, 35, 76, 192. Swamping was the term used for road construction and maintenance; chopping and sawing was the two-step process of felling a tree and sawing it into logs. Log marks date back into English history and were used in America from the colonial period. In Michigan, logs were initially marked once on the bark for identification, but increased volume made this system inadequate. Double log marking, akin to cattle branding, replaced simple bark marks. These symbols had to be registered by county. Ralph Clement Bryant, *Logging: The Principles and General Methods of Operation in the United States* (New York, 1913), 482, 486, 505; Clifford Allen, ed., *Michigan Log Marks* (East Lansing, 1941), 7–12. The latter book contains drawings of many marks registered in Michigan.

14. *Port Huron Observer*, Apr. 1, 1848, Dec. 9, 1848.

15. *The Weekly Observer* (Fentonville), Feb. 9, 1853.

16. Hotchkiss, *History of the Lumber Industry*, 59.

17. Ibid., 110; *Lumberman's Gazette* (Bay City), Apr. 6, 1881; Crapo, notebooks, undated entry, handco-

pied from the *Saginaw Enterprise*, Feb. 22, 1886, Crapo Papers. The content of a log calculated in board feet was, particularly in the antebellum period, a rough approximation. To remedy this problem, a variety of guides were prepared for scalers to use. For consistency, this work will make use of Clark's International Log rule, one of the most popular of the early formulas.

18. Quoted in Richard G. Wood, *A. History of Lumbering in Maine, 1820–1861* (Orono, Maine, 1935), 85; *Lumberman's Gazette*, Oct. 8, 1879; James Glasgow, "Muskegon, Michigan: The Evolution of a Lake Port" (Ph.D. diss., University of Chicago, 1939), 13–14.

19. Rector, *Log Transportation in the Lakes States Lumber Industry*, 72. The description of the logging process is drawn from Rector, 72–79, 191; *Lumberman's Gazette*, Apr. 6, 1881; James Cooke Mills, *History of Saginaw County, Michigan*, 2 vols. (Saginaw, 1918), II, 402.

20. One log processed at the E. B. Clarke mill, for example, produced 2,700 feet of lumber, nearly fourteen times the average amount. *Port Huron Observer*, Sept. 9, 1848.

21. *Lumberman's Gazette*, Apr. 6, 1881.

22. There are a few examples of horse tramways or railroads, but these were isolated, and obviously not very successful, experiments. J. D. Pierson, "Letter to the Editor," *Michigan History Magazine*, 11, (1927), 668; *History of Ottawa County, Michigan, with Illustrations and Biographical Sketches of Some of Its Prominent Men and Pioneers* (Chicago, 1882), 104.

23. Beatrice Corbett, "Susan Moulter Fraser McMaster," *Inland Sease*, 31 (1975), 195; Hotchkiss, *History of the Lumber and Forest Industry*, 121.

24. Rector, *Log Transportation in the Lakes States Lumber Industry*, 35, 76, 192.

25. Engberg, "Labor in the Lakes States Lumber Industry, 1830–1930," 317–18; St. Mary's Falls Ship Canal

Co., *560,000 Acres Pine Lands, in the State of Michigan, with Lumber Statistics and Other Valuable Information Concerning the Pine Lands of the St. Mary's Falls Ship Canal Company* (Detroit, 1857), 12–13.

26. Hotchkiss, *Industrial Chicago,* 255; I Kings, 5: 15–24.

27. Hotchkiss, *Industrial Chicago,* 255; _____, *History of the Lumber and Forest Industry,* 285.

28. Arthur Martin Weimer, "An Economic History of Alma, Michigan" (Ph.D. diss., University of Chicago, 1934), 90.

29. *Lumberman's Gazette,* Feb. 1873; *History of Wexford County, Michigan: Embracing a Concise Review of Its Early Settlement, Industrial Development and Present Conditions* (n.p., 1903), 222.

30. Rector, *Log Transportation in the Lakes States Lumber Industry,* 183–86; Ralph W. Hidy, Frank Ernest Hill, and Allan Nevins, *Timber and Men: The Weyerhaeuser Story* (New York, 1963), 20.

31. Lloyd M. Atwood, "Cheboygan as a Nineteenth Century Lumber Area" (M.A. thesis, Wayne State University, 1947), 35; Clifford Allen, ed., *Michigan Log Marks,* 8–10; *Moore* vs. *Sanborn,* 2 Mich. 520, 1853.

32. Rector, *Log Transportation in the Lakes States Lumber Industry,* 101, Michigan *Acts,* 156, 165, 1851.

33. *Genesee Whig,* Mar. 4, 1854.

34. *Lake Huron Observer,* May 12, 1845.

35. *History of Muskegon County, Michigan,* 28; Allen, ed., *Michigan Log Marks,* 10–11.

36. Allen, ed., *Michigan Log Marks.* There were, of course, a few other unusual, colorful, and innovatively adaptive methods for moving logs from the river to the mill, such as the Gilbert brothers' horse tramway from Steams' Bayou to Grand Haven, *History of Ottawa County, Michigan,* 104.

37. Glasgow, "Muskegon, Michigan," 30; *Lake Huron Observer,* Apr. 12, 1845; *Lumberman's Gazette,* June

1873. The Muskegon figures are based on the calculation of 5,000 logs = 1,000,000 feet.

38. Hotchkiss, *History of the Lumber and Forest Industry*, 90; Crapo, notebooks, undated entry, hand-copied from the *Saginaw Enterprise*, Feb. 15, 1856, Crapo Collection; *Lumberman's Gazette*, June 1873. These figures are based on manufacturing output at the rate of 5,000 logs for every 1,000,000 feet. These are low estimates, because they do not include logs purchased for sawmills outside the state.

39. *Lake Huron Observer*, July 27, 1844, Apr. 21, 1845; *The Merchants' Magazine, and Commercial Review* 19 (1848), 28.

40. Undated receipt, George D. Hill Papers.

41. *Lumberman's Gazette*, Mar. 1873, Apr. 1873; Crapo, Notebooks, Jan. 3, 1856, Crapo Papers; Manuscript Census for the State of Michigan, 1850. The records of Hannah, Lay and Company do not show the same price level. In January of 1855, for example, the company purchased 400 logs for $100, or approximately $1.25 M. Undoubtedly, the complete manufacturing control exercised by the company over an extremely isolated area worked to deflate prices there. Hannah, Lay and Company, 1854–55 Daybook, Jan. 1855, Hannah, Lay and Company Manuscripts (Michigan Historical Collections, Bentley Historical Library, University of Michigan).

42. Mears, Account Book, Lumber Trade, 1852–53, Mears Collection. Since Mears operated in an isolated, noncompetitive situation, his log costs would probably be lower than those of manufacturers in Muskegon and Grand Haven. *History of Ottawa County*, 104.

43. St. Mary's Falls Ship Canal Company, *560,000 Acres Pine Lands*, 12–13.

CHAPTER 6

1. My measurements for manufacturing in Michigan in 1850 are based on the categories and procedures developed by Margaret Walsh and outlined in Appendix A of *The Manufacturing Frontier: Pioneer Industry in Antebellum Wisconsin, 1830–1860* (Madison, 1972). To adjust her categories to better reflect manufacturing in Michigan, "meat packing," "gas," "soap and candles," and "miscellaneous" have been deleted, and "wagons and carriages" has been expanded to "vehicles" to include railroad and boat construction.

All the data on Michigan's industries in 1850 has been drawn from U.S., 35th Cong., 2d sess., Senate Executive Doc. no. 39, *Abstract of the Statistics of Manufactures, According to the Returns of the Seventh Census.*

2. *Northwestern Lumberman* (Chicago), Sept. 23, 1893; James C. Mills, *History of Saginaw County, Michigan*, 2 vols. (Saginaw, 1918), I, 400–02.

3. *Northwestern Lumberman*, May 31, 1890, Sept. 23, 1893; *Lumberman's Gazette* (Bay City), Mar. 1873.

4. Mills, *History of Saginaw County*, I, 400–402.

5. George H. Hazelton, "Reminiscences of Seventeen Years Residence in Michigan, 1836–1853," *Michigan Pioneer and Historical Society Historical Collections* 21 (1892), 384, 410–11; George W. Hotchkiss, *History of the Lumber and Forest Industry of the Northwest*, (Chicago, 1898), 90.

6. *Lumberman's Gazette*, June, Nov. 1873.

7. *Genesee Whig* (Flint), July 1, 1854; *Port Huron Observer*, Aug. 28, 1847; *Lake Huron Observer*, May 24, 1844; *Grand Rapids Enquirer*, July 20, 1841; *Northwestern Lumberman*, Sept. 6, 1890, Feb. 13, 1892; Hotchkiss, *History of the Lumber and Forest Industry*, 290; _____, *Industrial Chicago: The Lumber Interests* (Chicago, 1894), 31; *History of Muskegon County, Michigan, with Illustrations and Biographical Sketches*

of Some of Its Prominent Men and Pioneers (Chicago, 1882), 24; Leo C. Lillie, *Historic Grand Haven and Ottawa County* (Grand Haven, Michigan, 1931), 149; Charles Mears, White Lake and Silver Lake Account Books, 1837–1841, Feb. 25, 1838, Charles Mears Collection (Chicago Historical Society).

8. St. Mary's Falls Ship Canal Company, *560,000 Acres Pine Lands, in the State of Michigan, with Lumber Statistics and Other Valuable Information Concerning the Pine Lands of the St. Mary's Falls Ship Canal Company* (Detroit, 1857), 12–13.

9. *Lumberman's Gazette*, Nov. 5, 1879; *Genesee Whig*, July 1, 1854; Hotchkiss, *History of the Lumber and Forest Industry*, 61–62. The range in capital-invested figures for the eight pine counties in 1850 was $300 to $85,000. Manuscript Census for the State of Michigan, 1850.

10. Mills, *History of Saginaw County*, I, 396; Ruth B. Bordin, "A Michigan Lumbering Family," *Business History Review*, 34 (1960): 66, 68.

11. Walsh, *The Manufacturing Frontier*, 216–17; Glenn Porter and Harold C. Livesay, *Merchants and Manufacturers: Studies in the Changing Structure of Nineteenth Century Marketing* (Baltimore, 1971), 68.

12. Manuscript Census for the State of Michigan, 1850, Ottawa, St. Clair, and Wayne counties.

13. For a discussion of logging wages in 1850, see chap. 11, pp. 274–75.

14. U.S., 35th Cong., 2d sess., Senate Executive Doc. no. 39, *Abstract of the Statistics of Manufactures, According to the Returns of the Seventh Census*, 73.

15. Amasa Brown Watson Papers, Clarke Historical Library, Central Michigan University.

16. For two clear examples of small loans and personal contacts, see Lillie, *Historic Grand Haven and Ottawa County*, 149; "The Jerome Family," *Michigan Pioneer and Historical Society Historical Collections* 11

(1877), 11. The lack of local credit was a problem for early businessmen in Wisconsin also. Walsh, *The Manufacturing Frontier*, 10–11.

17. Dun and Bradstreet Credit Reports, Baker Library, Harvard University, vol. 69, pp. 3, 10.

18. Frances Caswell Hanna, *Sand, Sawdust and Saw Logs: Lumber Days in Ludington* (Ludington, Michigan, 1955), 13. Ford lost his mill to Ludington for non-payment of debts in 1859. Ludington immediately leased the mill to Charles Mears.

19. *Lumberman's Gazette*, No. 5, 1879; *Northwestern Lumberman*, Nov. 20, 1886; Hotchkiss, *History of the Lumber and Forest Industry*, 114; Mills, *History of Saginaw County*, I, 156–58 and II, 244–47; Charles Richard Tuttle, *General History of the State of Michigan, With Biographical Sketches* (Detroit, 1874), 141–43; *Michigan: A Centennial History of the State and Its People*, 5 vols. (Chicago, 1939), 5, 542–43; William Lee Jenks, *St. Clair County, Michigan: Its History and Its People*, 2 vols. (Chicago, 1912), I, 371; *Report of the Committee for Investigating the Affairs of the Old Colony Railroad Company, Appointed by the Stockholders, Dec. 26, 1849* (Boston, 1850), 62–70, Appendix 1–12; Dun and Bradstreet, vol. 69, p. 6. Irregularities and mismanagement were found in the Treasurer's Office of the Old Colony Railroad, and Fletcher resigned his position with the railroad at about the same time that the enterprise in Michigan began to fail.

20. Porter and Livesay, *Merchants and Manufacturers*, 8, 69, 76.

21. *Lumberman's Gazette*, Dec. 1873; *History of Bay County, Michigan, with Illustrations and Biographical Sketches of Some of Its Prominent Men and Pioneers* (Chicago, 1883), 78; Augustus H. Gansser, ed. and comp., *History of Bay County, Michigan, and Representative Citizens* (Chicago, 1905), 390; Hotchkiss, *History of the Lumber and Forest Industry*, 120.

22. Jenks, *St. Clair County*, I, 368. No records have been found of any of the partners having re-entered the industry elsewhere in the state.

23. *History of Allegan and Berrien Counties, Michigan, With Illustrations and Biographical Sketches of Their Prominent Men and Pioneers* (Philadelphia, 1880), 240–41.

24. *Lumberman's Gazette*, Nov. 1873.

25. Defebaugh emphasizes the importance of good water transportation for nineteenth-century lumber manufacturers. James E. Defebaugh, *History of the Lumber Industry of America*, 2 vols. (Chicago, 1906), I, 473.

26. The mill of W. B. Hibbard and N. D. Horton, for example, produced 3,600,000 feet in 1850, although its capacity was 5,000,000 feet. Jenks, *History of St. Clair County*, I, 368; Manuscript Census for the State of Michigan, 1850, St. Clair County. According to the census, in that year virtually all mills in the state were operating at less than full capacity.

27. There is one reference to a wind-propelled mill in Holland Township of Ottawa County that operated with "tolerable success," but the idea of harnessing the wind did not take hold outside the Dutch community. *History of Ottawa County*, 84. Most of the water-powered mills were located directly on the bank of a stream and did not rely on long races, or artificial channels, to alter the head of water. For this reason the majority of water wheels must have been of the undershot variety, the least efficient type, although a breast-type wheel may have been possible in some locations with sufficient water.

28. See Wilson Compton, *The Organization of the Lumber Industry: With Special Reference to the Influences Determining the Prices of Lumber in the United States* (Chicago, 1916), 36; Vernon L. Jensen, *Lumber and Labor* (New York, 1945), 48–49; Edmond S. Meany, Jr., "The History of the Lumber Industry in the Pacific

Northwest to 1917" (Ph.D. diss., Harvard University, 1935), chap. 9.

29. J. Richards, *A Treatise on the Construction and Operation of Wood-Working Machines: Including a History of the Origin and Progress of the Manufacture of Wood-Working Machinery* (London, 1872), 171–19.

30. *Lumberman's Gazette,* May 1873.

31. *Lumberman's Gazette,* Oct. 15, 1879; Mills, *History of Saginaw County,* I, 415–16; Hotchkiss, *History of the Lumber and Forest Industry,* 104–05; *Michigan Biographies,* 2 vols. (Lansing, 1924), I, 101; Silas Farmer, *The History of Detroit and Michigan,* 2d ed., 2 vols. (Detroit, 1889), II, 1219–25. Merrill began purchasing pinelands in Michigan in 1836 but did not close his operations in Maine until about 1850. The gang saw for the Saginaw mill came from Lowell, Massachusetts.

32. Richards, *A Treatise on the Construction and Operation of Wood-Working Machines,* 141, estimates that 3/8 of every 1″ of slab was lost as sawdust. Nathan Rosenberg, "America's Rise to Woodworking Leadership," in Brooke Hindle, ed., *America's Wooden Age: Aspects of Its Early Technology* (Tarrytown, N.Y., 1975), 54, emphasizes that early nineteenth-century American technology substituted abundant materials, in this case timber, for both capital and labor, more scarce factors of production.

33. *Lumberman's Gazette,* Oct. 15, 1879.

34. Victor S. Clark, *History of Manufactures in the United States, 1607–1860* (Washington, 1916), 421.

35. Will Holmes, "Early American Sawmills," Eleutherian Mills-Hagley Foundation Research Report, 1960, pp. 12–14.

36. *Lumberman's Gazette,* Mar. 30, 1881. Another source credits William T. Powers of Grand Rapids with first using a circular saw in 1852. *Michigan Biographies,* II, 101.

37. Hotchkiss, *History of the Lumber and Forest In-*

dustry, 127. For biographical information on Fraser, see *History of Bay County,* 66–68; *Michigan Biographies,* II, 15–16; Hotchkiss, *Industrial Chicago,* 352.

38. *Wolverine Citizen* (Flint), May 26, Dec. 8, 1855.

39. Rosenberg, "America's Rise to Woodworking Leadership," 47; Rodney C. Loehr, "Saving the Kerf: The Introduction of the Bank Saw Mill," *Agricultural History* 23 (1949), 169.

40. Rosenberg, "America's Rise to Woodworking Leadership," 47; *Lumberman's Gazette,* Mar. 30, 1881; Loehr, "Saving the Kerf," 168–69.

41. For a brief, nontechnical description of the manufacturing sequence in a one-saw mill, see "American Sawmills," *The Penny Magazine* (Boston), Apr. 2, 1842.

42. Richards, *A Treatise on the Construction and Operation of Wood-working Machines,* 119. For representative contemporary accounts of sawmill equipment, see *Port Huron Observer,* June 19, 1847; *Lumberman's Gazette,* Nov. 1873; Nov. 5, 1879; Hotchkiss, *History of the Lumber and Forest Industry,* 64, 68–70, 110; *History of Allegan and Berrien Counties,* 240–41; *History of Bay County,* 51–52; Henry H. Crapo, Notebooks, undated entry, ca. late 1855, Henry H. Crapo Papers (Michigan Historical Collections, Bentley Historical Library, University of Michigan). Crapo noted that the forty steam mills on the Saginaw River averaged four saws per mill.

43. Truman B. Fox, *History of Saginaw County, From the Year 1819 down to the Present Time. Compiled from Authentic Records and other Sources: Traditionary Accounts, Legends, Anecdotes, and C. With Valuable Statistics, and Notes of its Resources and General Information Concerning its Advantages: Also, A Business Directory of Each of the Three Principal Towns of the County* (East Saginaw, Michigan, 1858,), 29.

44. The cost of steam was not so high if it was balanced against the cost of constructing and maintaining a race, which would have offered the manufacturer some

protection against low water but little help in floods. Peter Temin, "Steam and Water Power in the Early Nineteenth Century," *Journal of Economic History* 26 (1966), 197–99.

45. Louis C. Hunter, "Waterpower in the Century of the Steam Engine," in Hindle, ed., *America's Wooden Age*, 160–92, discusses the transfer from water to steam power and notes that the size of an operation was a key factor in choice of power.

46. U.S., 25th Cong., 3d sess., House of Representatives Doc. 21, *Steam-Engines* (Washington, 1839), 346–48.

47. Manuscript Census for the State of Michigan, 1850. Returns for the state census of 1854 are incomplete, but they indicate a further increase to more than 75.

48. *Census and Statistics of the State of Michigan, 1854.*

49. *Lumberman's Gazette*, Feb. 1873.

50. *Lumberman's Gazette*, Jan. 4, 1877; George B. Engberg, "Labor in the Lake States Lumber Industry" (Ph.D. diss., University of Minnesota, 1949), 429; *History of Bay County*, 49; Compton, *The Organization of the Lumber Industry*, 17.

CHAPTER 7

1. George W. Hotchkiss, *History of the Lumber and Forest Industry of the Northwest* (Chicago, 1898), 90; George N. Fuller, ed., *Messages of the Governors of Michigan*, 3 vols. (Lansing, 1925–1926), II, 284.

2. *Lake Huron Observer*, (Port Huron), May 10, 1844.

3. *The Merchants Magazine and Commercial Review* 19 (1848), 19–40.

4. George W. Hotchkiss, *Industrial Chicago: The Lumber Interests* (Chicago, 1894), 32. Hotchkiss' calcu-

lation would include all sources of supply, but since shipments from Wisconsin were minor, his estimate can be taken as primarily lumber from Michigan.

5. Bessie Louise Pierce, *A History of Chicago*, 3 vols. (New York, 1937–1957), I, 133–34; William Vipond Pooley, *the Settlement of Illinois from 1830 to 1850* (Madison, 1908), 544; Hotchkiss, *Industrial Chicago*, 32; *The Pinelands and Lumber Trade of Michigan, Exhibiting the Extent, Quality and Advantages, Compiled from Official and Authentic Sources* (Detroit, 1856), 6.

6. Henry H. Crapo, Notebooks, Jan. 4, 1856, Henry H. Crapo Papers (Michigan Historical Collections, Bentley Historical Library, University of Michigan).

7. Charles J. Wolfe, "Hannah, Lay and Company: A Study in Michigan's Lumber Industry" (M.A. thesis, Wayne State University, 1938), 7–8, 10–11.

8. Wolfe, "Hannah, Lay and Company," 10–11; *The Pinelands and Lumber Trade of Michigan*, 6.

9. *The Pinelands and Lumber Trade of Michigan*, 6; *The Saginaw Enterprise*, Feb. 15, 1856 reported virtually the same percentage of production marketed at Chicago in 1855. Quoted in Crapo, Notebooks, undated entry, ca. early 1856, Crapo Papers.

10. Quoted in Crapo, Notebooks, undated entry, ca. early 1886, Crapo Papers. Actual production totaled 552,771,200 feet. *The Pinelands and Lumber Trade of Michigan*, 6.

11. *The Western Farmer, Containing Original and Selected Articles Relative to Agriculture and Domestic Economy, With Various Statistics Relative to Michigan*, Oct. 1, 1841; Harry L. Spooner, "Letter to the Editor," *Michigan History Magazine* 20 (1936), 262–63; _____, "The First White Pathfinder of Newaygo County, Michigan," unpublished ms., Library of Michigan, Lansing, Michigan, 38–39, 45; *Port Huron Observer*, Apr. 1, Dec. 9, 1848; St. Mary's Falls Ship Canal Company, *560,000 Acres Pine Lands, in the State of*

Michigan, with Lumber Statistics and Other Valuable Information Concerning the Pine Lands of the St. Mary's Falls Ship Canal Company (Detroit, 1851), 10; James Glasgow, "Muskegon, Michigan: The Evolution of a Lake Port" (Ph.D. diss., University of Chicago, 1939), 26; Hotchkiss, *Industrial Chicago,* 211, 546; Elmer A. Ripley, "The Development of Chicago and Vicinity as a Manufacturing Center Prior to 1880" (Ph.D. diss., University of Chicago, 1911), 51; Francis Caswell Hanna, *Sand, Sawdust and Saw Logs: Lumber Days in Ludington* (Ludington, Mich., 1955), 12–19; William O. Van Eyck, "Letter to the Editor," *Michigan History Magazine* 16 (1932), 225–26; Charles Mears, 1837–45 Account Books, Charles Mears Collection (Chicago Historical Society).

12. Quoted in Crapo, Notebooks, undated entry ca. early 1856, Crapo Papers.

13. U.S., *Compendium of the Enumeration of the Inhabitants and Statistics of the United States* (Washington, 1841), 92–93; *Statistical View of the United States . . . Being a Compendium of the Seventh Census* (Washington, 1854), 102, 258–59.

14. *Port Huron Observer,* Jan. 6, 1849.

15. James Cooke Mills, *History of Saginaw County, Michigan,* 2 vols. (Saginaw, 1918), I, 402; Charles Sumner Van Tassel, *Story of the Maumee Valley, Toledo and the Sandusky Region,* 4 vols. (Chicago, 1929), II, 1368–69; Hotchkiss, *History of the Lumber and Forest Industry,* 105–06; H. Hazelton, "Reminiscences of Seventeen Years Residence in Michigan, 1836–1853," *Michigan Pioneer and Historical Society Historical Collections* 21 (1892), 406; *Lumberman's Gazette* (Bay City), Feb. 8, 1882; *the Merchants' Magazine, and Commercial Review* 6 (1942), 345, *Port Huron Observer,* Dec. 9, 1848.

16. Charles Cist, *Sketches and Statistics of Cincinnati in 1851* (Cincinnati, 1851), 181; *A Review of the Trade and Commerce of Cincinnati: For the Commercial Year*

Ending Aug. 31st, 1852 (Cincinnati, 1852), 13; *A Review of the Trade and Commerce of Cincinnati . . . 1854* (Cincinnati, 1854), 11; *A Review of the Trade and Commerce of Cincinnati . . . 1855* (Cincinnati, 1855), 20.

17. *Port Huron Observer*, Dec. 30, 1848.

18. Unsigned letter, Aug. 22, 1842, William Lee Jenks Manuscript Collection (Burton Historical Collection, Detroit Public Library); *Lumberman's Gazette*, Apr. 1873; *Northwestern Lumberman* (Chicago), Nov. 19, 1892; Arthur Scott White, "Early Days Around Alpena," *Michigan History Magazine* 9 (1925), 357.

19. *History of Bay County, Michigan, with Illustrations and Biographical Sketches of Some of Its Prominent Men and Pioneers* (Chicago, 1883), 38–39; Hotchkiss, *History of the Lumber and Forest Industry*, 48, 94; *The Western Farmer*, Feb. 2, 1841; *Northwestern Lumberman*, May 31, 1890; Mills, *History of Saginaw County*, I, 396 and II, 322; Ormond S. Danford, "The Social and Economic Effects of Lumbering on Michigan, 1835–90," *Michigan History Magazine* 26 (1942), 349; Ronald Shaw, "Michigan Influences upon the Formative Years of the Erie Canal," *Michigan History Magazine* 37 (1953), 12.

20. *The Pinelands and Lumber Trade of Michigan*, 10; Victor S. Clark, *History of Manufactures in the United States, 1607–1860* (Washington, 1916), 467; James E. Defebaugh, *History of the Lumber Industry of America*, 2 vols. (Chicago, 1906), II, 55, 325, 408–10, 412.

21. *The Pinelands and Lumber Trade of Michigan*, 10.

22. Defebaugh, *History of the City of Buffalo and Erie County*, 2 vols. (Syracuse, 1884), I, 418, R. E. Morse to George D. Hill, June 4, 1855, George D. Hill Papers (Michigan Historical Collections, Bentley Histori-

cal Library, University of Michigan); *Lumberman's Ga-zette*, Jan. 1873.

23. *Lake Huron Observer,* Apr. 12, 1844; *Detroit Daily Advertiser,* Aug. 29, Oct. 3, 1839; July 18, 1840; Leo C. Lillie, *Historic Grand Haven and Ottawa County* (Grand Haven, Mich., 1931), 241. Undoubtedly there were contract sales that required no marketing on the part of the manufacturer, but such arrangements were probably quite rare before 1850. Compare, for example, the representative cases of James McCormick in 1841 and T. Barren in 1851. McCormick had to ship his lumber from Saginaw County to Detroit and then find a buyer, while Barron was selling at least part of his product on order at his St. Clair County mill, saving all distribution costs. *History of Bay County,* 69; Hiram Walker to T. Barron, June 5, 1851, Jenks Collection.

24. *Lake Huron Observer,* Aug. 3, 1844; James Abbott to Horace Bunce, Nov. 6, 1845, Feb. 23, 1847, Jenks Collection.

25. *Detroit Daily Advertiser,* May 4, 1840; Hazelton, "Reminiscences of Seventeen Years of Residence in Michigan," 384; *History of Allegan and Berrien Counties, Michigan with Illustrations and Biographical Sketches of their Prominent Men and Pioneers* (Philadelphia, 1880), 330; Lillie, *Historic Grand Haven and Ottawa Counties,* 241; Crapo, Notebooks, undated entry, ca. early 1856, Crapo Papers; William Lee Jenks, *St. Clair County, Michigan: Its History and Its People,* 2 vols. (Chicago, 1912), I, 365–66 and II, 874–75; *Michigan Biographies,* 2 vols. (Lansing, 1924), II, 74.

26. Crapo, Notebooks, Jan. 4, 1856, Crapo Papers.

27. Ibid.; *Detroit Daily Advertiser,* Dec. 18, 1839; Abbott to Bunce, Feb. 23, 1847, Jenks Collection; Hotchkiss, *History of the Lumber and Forest Industry,* 673.

28. Hotchkiss, *Industrial Chicago,* 27, 171–72, 208, 337–38; Carrie E. Mears, "Charles Mears, Lumber-

man," *Michigan History Magazine* 30 (1946), 568; Mears, 1837–45 Account Books, Mears Collection.

29. Hotchkiss, *History of the Lumber and Forest Industry*, 262; White, "Early Days Around Alpena," 357; *History of Bay County*, 46.

30. *History of Muskegon County, Michigan, with Illustrations and Biographical Sketches of Some of Its Prominent Men and Pioneers* (Chicago, 1882), 116; Lillie, *Historical Grand Haven and Ottawa County*, 270–71.

31. *History of Muskegon County*, 69–72; *Michigan Biographies*, I, 226–27; Hotchkiss, *History of the Lumber and Forest Industry*, 169–71, 192–94; *History of Ottawa County, Michigan, with Illustrations and Biographical Sketches of Some of Its Prominent Men and Pioneers* (Chicago, 1882), 99; *Portrait and Biographical Record of Muskegon and Ottawa Counties, Michigan* (Chicago, 1893), 371–72; Lillie, *Historic Grand Haven and Ottawa County*, 241; *Northwestern Lumberman* Nov. 14, 1891.

32. Hotchkiss, *Industrial Chicago*, 40; *Lumberman's Gazette*, Mar. 30, 1881; Spooner, "First White Pathfinders of Newaygo County," 38–39, 45; *Lake Huron Observer*, May 12, 1845. See also Bordin, "A Michigan Lumbering Family," for a description of the sale of a full year's production to a Chicago lumberyard in 1855 (p. 69).

33. The contract arrangement appears to have worked to the disadvantage of the buyer less frequently than to the seller, probably because the buyer was better aware of the market situation.

34. Hotchkiss, *History of the Lumber and Forest Industry*, 250, 668; _____, *Industrial Chicago*, 27–28, 171–72, 175, 568; James W. Norris, *Norris' Business Directory and Statistics of the City of Chicago for 1846* (Chicago, 1883), passim.

35. Hotchkiss, *Industrial Chicago*, 25.

36. Ibid., 39–44, 206, 220; Norris, *Directory*, 46;

Richard G. Wood, *A History of Lumbering In Maine, 1820–1861* (Orono, Maine, 1935), 229.

37. Hotchkiss, *Industrial Chicago*, 211; Eli Bates to Charles Mears, Aug. 22, 1851, Apr. 24, 1853, Mears Collection. Francis B. Stockbridge and Artemus Carter also opened a yard in Chicago in the late 1840s, supplying it with lumber from their mills at Saugatuck. Hotchkiss, *Industrial Chicago*, 272; *Michigan Biographies*, II, 327.

38. Hotchkiss, *History of the Lumber and Forest Industry*, 231, _____, *Industrial Chicago*, 403; *Lumberman's Gazette*, Nov. 19, 1892. These firms are meant to be illustrative rather than inclusive. Inadequate records, a rapid rate of change in lumber dealers, and the fluid nature of partnerships make an exact accounting impossible. George C. Norton, for instance, was a partner in a succession of at least three firms between 1851 and 1855. Hotchkiss, *Industrial Chicago*, 58, 337–38.

39. *Michigan Biographies*, I, 226–27; *History of Muskegon County*, 69–72; Dun and Bradstreet Credit Reports (Baker Library, Harvard University), vol. 60. An alphabetical list of names is in the front of each volume.

40. "A. H. Mershon," *Michigan Pioneer and Historical Society Historical Collections* 8 (1885), 73–74.

41. Hotckiss, *History of the Lumber and Forest Industry*, 266–67; 686, 689; _____, *Industrial Chicago*, 266, 328; Wolfe, "Hannah, Lay and Company," 14–16; *Representative Men of Michigan*, II, 9. Many yards, especially those owned by a manufacturer or located in an urban center, operated at both wholesale and retail levels. Hannah, Lay & Company for example, would sell in quantity to dealers in the interior and retail to local customers.

42. Crapo, Notebooks, Jan. 5, 1856, Crapo Papers.

43. Hotchkiss, *Industrial Chicago*, 271.

44. Hotchkiss, *History of the Lumber and Forest Industry*, 673–74; _____, *Industrial Chicago*, 40; *History of Muskegon County*, 32.

45. Hazelton, "Reminiscences of Seventeen Years Resi-

dence in Michigan," 406; "Historical Notes," *Michigan History Magazine* 16 (1932), 501; *Lumberman's Gazette*, Apr. 1873 and Feb. 8, 1882.

46. *Lumberman's Gazette*, Jan. 1873; Hotchkiss, *History of the Lumber and Forest Industry*, 48; R. E. Morse to George D. Hill, June 4, 1855, Hill Papers.

47. Crapo, Notebooks, undated entry, ca. early 1856, Crapo Papers; Mills, *History of Saginaw County*, I, 416–17; Hotchkiss, *History of the Lumber and Forest Industry*, 109–11.

48. Crapo, Notebooks, Jan. 3, 4, 5, 1856, Crapo Papers; Hannah, Lay and Company, 1854–55 Daybook, Hannah, Lay and Company Records (Michigan Historical Collections, Bentley Historical Library, University of Michigan); White River Daybook, 1850, Charles B. Mears Papers (Michigan Historical Collections, Bentley Historical Library, University of Michigan; Z. W. Bunce, Ledger, 1853, Jenks Manuscript Collection; *Merchants Magazine and Commercial Review* 18 (1847), 521; *Lumberman's Gazette*, Apr. 1873, Mar. 30, 1881; *Detroit Daily Advertiser*, 1840–; *Lake Huron Observer*, 1849; *History of Musekegon County*, 32; Hotchkiss, *History of the Lumber and Forest Industry*, 90, 110, 127, 671, 677; *Detroit Free Press*, May 7, 1849, quoted in Carl Addison Leach, "Paul Bunyan's Land and the First Sawmills in Michigan," *Michigan History Magazine* 20 (1936), 32; *Northwestern Lumberman*, Sept. 23, 1893; William H. Sweet, "Brief History of Saginaw County," *Michigan Pioneer and Historical Society Historical Collection* 28 (1900), 28, 498.

49. Export values of Michigan lumber in 1847 as reported by a correspondent to the *Merchant's Magazine and Commercial Review* confirm the price levels recorded by the census enumerators.

Detroit	$10.00	Saginaw	$7.03
Algonac	8.59	Ottawa	6.25–7.20
St. Clair Co.	8.00–8.20	Allegan	6.00

50. Vernon L. Jensen, *Lumber and Labor* (New York,

1945), 26–27; *Port Huron Observer,* Apr. 21, 1849.

51. *Northwestern Lumberman,* July 28, 1888.

52. *Merchants Magazine and Commercial Review* 18 (1848), 169. See also *Detroit Daily Advertiser,* June 1, 1839, Aug. 28, 1840; *Lake Huron Observer,* Dec. 30, 1844. The Michigan lumber region long remained a lucrative market for Chicago's "surplus products." *Annual Review of the Business of Chicago for the Year 1852* (Chicago, n.d.), 9–10.

53. Bates to Mears, Aug. 22, 1851, Mears Collection.

54. St. Mary's Falls Ship Canal Company, *560,000 Acres Pine Lands,* 13; *Genesee Whig,* Apr. 22, 1844; Hotchkiss, *History of the Lumber and Forest Industry,* 90, 110; *The Pinelands and Lumber Trade of Michigan,* 6. Mills, *History of Saginaw County,* I, 416; *Merchants Magazine and Commercial Review* 30 (1854).

55. Hotchkiss, *Industrial Chicago,* 38.

56. *Annual Review of the Commerce, Manufactures, Public and Private Improvement of Chicago, for the Year 1854: Several Articles Published in the Daily Democratic Press* (Chicago, 1855); *Fourth Annual Review of the Commerce, Manufactures, and the Public and Private Improvements of Chicago, for the Year 1855: Compiled from Several Articles Published in the Daily Democratic Press* (Chicago, 1856), 16; *Genesee Whig,* Apr. 22, 1854. In 1848 James Fraser found that his cargo of circular-sawn lumber commanded $1.00 to $1.50 above average price. *Lumberman's Gazette* Mar. 30, 1881.

Appropriations bills of Aug. 30, 1852 and July 8, 1856 provided $65,000 for deepening the channel over the St. Clair Flats. Several smaller improvements that directly benefitted the lumberman were included in the 1852 bill:

New Buffalo harbor	$10,000
St. Joseph harbor	10,000
Grand River harbor	2,000

U.S., 49th Cong., 2d sess., Sen. Misc. Doc. 91, *Laws of the United States Relating to the Improvement of Rivers and Harbors from August 11, 1790 to March 3, 1887, with a Tabulated Statement of Appropriations and Allotments* (Washington, 1887), 100–05, 113–14. These were the only federal appropriations for improvements of rivers and harbors in the lumbering region in the antebellum period.

57. *Lake Huron Observer*, July 27, 1844, Jan. 13, 1845.

58. Hotchkiss, *History of the Lumber and Forest Industry*, 223.

59. Wolfe, "Hannah, Lay and Company," 66.

60. St. Mary's Falls Ship Canal Company, *560,000 Acres Pine Lands*, 13.

CHAPTER 8

1. Henry H. Crapo to William Crapo, quoted in Martin D. Lewis, *Lumberman from Flint: The Michigan Career of Henry H. Crapo, 1855–1869* (Detroit, 1958), 86. See also Henry H. Crapo, Journals, Dec. 10–11, 1860, Jan. 8–9, 1862, Henry H. Crapo Manuscripts (Michigan Historical Collections, Bentley Historical Library, University of Michigan); Edward Ferry to Montague Ferry, Mar. 16, 1863, Ferry Family Papers (Michigan Historical Collections, Bentley Historical Library, University of Michigan); Charles Mears, Diaries, Jan. 1–28, 1850, Mears Papers (Michigan Historical Collections, Bentley Historical Library, University of Michigan); David Ward, *The Autobiography of David Ward* (New York, 1912), 127–28. The quotation is from Lewis.

2. H. H. Crapo to W. Crapo, Oct. 16, 1859, Sept. 28, 1860, and Nov. 25, 1860, Crapo Papers; Lewis, *Lumberman from Flint*, 38, 49, 102. The quotation is from the letter of Nov. 25, 1860. For an example of the terms of one logging agreement, see Crapo, Notebooks, undated

entry, 1856, of contract between Crapo and George H. Hoffman and Harvey Parnes, Crapo Papers.

3. Crapo, Notebooks, undated entry, 1856, Crapo Papers.

4. Manuscript Census for the State of Michigan, Manistee and Muskegon counties.

5. Arthur S. Draper, "Reminiscences of the Lumber Camp," *Michigan History Magazine* 14 (1930), 447–48.

6. C. Briggs to Cyrus Woodman, Mar. 19, 1864, Michigan Pine Lands Association Papers (Burton Historical Collections of the Detroit Public Library). See also Ward, *Autobiography,* 106–07, for use of jobbers by an independent logger.

7. Procter, Diaries, Sept. 26, Oct. 19–Dec. 21, 1870, Procter Diaries (Michigan Historical Collections, Bentley Historical Library, University of Michigan).

8. George W. Hotchkiss, *History of the Lumber and Forest Industry of the Northwest* (Chicago, 1898), 76–77, 109, 257–58, 337; James Cooke Mills, *History of Saginaw County, Michigan,* 2 vols. (Saginaw, 1918), II, 17–18; *Portrait and Biographical Album of Newaygo County, Michigan* (Chicago, 1884), 226; *Portrait and Biographical Record of Muskegon and Ottawa Counties, Michigan* (Chicago, 1893), 228, 331; Harry L. Spooner, "The First White Pathfinders of Newaygo County, Michigan," unpublished ms., Library of Michigan, Lansing, Michigan, 82; _____, Lumbering in Newaygo County (White Cloud, Mich., n.d.), 5; *American Lumberman* (Chicago), June 3, 1905; *Mecosta County Pioneer* (Big Rapids), June 5, 1862.

9. H. H. Crapo to W. Crapo, Feb. 25, 1860, Crapo Papers.

10. Ward, *Autobiography,* 104, 127–28; *Northwestern Lumberman,* Feb. 6, July 26, 1892; *Lumberman's Gazette,* Aug. 1873, Mar. 3, 1880; *Detroit Daily Advertiser,* Feb. 29, 1860; Briggs to Woodman, Mar. 19, 1864, Michigan Pine Lands Association Papers; Crapo, Diaies, undated entry handcopied from the *Saginaw Enter-*

prise, Feb. 15, 1856, Crapo Papers.

11. *Detroit Daily Advertiser,* Feb. 29, 1860, Jan. 24, 1861; *Detroit Advertiser & Tribune,* Dec. 8, 1862; *Lumberman's Gazette,* Mar. 3, 1880; Charles J. Wolfe, "Hannah, Lay and Company: A Study in Michigan's Lumber Industry" (M.A. thesis, Wayne State University, 1938), 56; Ward, *Autobiography,* 100, 102–03, 127–28, Hotchkiss, *History of the Lumber and Forest Industry,* 113, 162, 347.

12. *The Merchants' Magazine* 42 (1860), 677–79; *Detroit Daily Advertiser,* Jan. 1860; Ward, *Autobiography,* 106–07; Mills, *History of Saginaw County,* I, 179; *Northwestern Lumberman,* Feb. 6, July 26, 1890; James O. Whittemore noted in 1866 the development of logging on the Au Gres and Au Sable Rivers (Diary, Jan. 4, copied by M. L. Whittemore, Clarke Historical Library, Central Michigan University).

13. Clarence Lewis Northrup, "Pioneer Days in Wexford County," *Michigan History Magazine* 5 (1921); Hotchkiss, *History of the Lumber and Forest Industy,* 208.

14. *Lumberman's Gazette,* Oct. 4, 1877.

15. *Detroit Daily Advertiser,* Dec. 21, 1859.

16. *The Merchants' Magazine* 54 (1866), 104; H. H. Crapo to W. Crapo, Jan. 7, 1859, Crapo Papers; *Detroit Daily Advertiser,* Dec. 21, 1859.

17. *Detroit Daily Advertiser,* Feb. 6, 1860.

18. The descripltion of logging in 1859–60 has been drawn from newspaper accounts from around the state as reported in the *Detroit Daily Advertiser,* Jan. 5, Jan. 7, Jan. 21, Feb. 6, Feb. 13, Mar. 22, 1860.

19. Briggs to Woodman, Mar. 19, 1864, Michigan Pine Lands Association Papers; *Detroit Daily Advertiser,* May 7, 1859. Hannah Lay & Company the largest firm north of Manistee, is representative of large-scale firms that did no summer logging before 1870. Wolfe, "Hannah, Lay and Company," 56.

20. *Detroit Daily Advertiser,* May 7, 1859, Apr. 17,

1861; Rector, *Log Transportation in the Lakes States Lumber Industry*, 41.

21. Roy M. Overpack, "The Michigan Logging Wheels," *Michigan Magazine of History* 35 (1951), 222–225; Bruce Catton, *Michigan: A Bicentennial History* (New York, 1976), 147.

22. Procter, diaries, Oct. 27, Dec. 11, 1870, Procter Diaries; *Northwestern Lumberman* (Chicago), Sept. 19, 1891; Ralph Clement Bryant, *Logging: Its Manufacture and Distribution* (New York, 1922), 93; William G. Rector, *Log Transportation in the Lakes States Lumber Industry, 1840–1918. The Movement of Its Logs and Its Relationship to Land Settlement, Waterway Development, Railroad Construction, Lumber Production and Prices* (Glendale, Cal., 1853), 206–07; *Detroit Daily Advertiser*, Feb. 22, 1860.

23. H. H. Crapo to Arnold and Prescott, Feb. 25, 1860, Crapo Papers; Rector, *Log Transportation in the Lakes States Lumber Industry*, 41; U.S., *Cong. Globe*, 41st Cong., 2nd sess., Appendix, May 24, 1870, p. 371.

24. H. H. Crapo to Arnold and Prescott, Feb. 25, 1860, Crapo Papers; Procter, Diaries, Feb. 25, 1869, Procter Diaries; Ward, *Autobiography*, 101–03.

25. *Detroit Daily Advertiser*, June 19, 1861, May 1, 1862; Lumberman's Gazette, May 13, 1885; Rector, *Log Transportation in the Lakes States Lumber Industry*, 27–28. The danger of logs jamming was greatest at the outset of the drive, when the rollway was broken. For a contemporary description of a drive by a worker, see Proctor, Diaries, Mar. 27–Apr. 25, 1869, Procter Diaries.

26. Richard G. Wood, *A History of Lumbering in Maine, 1820–1861* (Orono, Me., 1935), 170–71; Bryant, *Logging*, 84–85.

27. H. H. Crapo to W. Crapo, Mar. 25, Apr. 1, 1860, Crapo Papers; *Detroit Daily Advertiser*, Mar. 21, Mar. 24, Apr. 4, Apr. 9, Apr. 17, June 5, June 18, 1860.

28. *East Saginaw Courier*, quoted in *Detroit Daily*

Advertiser, Feb. 21, 1860; Clifford Allen, ed., *Michigan Log Marks* (East Lansing, 1941), 11, Paul W. Ivey, *The Pere Marquette Railroad Company: An Historical Study of the Growth and Development of One of Michigan's Most Important Railway Systems* (Lansing, 1919), 218; Bernard C. Korn, "Eber B. Ward: Pathfinder of American Industry" (Ph.D. diss., Marquette University, 1942), 210; *Detroit Daily Advertiser*, Feb. 6, 1860.

29. Hotchkiss, *History of the Lumber and Forest Industry*, 162; *History of Saginaw County* I, 179; Allen, ed., *Michigan Log Marks* 19; James Glasgow, "Muskegon, Michigan: The Evolution of a Lake Port" (Ph.D. diss., University of Chicago, 1939), 34, 35. Whittemore, for example, noted that his father's project to clear the upper Tawas required cutting out timber buried in the water so long that sod had covered them to create small islands (Whittemore, diary, Jan. 8, 1866).

30. Allen, *Michigan Log Marks*, 12–13; *Ames vs. Port Huron Log & Driving Company* 6 (Michigan, 1859), 266; George N. Fuller, ed., *Messages of the Governors of Michigan*, 3 vols. (Lansing, 1925–26), II, 491; *Acts of the Legislature of the State of Michigan*, 40, 1855, 263, 1861.

Legislative acts also settled disputes that pitted one lumberman against another, establishing procedures for future operations. For example, a section of the act of 1861 cited above established rules for handling log jams. If a lumberman caused a jam on a river through neglect and did not break it immediately, another individual could act and then recover costs from the negligent party. Another major source of conflict was the establishment of log ownership in a large drive. In 1859 the legislature required that logs floated on the Muskegon be marked on an end with the owner's symbol, duly registered with the county clerk. In subsequent legislation in 1867, this requirement was extended to all rivers.

31. *Detroit Daily Advertiser*, Apr. 17, 1861; *American Lumberman*, I, 239–42, III, 221–24; Announcement of log sale, Aug. 10, 1857, Port Huron Log Driving and Booming Company, George D. Hill Manuscript Collection (Michigan Historical Collections, Bentley Historical Library, University of Michigan); Hotchkiss, *History of the Lumber and Forest Industry*, 142, 184–86; Allen, ed., *Michigan Log Marks*, 23–24; Wood, *A History of Lumbering in Maine*, 128; Mills, *History of Saginaw County*, I, 400, 402; *History of Muskegon County, Michigan, with Illustrations and Biographical Sketches of Some of the Prominent Men and Pioneers* (Chicago, 1882), 29.

32. *Lumberman's Gazette*, Dec. 1873, Jan. 28, 1879; Rector, *Log Transportation in the Lakes States Lumber Industry*, 128; Allen, ed., *Michigan Log Marks*, 13.

33. *Lumberman's Gazette*, Jan. 28, 1879, Mar. 3, 1880, Nov. 29, 1882; Hotchkiss, *History of the Lumber and Forest Industry*, 142; Mills, *History of Saginaw County*, I, 400; Rector, *Log Transportation in the Lakes States Lumber Industry*, 128; Allen, ed., *Michigan Log Marks*, 11, 31, 40; Tittabawassee Boom Company, Dun and Bradstreet Credit Reports, Baker Library, Harvard University, vol. 60. There is an alphabetical index of names at the beginning of each volume of the credit reports.

34. Rector, *Log Transportation in the Lakes States Lumber Industry*, 128.

35. *Lumberman's Gazette*, Jan. 4, Jan. 18, 1882; *Northwestern Lumberman*, Aug. 8, 1891; Rector, *Log Transportation in the Lakes States Lumber Industry*, 128; Hotchkiss, *History of the Lumber and Forest Industry*, 262, 265; Allen, ed., *Michigan Log Marks*, 42–43, 58–59, 71.

36. *Detroit Daily Advertiser*, July 13, July 16, 1862; Hotchkiss, *History of the Lumber and Forest Industry*,

76–77, 144; Rector, *Log Transportation in the Lakes States Lumber Industry*, 166.

37. Ivey, *The Pere Marquette Railroad Company*, 215, 235, 250; Hotchkiss, *History of the Lumber and Forest Industry*, 101, Willis F. Dunbar, *All Aboard! A History of Railroads in Michigan* (Grand Rapids, 1969), 79, 116; William G. Rector, "Railroad Logging in the Lakes States," *Michigan History Magazine* 36 (1952), 352–54; Daniel Cary, "Michigan's Foremost Unique Logger," *Michigan History Magazine* 32 (1948), 301; Charles M. Davis, "Lumbering in the High Plains," in Charles M. Davis, ed., *Readings in the Geography of Michigan* (Ann Arbor, 1964), 102; Catton, *Michigan*, 146–47. For a brief, clear description of the growth of railroads in Michigan and an assessment of the influence of the lumber industry on railroad buildings in the state, see Dunbar, *All Aboard!*, chapters 3, 4, 5, and 7.

38. *The Merchants' Magazine* 54 (1866), 102; Wilson Compton, *The Organization of the Lumber Industry: With Special Reference to the Influences Determining the Prices of Lumber in the United States* (Chicago, 1916), 116; Crapo, Notebooks, Jan. 4, 1856, list of logging contractors, n.d., 1863, Journals, Apr. 17, 1860, H. H. Crapo to W. Crapo, Sept. 9, Sept. 28, Oct. 31, 1860, Crapo Papers; Sweetser & Sanborn to George D. Hill, May 23, 1857, Mark Norris to George D. Hill, Aug. 3, 1867, Hill Manuscript Collection; Mears, 1864 Middlesex Ledger, Mar. 18, Apr. 5, 1864, 1866–67 Middlesex Daybook, Maxwell Sands Account, 1868–70 Lincoln Daybook, undated entry, 1870, Mears Papers; S. S. Hastings to Woodman, n.d., 1865, Michigan Pine Lands Association Papers; Case Lumber Company, 1866–67 Mill Account Book, May 15, 1867, William L. Case Papers (Michigan Historical Collections, Bentley Historical Library, University of Michigan), *American Lumberman*, Jan. 14, 1905; *Lumberman's Gazette*, Aug. 1873, Jan. 19, 1881; *Northwestern Lumberman*, Sept. 26,

1891; Rector, "Railroad Logging," 351–52; U.S., *Cong. Globe*, 41st Cong., 2d sess., Appendix, May 24, 1870, p. 371; Hotchkiss, *History of the Lumber and Forest Industry*, 117, 160.

39. The manuscript census for Michigan in 1870 has only partially survived. Records for all counties alphabetically preceding Emmet and for scattered other counties are not available. For this study, it is particularly unfortunate that the returns for Alpena, Bay, Manistee, and Wayne counties are missing.

CHAPTER 9

1. James E. Defenbaugh, *History of the Lumber Industry in America*, 2 vols. (Chicago, 1906–07), I, 490–92.

2. Wilson Compton, *The Organization of the Lumber Industry: With Special Reference to the Influences Determining the Prices of Lumber in the United States* (Chicago, 1916), 88, 112; Vernon H. Jensen, *Lumber and Labor* (New York, 1945), 29; William G. Rector, *Log Transportation in the Lakes States Lumber Industry 1840–1918. The Movement of Its Logs and Its Relationship to Land Settlement, Waterway Development, Railroad Construction, Lumber Production, and Prices* (Glendale, Cal., 1953), 38; Martin D. Lewis, *Lumberman from Flint: The Michigan Career of Henry H. Crapo, 1855–1869* (Detroit, 1958), 57–58.

3. Henry H. Crapo, Notebooks, Jan. 5, 1856, Henry H. Crapo Papers (Michigan Historical Collections, Bentley Historical Library, University of Michigan).

4. Sweetser & Sanborn to George D. Hill, Aug. 10, 1857, George D. Hill Manuscript Collection (Michigan Historical Collections, Bentley Historical Library, University of Michigan).

5. G. Lister to Hill, Aug. 21, 1857, Johnson & Taintor to Charles L. May & Co., April 25, 1857, Hill Papers; Crapo, Notebooks, Jan. 4, Dec. 3, 1856, Mar. 20, 1857, undated talk with Aaron Watrous, Crapo Papers; *Detroit Daily Advertiser*, Aug. 14, Sept. 1, Sept. 18, 1857.

6. Quoted in Lewis, *Lumberman from Flint*, 68, 71–72; George W. Hotchkiss, *Industrial Chicago: The Lumber Interests* (Chicago, 1894), 408; *Portrait and Biographical Record of Muskegon and Ottawa Counties* (Chicago, 1893), 325; *First Annual Statement of the Trade and Commerce of Chicago, for the Year Ending Dec. 31, 1858* (Chicago, 1859), 32; *Detroit Daily Advertiser*, Apr. 6, Apr. 18, Apr. 27, Dec. 29, 1858; Ruth R. Bordin, "A Michigan Lumbering Family," *Business History Review*, 34 (1960): 72.

7. H. H. Crapo to W. Crapo, Oct. 16, Nov. 21, 1859, Crapo Papers; *Detroit Daily Advertiser*, Mar. 23, 1859–Nov. 12, 1859, Jan. 27, 1860; Charles H. Mears, Diaries, Apr. 12, May 6, 1859, Charles H. Mears Papers (Michigan Historical Collections, Bentley Historical Library, University of Michigan); *Second Annual Statement of the Trade and Commerce of Chicago, for the Year Ending Dec. 31, 1859* (Chicago, 1860), 61–62; David Ward, *The Autobiography of David Ward* (New York, 1912), 106. The quotation is from Crapo letter of Nov. 21, 1859.

8. Statement of Accounts, 1857–Dec. 1, 1859, prepared by H. H. Crapo and dated Mar. 3, 1860, in response to a letter of J. P. Arnold, Feb. 23, 1860, Crapo Papers.

9. W. W. Crapo to W. Crapo, Oct. 5, 1859, Crapo Papers; *Detroit Daily Advertiser*, Jan. 6, 1860.

10. *Detroit Daily Advertiser*, Jan. 23, 1860–Nov. 16, 1860; H. H. Crapo, May 27, June 3, Aug. 23, Oct. 25, 1860, H. H. Crapo to Arnold & Prescott, Mar. 3, 1860, Crapo Papers; *Lumberman's Gazette* (Bay City), Jan. 19, 1881; *Third Annual Statement of the Trade and*

Commerce of Chicago, for the Year Ending Dec. 31, 1860 (Chicago, 1861), 40–41.

11. *Detroit Daily Advertiser,* Dec. 23, 1860, Apr. 5, Oct. 25, 1861, Jan. 27, 1862; Herbert Brinkes, "The Effect of the Civil War in 1861 on Michigan Lumbering and Mining Industries," *Michigan Magazine of History* 44 (1960), 102, 105–06; *Lumberman's Gazette,* Aug. 1873; Ward, *Autobiography,* 107 *Fourth Annual Statement of the Trade and Commerce of Chicago, for the Year Ending Dec. 31, 1861* (Chicago, 1862), 39.

12. Anita Shafer Goodstein, *Biography of a Businessman: Henry W. Sage, 1814–1897* (Ithaca, 1962), 77.

13. *Detroit Daily Advertiser,* Mar. 25, 1862–July 28, 1862; *Detroit Advertiser & Tribune,* Sept. 13–Nov. 19, 1862; George W. Hotchkiss, *History of the Lumber and Forest Industry of the Northwest* (Chicago, 1898), 117, 678–79; Goodstein, *Biography of a Businessman,* 79.

14. Ward, *Autobiography,* 117–18, 127–28; Rector, *Log Transportation in the Lakes States Lumber Industry,* 37; _____, "Railroad Logging in the Lakes States," *Michigan History Magazine* 36 (1952), 351–52; Hotchkiss, *History of the Lumber and Forest Industry,* 68, 90, 679; *Detroit Advertiser & Tribune,* Dec. 22, 1863; *Lumberman's Gazette,* Jan. 19, 1881; Case Lumber Company, Mill Account Book, Nov. 1867, William L. Case Papers (Michigan Historical Collections, Bentley Historical Library, University of Michigan); Mears, Lincoln Daybook, Apr. 6, 1862, 1870 passim, Middlesex ledgers, May 1864, Nov. 1864, May 1867, Sept. 1867, Dec. 1867, Apr. 1868, Pentwater Mill, balance statement, Mears Papers; *Annual Reports of the Chicago Board of Trade, 1864–70*; James O. Whittemore, diary, copied by M. L. Whittemore, Jun. 7, 1866, Clarke Historical Library, Central Michigan University. For a comparison of capacity and output for Saginaw mills, see Hotchkiss, *History of the Lumber and Forest Industry,* 89, 96, 100–02 and the Manuscript Census for the State

of Michigan, 1870, Saginaw County.

15. *Detroit Daily Advertiser*, Mar. 19, Oct. 11, 1860, Dec. 23, 1861; *Lumberman's Gazette*, Jan., Feb., Mar. 1873; Milton O. Nelson, "The Lumber Industry of America," *Review of Reviews* 36 (1907), 570; Hotchkiss, *History of the Lumber and Forest Industry*, 89, 96, 101–02; Mills, *History of Saginaw County* I, 410; Bernard C. Korn, "Eber Brock Ward: Pathfinder of American Industry" (Ph.D. diss., Marquette University, 1942), 222; Compton, *The Organization of the Lumber Industry*, 40.

16. Manuscript Census for the State of Michigan, 1870.

17. *Lumberman's Gazette*, Jan. 4, Jan. 11, 1877, Feb. 25, 1884; *Northwestern Lumberman* (Chicago), July 27, 1886; Hotchkiss, *History of the Lumber and Forest Industry*, 97; Compton, *The Organization of the Lumber Industry*, 38.

18. *Detroit Daily Advertiser*, Dec. 29, 1858, July 28, 1859, July 1, Oct. 11, 1860, Dec. 23, 1861; *Detroit Advertiser & Tribune*, Nov. 7, 1862, *Lumberman's Gazette*, Jan., Feb., Mar., 1873, Apr. 1877, Oct. 1, Oct. 15, Nov. 5, 1879, Apr. 15, 1885; Nelson, "The Lumber Industry of America," 570; Hotchkiss, *History of the Lumber and Forest Industry*, 96, 102. *Michigan Pioneer and Historical Society Historical Collections* I (1874), 290; Compton, *The Organization of the Lumber Industry*, 37; Crapo, Notebooks, conversation with John Brooks, recorded Oct. 18, 1856, Crapo Papers.

19. *Lumberman's Gazette*, Jan., Feb., Mar. 1873, Oct. 15, 1879; Hotchkiss, *History of the Lumber and Forest Industry*, 96–97, 102.

20. *History of Muskegon County*, 25; *Michigan Pioneer and Historical Society Collections* I (1874), 290.

21. Manuscript Census for the State of Michigan, 1870, Saginaw and Grand Traverse Counties.

22. Manuscript Censuses for the State of Michigan, 1850, 1860, and 1870.

23. Manuscript Census for the State of Michigan, 1870, Saginaw and Genesee counties.

24. A representative example of a modest-sized manufacturer would be Ira Chaffee of Allegan. According to the correspondents for the credit-reporting firm of R. G. Dun and Company, he experienced cash problems throughout the late 1850s. (Dun & Bradstreet Credit Reports, vol. 3, Allegan County, entry for Ira Chaffee [Baker Library, Harvard University]. An alphabetical index of names is located at the beginning of each volume of the credit reports.)

25. H. H. Crapo to Arnold & Prescott, Feb. 25, 1860, Crapo Papers.

26. Arnold put up the $150,000 and held $50,000 notes from the other two partners.

27. Charles J. Wolfe, "Hannah, Lay and Company: A Study in Michigan's Lumber Industry" (M.A. thesis, Wayne State University, 1938), 70. For a sense of the size and stability of large-scale firms in the 1860s, see the Dun & Bradstreet reports for Saginaw, St. Clair, Bay, Allegan, and Ottawa counties.

28. Hotchkiss, *History of the Lumber and Forest Industry*, 176–77; Glenn Porter and Harold C. Livesay, *Merchants and Manufacturers: Studies in the Changing Structure of Nineteenth-Century Marketing* (Baltimore, 1971), 8, 25.

29. Crapo, Notebooks, Jan. 4, 1856, Crapo Papers.

30. H. H. Crapo to Prescott & Arnold, Mar. 3, 1860, Statement of Accounts, 1857–59, Crapo Papers. The partners had agreed that receipts would be used in the following order: (1) Crapo's salary and commission; (2) current operating expenses: (3) installment payments for timberland; (4) income to partners.

31. Mears, Profit and Loss Statement for 1866, Mid-

dlesex daybook, 1866–67, Mears Papers.

32. U.S., *Congressional Globe*, 41st Cong., 2d sess., Appendix, 371.

33. Manuscript Census for the State of Michigan, 1870, Saginaw County.

CHAPTER 10

1. James Glasgow, "Muskegon, Michigan: The Evolution of a Lake Port" (Ph.D. diss., University of Chicago, 1939), 37.

2. Henry H. Crapo to William Crapo, Nov. 13, 1860, Henry H. Crapo Papers (Michigan Historical Collections, Bentley Historical Library, University of Michigan).

3. Willis Compton, "The Price Problem in the Lumber Industry," *American Economic Review* 7 (1917), 588.

4. Chicago Board of Trade, *Annual Reports, 1857–1869*. These summaries were published for the calendar year during 1857–62 and 1869; between 1863 and 1868 they were compiled on an annual basis each March.

5. Charles Mears, Diaries, Dec. 1, Apr. 19, 1858, Charles Mears Papers (Michigan Historical Collections, Bentley Historical Library, University of Michigan); *Detroit Daily Advertiser*, Jan. 27, 1860; *Annual Statement of the Trade and Commerce of Buffalo, for the Year Ending December 31, 1869* (Buffalo, 1870), 127; Dun & Bradstreet Credit Reports, vol. 64, Saginaw County, H. Raymond, and vol. 69, St. Clair County, W. B. Hibbard & Co. (Baker Library, Harvard University). An alphabetical index of names is located at the beginning of each volume of the credit reports.

6. H. H. Crapo to W. Crapo, Oct. 16, 1859, Notebooks, June 20–29, 1859, Journals, July 18–19, 1861, Crapo Papers; Articles of Agreement between Z. W. Bunce & Sons and Peter Gilchers, Apr. 4, 1856, William

L. Jenks Manuscript Collection (Burton Historical Collection, Detroit Public Library); *Detroit Daily Advertiser*, June 11, June 25, 1860; Oliver Raymond, "Port Sanilac Settlers," *Michigan Magazine of History* 33; (1949), 169; *Annual Statement of the Trade and Commerce of Cincinnati for the Commercial Year Ending August 31st, 1860* (Cincinnati, 1860), 6, 26; *Annual Statement of the Trade, Commerce and Manufacturers of the City of Cleveland, for the Year 1867* (Cleveland, 1868), 7, 10, 13, 30; *The Morning Expresses' Annual Statement of the Trade and Commerce of Buffalo for the Year 1861* (Buffalo, 1861), 32; *Annual Statement of the Trade and Commerce of Buffalo, 1869*, 126; Dun & Bradstreet Credit Reports, vol. 62, Sanilac County, Woods, Nims & Co., vol. 64, Saginaw County, Valorous Paine, John D. Rust & Co., vol. 69, St. Clair County, R. B. Hubbard & Co.

7. *Detroit Daily Advertiser*, Sept. 7, 1859, Aug. 7, 1860, May 9, 1862; David Ward, *The Autobiography of David Ward* (New York, 1912), 106; H. H. Crapo to W. Crapo, June 6, 1860, Crapo Papers. It may have been that delays on the Erie Canal and the increasing costs of handling at Buffalo prompted some manufacturers to ship to Albany by way of Lake Ontario and Oswego. For a fuller description of the lumber trade at Buffalo, Oswego, and Albany, see the trade and commerce reports for Buffalo, 1858–1869. The *Commercial Advertiser* published annual reports for the years 1858–1861; after that date Buffao's board of trade assumed the responsibility.

8. Mears, Diaries, July 6, 1859, Mears Papers; George W. Hotchkiss, *Industrial Chicago: The Lumber Interests* (Chicago, 1894), 187.

9. *Detroit Daily Advertiser*, Apr. 11, 1859; Crapo, Journals, May 29, 1859, Crapo Papers.

10. *Detroit Daily Advertiser*, Sept. 7, 1859; *Northwestern Lumberman* (Chicago), Sept. 5, 1891; Crapo,

Notebooks, undated entry, 1858, and H. H. Crapo to W. Crapo, Nov. 6, Dec. 17, 1859, Crapo Papers; Memorandum of Agreement between S. P. Mend and C. L. May & Co., Aug. 10, 1857, George D. Hill Papers (Michigan Historical Collections, Bentley Historical Library, University of Michigan).

11. "Autobiography of Everett S. Hotchkiss: Remembrances of Bay City, Michigan in the 1860s and 1870s" (unpublished typescript, Michigan Historical Collections, Bentley Historical Library, University of Michigan), 6; G. L. Lister to G. D. Hill, July 13, 1857, Chas. M. Taintor to G. D. Hill, Mar. 7, 1857, Hill Papers; Article of Agreement between Z. W. Bunce & Sons and Peter Gilcher Apr. 4, 1856, Jenks Collection; *Northwestern Lumberman*, May 31, Sept. 6, 1890, Oct. 3, Nov. 21, 1891; George W. Hotchkiss, *History of the Lumber and Forest Industry of the Northwest*, (Chicago, 1898), 149; Dun & Bradstreet Credit Reports, vol. 80, Wayne County, D. Whitney & Co. and William Wainer.

12. The Dun & Bradstreet Reports for Iosco, Alcona, Alpena, Huron, Sanilac, and Saginaw counties are particularly useful in illustrating the large number of integrated firms marketing exclusively in the East, particularly in New York and Ohio. Dun & Bradstreet, vols. 2, 4, 24, 62, 64. For additional examples of integrated firms, see *Detroit Daily Advertiser*, Mar. 28, 1860, Dec. 23, 1861; *American Lumberman* (Chicago), July 8, 1905; Crapo, Notebooks, undated entry, 1855, Crapo Papers; Bernard C. Korn, "Eber Brock Ward: Pathfinder of American Industry" (Ph.D. diss., Marquette University, 1942), 226; Hotckiss, *History of the Lumber and Forest Industry*, 45–46.

13. H. H. Crapo to Arnold & Prescott, Feb. 25, 1860, H. H. Crapo to W. Crapo, May 27, July 24, Oct. 25, 1860, Notebooks, undated entry on profits by grade for shipment to Albany, 1855, Crapo Papers; *Detroit Daily Advertiser*, June 6, 1859, Feb. 11, 1862; *Northwestern Lumberman*, July 5, 1890.

14. H. H. Crapo to W. Crapo, Sept. 9, 1860, Crapo Papers.

15. H. H. Crapo to W. Crapo, Jan. 7, Oct. 5, Oct. 16, 1859, Feb. 25, May 6, May 27, June 3, June 7, Aug. 12, Oct. 25, 1860, Notebooks, June 2–20, 1859, Journals, July 18–19, 1861, Crapo Papers.

16. Mears, diaries, Jan. 30–Feb. 3, July 30, 1857, Apr. 17, Apr. 17, 1858, Mears Papers.

17. Mears, diaries, Mar. 13, 1859, Mears Papers; *Detroit Daily Advertiser,* June 14, 1859, May 15, Oct. 31, 1860, Apr. 16, 1862; *Lumberman's Gazette* (Bay City), Apr. 19, 1877; *Northwestern Lumberman,* July 4, 1891; *Ninth Annual Statement of the Trade and Commerce of Chicago,* 1867, 26. Aaron Watrous calculated that the shipping costs ($3.00) from his mill to Saginaw accounted for 29 percent of his total shipping costs ($10.25) to Albany in 1856. Crapo, Notebooks, Watrous entry, Jan., 1856, Crapo Papers.

18. *Lumberman's Gazette,* Apr. 22, 1885; *Northwestern Lumberman,* July 4, 1891; Hotchkiss, *History of the Lumber and Forest Industry,* 234; Wilson Compton, *The Organization of the Lumber Industry: With Special References to the Influences Determining the Prices of Lumber in the United States* (Chicago, 1916), 37.

19. H. H. Crapo to W. Crapo, Aug. 3, Aug. 5, 1860, Crapo Papers; *Detroit Advertiser & Tribune,* Aug. 16, 1862; *Annual Statement of the Trade and Commerce of Buffalo, 1863,* p. 41; *Annual Statement of the Trade and Commerce of Buffalo, 1865* p. 43.

20. Information on shipping costs has been drawn from many sources, including Crapo, Notebooks, Watrous entry, Jan. 1, 1856, Jan. 2, 1856, undated entry, 1858, Crapo Papers; U.S., *Cong. Globe,* 41st Cong., 2d sess., App., p. 371. *The Detroit Daily Advertiser* and, after mid-1862 its successor, the *Detroit Advertiser & Tribune* carried a column on freight notes during the shipping season.

21. For a brief and sprightly description of the devel-

opment of shipping on the Great Lakes, see Bruce Catton, *Michigan: A Bicentennial History* (New York, 1976), 124–27.

22. *Detroit Daily Advertiser*, Sept. 11, 1861; *Detroit Advertiser & Tribune*, Aug. 16–Nov. 17, 1862, July 2, 1869; *Tuscola Advertiser*, Aug. 12, 1869; *American Lumberman* I, 136.

23. *Autobiography of E. S. Hotchkiss*, 6; Detroit *Daily Advertiser*, Apr. 30, June 2, Dec. 12, 1859; Glasgow, "Muskegon, Michigan," 27; *Michigan Pioneer and Historical Society Historical Collection* I (1874–76), 299–300; Francis C. Hannah, "The Harbor at Ludington," *Michigan History Magazine* 35 (1951), 409; U.S. 49th Cong., 2d sess., Sen. Misc. Doc. 91, *Laws of the United States Relating to the Improvement of Rivers and Harbors from August 11, 1790 to March 3, 1887*, pp. 11–68; Mears, diaries; Jan. 5, Jan. 31, Feb. 1, 1856; Aug. 17–18, 1860, Mears Papers; George N. Fuller, ed., *Messages of the Governors of Michigan*, 3 vols. (Lansing, 1925–26), II, 392; Michigan *Acts*, 167, Mar. 15, 1861.

24. Paul Wesley Ivey, *The Pere Marquette Railroad Company, An Historical Study of the Growth and Development of One of Michigan's Most Important Railway Systems* (Lansing, 1919), 225. Glasgow's findings for Muskegon support Ivey's study. Although rail connections between Muskegon and Chicago were completed in 1872, lumbermen there made little use of the railroad in marketing until the early 1880s. Glasgow, "Muskegon, Michigan," 43.

25. Crapo, Journals, Aug. 26–27, 1858, H. H. Crapo to W. Crapo, May 27, 1860, Crapo Papers; Mears, Diaries, July 22, 1857, Mears Papers; *Detroit Daily Advertiser*, June 18, 1860; *Detroit Advertiser & Tribune*, Dec. 8, 1862; Korn, "Eber Brock Ward," 203, 205; Dennis G. Cooper and Floyd A. Stilgenbauer, "The Urban Geography of Saginaw, Michigan," in Eugene S. McCartney and Robert Burnett Hall, eds., *Michigan Papers in Geogra-*

phy 5 (1935), 303; W. O. Hedrick, "A Sketch of Some of the Institutional Beginnings in Michigan," *Michigan History Magazine* 5 (1921), 205–07; Hotchkiss, *History of the Lumber and Forest Industry*, 334; Ivey, *the Pere Marquette Railroad Company;* Willis F. Dunbar, *All Aboard! A History of Railroads in Michigan* (Grand Rapids, 1968), chaps. 3–6.

26. *Annual Statement of the Trade and Commerce of Buffalo, 1869*, p. 124; *Eighth Annual Statement of the Trade and Commerce of Chicago, 1866*, pp. 59–61; *Eleventh Annual Statement of the Trade and Commerce of Chicago, 1869*, p. 50.

CHAPTER 11

1. Quoted in *Weekley Observer* (Fentonville), Mar. 30, 1854.

2. *Detroit Advertiser & Tribune*, Sept. 18, 1862.

3. George Barker Engberg, "Labor in the Lake States Lumber Industry, 1830–1930" (Ph.D. diss., University of Minnesota, 1949), 61–67; Leo C. Lillie, *Historic Grand Haven and Ottawa County* (Grand Haven, Mich., 1931), 262–63; *History of Allegan and Barry Counties, Michigan, with Illustrations and Biographical Sketches of Their Prominent Men and Pioneers* (Philadelphia, 1880), 152, 170; *Northwestern Lumberman* (Chicago), Nov. 19, 1892; *Lake Huron Observer* (Port Huron), Mar. 10, 1845.

4. Frances Caswell Hanna, *Sand, Sawdust and Saw Logs: Lumber Days in Ludington* (Ludington, Mich., 1955), 9–10; Vernon H. Jensen, *Lumber and Labor* (New York, 1945), 53–55; Engberg, "Labor in the Lake States Lumber Industry," 26, 28, 101–03; Edward Vincent, Diary, 1864 (Clarke Historical Library, Central Michigan University); Employment Agreement between

Charles Mears and Thomas Ockerby, n.d., Charles
Mears Collection (Chicago Historical Society); Charles
Mears, Lincoln Daybook, Sept. 1861, Diaries, Oct. 28,
30, 1857, May 31, 1858, June 9, 1860, Charles Mears
Papers (Michigan Historical Collection, Bentley Historical Library, University of Michigan); Henry H. Crapo to
William Crapo, Nov. 27, 1860, Henry H. Crapo Papers
(Michigan Historical Collections, Bentley Historical Library, University of Michigan); James Cooke Mills, *History of Saginaw County, Michigan*, 2 vols. (Saginaw,
1918), I, 147.

5. George Blackburn and Sherman L. Ricards, Jr., "A
Demographic History of the West: Manistee County,"
Michigan, 1860," *Journal of American History* 57 (1970–
71), 604–09; *Portrait and Biographical Album of Osceola
County, Containing Portraits and Biographical Sketches
of Prominent and Representative Citizens of the County*
(Chicago, 1884), 356–57; Edward Vincent, Diary, Dec.
8, 1864; Manuscript Census for the State of Michigan,
1860; U.S., Bureau of the Census, Ninth Census, 1870,
vol. 3. *The Statistics of Wealth and Industry in the
United States.*

6. Engberg, "Labor in the Lakes States Lumber In-
dustry," 46, 55; _____, "Who Were the Lumber-
jacks?" *Michigan History Magazine* 22 (1948), 241–43;
Detroit Advertiser & Tribune, Sept. 18, 1862; Andrew J.
Perjuda, "Sources and Dispersal of Michigan's Popula-
tion," *Michigan History Magazine* 32 (1948), 364; Carl-
ton C. Qualey, "Pioneer Scandinavian Settlement in
Michigan," *Michigan History Magazine* 24 (1940), 438;
Charlotte Erickson, "British Immigrants in the Old
Northwest, 1815–1860," in David M. Ellis, ed., *The
Frontier in American Development: Essays in Honor of
Paul Wallace Gates* (Ithaca, 1969), 333–34; Marcus Lee
Hansen, *The Mingling of the Canadian and American
People* (New Haven, 1940), 130–31, 152–53. Blackburn

and Ricards found a higher percentage of foreign-born in Manistee County in 1860 than would have been true of the state as a whole; Blackburn and Ricards, "A Demographic History of the West," 613–18.

7. Engberg, "Lumber in the Lakes States Lumber Industry," 103. This study emphasizes the importance of an interoccupational flow of workers. For good descriptions of early interoccupational mobility, see also Engberg, "Who Were the Lumberjacks?," 244–45; Arthur M. Weimer, "An Economic History of Alma, Michigan" (Ph.D. diss., University of Chicago, 1934), 49; Harry L. Spooner, *Lumbering in Newaygo County* (White Cloud, Mich., n.d.), 1; David E. Shob, *Hired Hands and Plowboys: Farm Labor in the Midwest, 1815–1860* (Urbana, 1975), 150–172.

8. H. H. Crapo to W. Crapo, Nov. 27, 1860, Crapo Papers.

9. H. H. Crapo to Arnold & Prescott, Feb. 25, 1860, Journals, Labor Agreements of Feb. 1858, July 18, 1860, Crapo Papers; blank contract, Charles Mears Collection (Burton Historical Collection of the Detroit Public Library), which reads as follows:

In consideration of the agreements hereinafter made, I hereby agree to work for _____ in Chicago, or at either of his Lumbering Establishments in Michigan, _____ for the sum of _____ with board _____ and to work as follows: from sunrise till sunset when the days are more than twelve hours long, twelve hours when there are twelve hours of daylight, and not less than eleven hours at any season of the year; also, to furnish myself with a good axe, and assist in loading and discharging vessels, if able, whenever required, and to do all I can to forward the work and promote the interest of my employer. I also, further agree to abstain entirely from the use of all intoxicating Liquors, except purely for medicinal purposes or forfeit my wages.

In consideration of the faithful fulfillment of the above contract said _____ agrees to pay the amount herein specified.

10. Jensen, *Lumber and Labor*, 49–50; Engberg, "Labor in the Lakes States Lumber Industry," 69, 90, 101–02; _____, "Who Were the Lumberjacks?," 239–40.

11. For a full discussion of the "Products of Industry" manuscript censuses for 1850 and 1860 and an assessment of their reliability, see Margaret Walsh, *The Manufacturing Frontier: Pioneer Industry in Antebellum Wisconsin, 1830–1860* (Madison, 1972), Appendix A, 221–29; _____, "The Census as an Accurate Source of Information: The Value of Mid-Nineteenth Century Manufacturing Returns," *Historical Methods Newsletter* 3 (1970), 3–13.

12. Manuscript Census for the State of Michigan, 1850, 1860, 1870. Information was available for 171 mills in 1850, 352 mills in 1860, and 309 mills in 1870.

13. Jensen, "Lumber and Labor," 53; Joseph F. Proctor, Diaries, Oct. 23–Nov. 2, 1870, Joseph F. Proctor Diaries (Michigan Historical Collections, Bentley Historical Library, University of Michigan); Willis C. Ward, "Reminiscences of Michigan's Logging Days," *Michigan History Magazine* 20 (1937), 302–06.

14. *Lumberman's Gazette* (Bay City), Apr. 6, 1881.

15. *Lumberman's Gazette*, Jan. 1874; David Ward, *Autobiography of David Ward* (New York, 1912), 100, 102–03, 110; Ward, "Reminiscences of Michigan's Logging Days," 302–06; Arthur Scott White, "Early Days Around Alpena," *Michigan History Magazine* 9 (1925), 359–60; *Northwestern Lumberman*, June 6, 1891; Crapo, Notebooks, handcopied from *Saginaw Enterprise*, Feb. 22, 1856, Crapo Papers; Hannah, Lay and Company, 1854–55 Daybook, Hannah, Lay and Company Papers (Michigan Historical Collections, Bentley Historical Library, University of Michigan); Joseph R. Conlin, " 'Old Boy, did you get enough of Pie?' A Social

History of Food in Logging Camps," *Journal of Forest History*, 23 (1979): 168–69.

16. *American Lumberman* (Chicago), July 15, 1905; George W. Hotchkiss, *History of the Lumber and Forest Industry of the Northwest* (Chicago, 1898), 177–79; *Portrait and Biographical Album of Osceola County*, 331–33; Beatrice Corkett, "Susan Moulter Fraser McMaster," *Inland Seas* 31 (1975), 195.

17. Quoted in Engberg, "Labor in the Lakes States Lumber Industry," 229.

18. *Tuscola Advertiser*, Feb. 25, 1869.

19. Ibid., Jan. 14, 1869.

20. *The Merchants' Magazine and Commercial Review* 54 (1866): 103; Ward, "Reminiscences of Michigan's Logging Days," 308; Hanna, *Sand, Sawdust and Saw Logs*, 9–10; Mears, blank labor contract, Mears Collection (Burton Historical Collections, Detroit Public Library); Engberg, "Labor in the Lake States Lumber Industry," 272; Jensen, *Lumber and Labor*, 53–55. The ban against alcohol was easier to enforce after 1853, when Michigan adopted prohibition. The state remained "dry" for twenty years. (Michigan *Acts* 66, 1853; F. B. Streeter, "History of Prohibition Legislation in Michigan," *Michigan History Magazine* 2 (1917), 289–309).

21. Engberg, "Labor in the Lakes States Lumber Industry," 317–18; Carrie E. Mears, "Charles Mears, Lumberman," *Michigan History Magazine* 30 (1946), 540; Charles J. Wolfe, "Hannah, Lay and Company: A Study in Michigan's Lumber Industry" (M.A. thesis, Wayne State University, 1938), 30, 36; Charles Mears, White River Daybook, 1850–1853, Dec. 1851 entries for Jacob Loaf, Aug. 28, 1852 entry for Max Michal, Charles Mears Papers (Michigan Historical Collections, Bentley Historical Library, University of Michigan).

22. Engberg, "Labor in the Lakes States Lumber Industry," 228. For an example of the variety and frequency of industrial accidents, see the *Detroit Advertiser*

& *Tribune*, July–Nov. 1862. During this period ten major accidents were reported.

23. H. H. Crapo to W. Crapo, Oct. 5, 1859, Crapo Papers; *Detroit Daily Advertiser*, July 24, 1862; *Lumberman's Gazette*, July 24, 1885; Engberg, "Labor in the Lakes States Lumber Industry," 230.

24. Crapo, Journals, June 29, 1864, Crapo Papers.

25. Engberg, "Labor in the Lakes States Lumber Industry," 274–75; Anita Shafer Goodstein, "Labor Relations in the Saginaw Valley Lumber Industry," *Bulletin of the Business History Society 27 (1953)*, 205–13; *Jeremy W. Kilar, "Community and Authority Response to the Saginaw Valley Strike of 1885," Journal of Forest History* 20 (1976), 67–69.

26. Jensen, *Lumber and Labor*, 58–59.

27. H. H. Crapo to W. Crapo, Feb. 12, Apr. 20, 1860, Journals, Sept. 29, 1859, Crapo Papers; Mears, Diaries, Jan. 7–Feb. 2, 1856, July 31, 1859, Aug. 15–30, 1860, Mears Papers (Michigan Historical Collections, Bentley Historical Library, University of Michigan); James Olin Whittemore, Diary, May 31, 1866, copied by M. L. Whittemore (Clarke Historical Library, Central Michigan University).

28. Anita Shafer Goodstein, *Biography of a Businessman: Henry W. Sage, 1814–1897* (Ithaca, 1962), 81; _____, "Labor Relations in the Saginaw Valley Lumber Industry," 197–98; Engberg, "Labor in the Lakes States Lumber Industry," 296; Mears to _____, June 4, 1865, Mears Papers (Michigan Historical Collections, Bentley Historical Library, University of Michigan).

29. Harry L. Spooner, *The First White Pathfinders of Newaygo County, Michigan*, unpublished ms., Library of Michigan, 9; *Portrait and Biographical Record of Michigan and Ottawa Counties, Michigan* (Chicago, 1893), 376.

30. Manuscript Census for the State of Michigan, 1850, St. Clair and Ottawa counties.

31. Mears, White River Daybook, 1850–53, entries for Jacob Loaf, Max Michal, Francis Gaugen, Lars Knudson, John Lamieux, John A. Johnson, Thomas A. Wood, Mears Papers (Michigan Historical Collections, Bentley Historical Library, University of Michigan). Those rates were lower than those paid by Mears in 1842. See miscellaneous entries, 1842 and Aug. 2, 1843, Account Book, 1837–45; Hannah, Lay and Company, Daybook, Nov.–Dec. 1854, Jan.–Feb. 1855, Hannah, Lay Papers; Crapo, Notebooks, handcopied from the *Saginaw Enterprise*, Feb. 22, 1856, Crapo Papers.

32. H. H. Crapo to W. Crapo, July 24, 1860.

33. Excerpt from letter, Island Mill Lumber Company, Alpena, *Michigan History Magazine* 16 (1932), 93–94; Engberg, "Labor in the Lakes States Lumber Industry," 306; Mears, Wage Notations, Mar. 1856, Misc. Folder, Time Book, Big Sauble Mill, 1861–63, Nov. 1861, Daybook, Lincoln, Feb. 20, 1861, Ledger, Duck Lake, wage entries, 1863–66, Mears to _____, June 4, 1865, Mears Papers (Michigan Historical Collections, Bentley Historical Library, University of Michigan); Crapo, Journals, Hiring Entries, Oct. 1857, Oct. 18, Oct. 22, 1859, Crapo Papers; *Northwestern Lumberman*, Sept. 26, 1891; Wolfe, "Hannah, Lay and Company," 57; Hotchkiss, *History of the Lumber and Forest Industry*, 117.

34. Hotchkiss, *History of the Lumber and Forest Industry*, 110; *Lake Huron Observer*, Mar. 10, 1845; Manuscript Census for the State of Michigan, 1850.

35. Engberg, "Labor in the Lakes States Lumber Industry," 35.

36. Z. W. Bunce, Ledger, 1835–53, undated entries, 1853, William Jenks Collection (Burton Historical Collection, Detroit Public Library). Other sources indicate that the lower limit of wages was about $12.00 per month. See *Portrait and Biographical Record of Muskegon and Ottawa Counties*, 401; Anita Shafer Goodstein, *Biography of a Businessman*, 81; Crapo, Notebooks,

handcopied from *Saginaw Enterprise*, Feb. 22, 1856, Crapo Papers; Woods & Nims, Ledger, 1852–56, Merrill Lumber Company Records (Michigan Historical Collections, Bentley Historical Library, University of Michigan).

37. Goodstein, "Labor Relations in the Saginaw Valley Lumber Industry," 199; Mears, Lincoln Daybook, July 18, 1861 (Michigan Historical Collections, Bentley Historical Library, University of Michigan).

38. All wages are calculated on a twenty-six-day working month. Crapo, Notebooks, undated notation on Ballou mill, 1858 undated notation on conversation with George W. Bumell, 1856, Diaries, Feb. 18, 1857, Journals, Feb.–Apr. wage entries, 1857, Crapo Papers; Mears, Lincoln Daybook, July 18, Sept. 4, 1861, and passim 1862, 1863, Middlesex Daybook, wage notations, 1864, Middlesex Daybook, wage notations, 1866–67, Cash Blotter, Dec. 1865, Mears Papers (Michigan Historical Collections, Bentley Historical Library, University of Michigan); C. C. Trowbridge, Journal, Dec. 9, 1865, Trowbridge Papers (Burton Historical Collection, Detroit Public Library); *Detroit Daily Advertiser*, June 3, July 24, 1862; *Northwestern Lumberman*, June 14, 1890, Apr. 25, 1891; *Lumberman's Gazette*, Aug. 16, 1877; Goodstein, *Biography of a Businessman*, 81; Procter, diaries, Jan. 7, Mar. 18, Dec. 18, 1868, Dec. 9, 1869, Jan. 5, 1870, Procter Diaries.

39. Crapo, Journals, wage entries, Oct. 1857, H. H. Crapo to W. Crapo, Nov. 27, 1860, Crapo Papers; Bunce, Ledger, Dec. 17, 1853, Jenks Collection; Mears, White River Daybook, 1850–53, Mar. 2, 1850, Mears Papers (Michigan Historical Collections, Bentley Historical Library, University of Michigan).

40. "Reminiscences of Carrie Mears," undated typescript, and "Reminiscences of F. N. Royle," undated, Mears Papers (Chicago Historical Society); *Lumberman's Gazette*, Feb. 18, 1885; Wolfe, "Hannah, Lay and

Company," 57, Hotchkiss, *History of the Lumber and Forest Industry*, 234; Engberg, "Labor in the Lakes States Lumber Industry, 234; Engberg, "Labor in the Lakes States Lumber Industry," 83, 312.

41. U.S., 35 Cong., 2d sess., Senate Executive Doc. No. 39, 1859, *Abstract of the Statistics of Manufactures, According to the Returns of the Seventh Census*. All figures in this paragraph were drawn from this source.

42. *Northwestern Lumberman*, Mar. 12, 1892.

43. Categories and methodology employed in analyzing these entrepreneurs are based on Frederick W. Kohlmeyer's study of the Great Lakes lumbering elite. Kohlmeyer, "Northern Pine Lumbermen," *The Journal of Economic History* 16 (1956), 529–38. See also Frances W. Gregory and Irene D. Neu, "The American Industrial elite in the 1870's: Their Social Origins," in William Miller, ed., *Men in Business: Essays on the Historical Role of the Entrepreneur* (Harper Torchbook, New York, 1962), 193–204; Merle Curti, *The Making of an American Community: A Case Study of Democracy in a Frontier County* (Stanford, 1959), 227–37.

44. Mills, *History of Saginaw County*, I, 144–148; George W. Hotchkiss, *Industrial Chicago: The Lumber Interests* (Chicago, 1894), 250; Wolfe, "Hannah, Lay and Company."

45. *American Lumberman: The Personal History and Public and Business Achievements of One Hundred Eminent Lumbermen of the United States*, 3 vols. (Chicago, 1905–06), I, 211–13; Hotchkiss, *History of the Lumber and Forest Industry*, 267–68; *Michigan Biographies*, 2 vols. (Lansing, 1924), I, 262 and II, 344; Dun and Bradstreet Credit Reports for the State of Michigan, vol. 69, St. Clair County, Sanborn and Sweetzer (Baker Library, Harvard University). An alphabetical index of names is located at the beginning of every volume of the credit reports.

46. *Michigan Biographies*, II, 344; Dun and Brad-

street Credit Reports, vol. 69, St. Clair County, Sanborn and Sweetzer. The estimated joint worth of Sanborn and Sweetzer increased from $3,000 in 1851 when they began lumbering to $200,000 in 1856.

47. See, for example, Dun and Bradstreet Credit Reports: vol. 64, Saginaw County, John F. Rust & Co. (4 partners), Miller, Payne & Wright (3 partners), H. A. Braddock & Co. (9 partners); vol. 80, Wayne County, D. Whitney & Co. (5 partners); vol. 4, Alpena County, Cunningham, Robinson, Haines & Co. (3 partners); vol. 62, Sanilac County, Imlay, Smith, Kelley & Co. (4 partners); vol. 2 Alcona County, Western Colwell & Co. (4 partners).

48. Dun and Bradstreet Credit Reports, vol. 64, Saginaw County, Forest Valley Salt & Lumber Co.; vol. 60, Ottawa County, Port Sheldon Lumber Co.; vol. 40, Mason County, Pere Marquette Lumber Co.

Bibliography

Michigan has received less attention than the other important eastern and midwestern lumbering states of Maine, New York, Pennsylvania, Wisconsin, and Minnesota. Modern histories of the Wolverine state, such as Bruce Catton's *Michigan: A Bicentennial History* and Willis Dunbar's *Michigan: The Wolverine State,* contain chapters or sections on the lumber industry, and there have been booklet-length popular accounts also, as, for example, Irene M. Hargreaves and Harold M. Foehl's *The Story of Logging the White Pine in the Saginaw Valley* and Rolland H. Maybee's *Michigan's White Pine Era, 1840–1900.* Several authors have written biographies of Michigan lumbermen, and articles on a specific aspect or incident, but no volume has appeared that studies all phases of the industry throughout the state over an extended period of time.

The sources for a study of the lumber industry in Michigan, particularly in the antebellum period, are limited, scattered, and diverse. Several guides provide detailed information about archival collections, particularly *The National Union Catalog of Manuscript Collections,* published by the Library of Congress, and *Guide to Manuscripts in the Michigan Historical Collections of the University of Michigan* are the best sources for the holdings of repositories within the state.

The largest and richest manuscript collections for this study were located in the Michigan Historical Collections, Bentley Historical Library, University of Michigan. The size and quality of the deposits vary. One of the most significant collections is the Henry H. Crapo Papers, which contain seventy-one volumes of journals, notebooks, diaries, and correspondence of Crapo and his family for the years 1841–1902. The Crapo Papers provide an insight into the personal and business life of an important lumberman. The Charles Mears Collection is slightly smaller but equally valuable. It contains diaries, journals, daybooks, and ledgers, covering the years 1837–1876, of one of western Michigan's earliest lumbermen. The remaining records of Hannah, Lay & Company of Grand Traverse County, the largest and most important firm in the entire northwest corner of the lower peninsula, are also at Ann Arbor. Like the Mears papers, the Hannah, Lay & Company Papers contain little correspondence but extensive business records. This large collection has been thoroughly processed and classified to reduce its bulk and increase its usefulness. Other collections containing business records include the William L. Case Papers, the George D. Hill Papers, and the Merrill Lumber Company Papers. The latter collection, as well as the William B. Mershon Papers, is very large but does not contain much material for the years before 1870. The papers of the Ferry family, well-known lumbermen for several generations, are disappointing. The correspondence in the Hill Papers contains interesting information on a small-scale merchant and manufacturer. A scrapbook for the years 1856–1870 in the Albert Yates collection; the reminiscences of Willis C. Ward, son of David Ward, a very large operator; and the diaries of Joseph E. Procter, a skilled laborer, are also very useful.

The Burton Historical Collection of the Detroit Public Library is an important repository of manuscript materials on lumbering in Michigan, especially for the early nineteenth century. The William Lee Jenks Papers contain the largest amount of material, all very valuable. Jenks, a lawyer and the author of *St. Clair County Michigan: Its History and Its People*, collected a vast quantity of source material on a variety of subjects concerning Port Huron and St. Clair County for the period 1820 to 1958. Most important for a history of the lumber industry are the ledgers of the Z. W. Bunce mill (1835–53; 1859–76), records of the Black River Steam Mill Company for the years 1832–35, and other miscellaneous correspondence concerning lumbering. The remaining collections relating to lumbering at the Detroit Public Library include papers of Charles Mears, the Michigan Pine Lands Association, and C. C. Trowbridge, all of which contain information on timberland purchasing. The David Oakes and William Woodbridge collections provide some details of the industry and the level of technology in the early 1830s.

The Clarke Historical Library of Central Michigan University also contains important collections relating to the lumber industry. Most fall beyond the time period of this study, but a number are of considerable value in documenting the rise of Michigan's lumber industry. The Amasa Brown Watson Papers contain records of the Newaygo Company and are particularly useful for documenting land purchases in the 1850s and 1860s. Other collections rich in land records include the Amos Gould Collection, the John Ball Papers, and the Ball and McKee Papers. The latter two collections, which span the period 1815–1908, contain diaries, correspondence, and legal papers as well as land lists. The diary of James Olin Whittemore, transcribed by M. L. Whittemore, provides a description of lumbering activity in the Tawas Bay area.

A significant collection of materials on Charles Mears and his company is to be found at the Chicago Historical Society. Diaries (1856–63; 1871–75), financial records, land warrants, shipping records, and a small amount of correspondence, as well as biographical information compiled by his daughter, comprise the bulk of the deposit.